•]

This book is dedicated to my parents, Lonnie and June Tompkins. When I was a kid, Lonnie was a tough disciplinarian who made me tough enough to make it in the world. He taught me how to take orders and instilled in me the feeling that I would rather die than fail. I damn near did both. June always listened, always believed in me, and constantly assured me I would win. One of my proudest accomplishments is that I finally did.

To my wife Linda's parents, Don and Darlene Ballantyne. If they had not loaned Linda and me $10,000 at a critical time years ago, we would have had to sell the agency. We repaid that loan plus interest in 39 days. It is what kept us afloat through some pretty tough times.

To my clients. Although they are too numerous to mention, they believed in me in the very beginning of my career. If not for them, Western Agency, Inc., never would have survived. It is a sacred trust to me that we continue to serve them well, and I shall be forever grateful for their business.

To my staff. They are the glue that holds Western Agency, Inc., together and the engine that powers it. They are one of the best staffs anywhere in the Independent Agency system. As I said so many years ago, if there were an Olympics for Independent Agencies, my staff would take the gold.

And finally, to my wife Linda. She is my partner; she learned from scratch how to be the comptroller of Western Agency, Inc. She had to listen to my frustrations when times were not good and knew just when to tell me to shut up and get things fixed. She watched me grow into a person who could run an agency. But more than anything, she made it all work. I love her more than words can tell, and this is not my story; it is our story.

• FORWARD •

For insurance agents or anyone who works in the insurance industry, a regulator's perspective is not always asked for, nor welcomed. This is especially true when the Insurance Commissioner is considered the 'cop on the beat' to make sure that agents and companies are following ethical business practices and staying true to the state law. I consider the role as Commissioner also to be one of providing leadership that fosters a competitive marketplace. This leadership ensures that consumers have choices with whom they choose to do their business.

In this case the author of this book, Chuck Tompkins, has always had a good history with regulators, and I value his opinion as a business person, a colleague and a friend. I am honored that he has asked me to contribute to his book, and encourage readers to take his comments and suggestions to heart. The Western Agency has proved to be a premier service provider in North Dakota and has provided a very valuable service in the market place in our rural state. I have read his book, and his advice is important, practical, and true to his good business form.

I offer my own personal perspectives on the insurance marketplace and how it affects an insurance Agent, specifically, one that works in an independent agency, or owns their own independent agency. My time as North Dakota Insurance Commissioner has allowed me to interact with all types of agents, varying by personality, business ethics, aggressiveness, and type of business they write.

Times are changing in the insurance industry. Technological advances, company consolidation, and product advances are making the industry more competitive for companies and agents. These factors can also make it more difficult for consumers to wade through the choices, decipher the differences, and make the important decisions about how to protect their financial futures.

Independent insurance agents have had to react to these changes. Company decisions certainly can change the way an independent agent does business. If a company decides to exit the marketplace, change their policies, or adjust their marketing practices, the independent agent is left to scramble to keep up and make sure their customers are represented and aware of the decisions they need to make.

Some independent agents have chosen not to get ahead of the marketplace. They have refused to become more technologically advanced. Some have refused to create relationships with companies that would allow them to better market a product, potentially keep a market that they have lost, or negotiate a better contract for them that would have secured their agency into the future by better serving their customers with good choices.

Survival in the insurance business is going to get tougher and tougher. From a regulators standpoint, the agents that contact our office complaining about another agent tend to be the agents that have not prepared themselves for the changing environment of the business. They also tend to be the ones that have not had to work for the business, and now are having to play defense. In my opinion, those that lose in this game are clearly the consumers, whose agent has not kept up with those changing times.

As one of North Dakota's most successful independent insurance agents, Chuck Tompkins has made the necessary changes. He has adapted to the changing marketplace, has been innovative, and most of all he has been conscious of the consumers needs. His advice and counsel in this book are on the mark. He addresses, from a businessperson's point of view, the ups and downs of creating a successful agency.

As the Insurance Commissioner, I have the opportunity to travel the country representing North Dakota consumers and the nation's Insurance Commissioners. I always love to talk about the brand of agent in North Dakota. By and large, they are honest, hard working, and share the same goals as the regulators. The goal of making sure the consumer has a good product at a fair price from a solvent company that will be able to pay the necessary claims. Chuck Tompkins is one of those agents, and I am pleased he has shared his insights for the benefit of others in a very important industry.

Jim Poolman, Commissioner of Insurance, North Dakota

• CONTENTS •

• INTRODUCTION •

HOW DO YOU KNOW IF YOU SHOULD READ THIS BOOK?

• If you are in business for yourself or are thinking of going into business for yourself, you should read this book.

• If you have ever been in debt up to your eyeballs with nowhere to go, you should read this book.

• If you have ever made a major purchase on a credit card and had to haggle with the credit card company to raise your credit amount to pay for it, you should read this book.

• If you want to hear a story about a little business that made it, you should read this book.

• If you have ever purchased insurance of any kind, you should read this book.

• And finally, if you own or operate an Independent Insurance Agency, you should, FOR SURE, read this book.

Right from the start, when I first outlined my ideas for this book on an airplane flight, May 3, 1999, I never set out to write another SALES book. There are already hundreds of them on the market, most of them written by people who probably have sales ability far superior to mine. I have never considered myself a super salesman. Of course, all through this book are ideas I have used to help my company grow to the size it is now, but again, this is not a SALES book. I do have a tremendous feel for situations and people: how they feel and what they want. In other words, good instincts have helped me put together an absolutely excellent agency. I do not, however, consider myself a great sales guru. Furthermore, I did not sit down and write this book to make a big amount of money or because I needed another job. I wrote this book because it is a good story; I wrote it because I felt many people in the Independent Agency business could use this information. I hope it helps you.

What I do consider myself is an absolute expert on running and managing a midsize Independent Insurance Agency. In this regard, I feel I can offer you insights and techniques that can help you expand, grow, increase your profitability, and possibly, if your store is in trouble, help save your agency. It is for these reasons I believe I have something important to say. That is why this book came to be written.

If you own or operate a small or midsize Independent Insurance Agency, this book should be a good read for you. It is the story of an Independent Insurance Agency, Western Agency, Inc., that I started from scratch on December 15, 1976, in the little town of Minot, North Dakota. As you may know, North Dakota is a state where the entire population is only 650,000. North Dakota's economy is primarily dependent on the income of our farmers; and as you may have read, the 1980s were the worst farm income years the state had seen since the Great Depression of the 1930s. If you read anything about North Dakota in those years, you probably think I was living in an economic opportunity desert. However, nothing could have been further from the truth. It was in those years that I grew Western Agency, Inc., from nothing to $11,700,000 in premium. When you keep in mind that we do not write workmen's compensation insurance in North Dakota, that is pretty fair production. Western Agency, Inc., has an average commission of 15.8%, has a staff of 16, and is totally paid for. Along the way I have had lots of ups and downs. I have been within a few dollars of being broke; I have bought several small agencies: some buys good, some bad. I have been upside-down on expenses; I have run out of credit at the bank and borrowed from relatives to stay in business. I have been nominated for United States Professional Insurance Agents Association (PIA) Agent of the Year in 1997, was PIA agent of the year for North Dakota in 1996, and am past president of the North Dakota PIA. To say the least, it has been an interesting ride.

There are essentially three types of insurance agents available to the insurance buying public; the Telemarketing Agent, the Direct Writer/Captive Agent, and the Independent Agent. I started my career as a Direct Writer/Captive Agent for Nodak Mutual/Farm Bureau, and after a few years started my own agency becoming an Independent Agent. Being an Independent Insurance Agent has been a rewarding and exciting career. I consider my clients my friends, and many times the policies my staff and I sold them have saved them from economic ruin. When I look back over the years and the positive impact my staff and I have had on literally thousands of lives, it makes me happy and proud to have been lucky enough to make this exciting and important industry my career. There are very few jobs on this earth in which you can have such a huge impact on people's lives and still

3

make an outstanding income.

Probably the reason I am writing this book is I believe the word is stronger than the sword and I cannot go out and personally cut the heads off all the GEICOs of this world. I would like nothing better than to see this book help Independent Agents stay in business and prosper. This book is about the inner workings of an Independent Insurance Agency: its ups, downs, challenges, opportunities, and growth over the past 27 years. Along the way I imagine I have made virtually every mistake that can be made in the operation of an Independent Insurance Agency, but it seems to me that surviving these mistakes was what finally propelled the store to where it is today. Even in these crazy times for the insurance industry, it is still very possible to have an extremely profitable store. I firmly believe that you and your employees can make an excellent living. In the process you can take care of the insurance needs of your customers far better than any other insurance delivery system on the planet.

In my heart of hearts I am convinced that there is no better way to look after the insurance needs of John Q. Public than the Independent Agency system. I can see no way that the insurance product can effectively be delivered over the phone or Internet. Someone must take the time to sit down with clients and take care of their insurance needs and questions. Clients need to talk to someone who knows them, someone who understands what it is that needs to be insured and understands the marketplace. This someone can then choose the correct company to market the risk to and correctly draw up a contract to cover the risk adequately. Please remember, insurance is essentially a contract, one between the client and the company. This contract had better be drawn up correctly; or when the claim comes, the company will not, they cannot pay the loss. It is up to the agent to be sure this does not happen.

Some half-insurance-educated telemarketer thousands of miles away, talking to the client on a phone line, simply is incapable of properly caring for the needs of the client. Furthermore, when the losses come in, a local Independent Agent is able to be continually involved in the claim process, from reporting the loss to the successful settlement of the claim. If there are problems in getting the loss settled, the local agent can help to keep the claim process moving smoothly along. Telemarketers in faraway cities have no idea of how to help get a claim settled. Even if they did, they would not be allowed to become involved in the claim process. That is somebody else's job, right? Wrong.

Furthermore, the direct-writing agent, like the telemarketer-agent, is saddled by a culture that also strictly forbids their being involved in the settlement of losses. If they happen to be additionally shackled with a poor adjustor on a given loss, by and large they can do nothing but sit helplessly by while their clients get the short end of the stick. In our Independent Agency world, if we are having adjusting problems, we are able to move faster to see to it that our client is correctly served. We simply do not have to sit by and watch a poor adjustor do our client harm. Good adjustors are worth their weight in gold: to the client, to us, and to the company. A bad adjustor is one of the banes of our business. As Independent Agents we can do something about this that most other agents simply cannot.

In addition, as Independent Agents we have far more flexibility in how we advertise, sell our products, and how we pick companies to insure our clients. Having these types of tools and flexibility has enabled me to compete successfully with direct writers and insurance telemarketers for years. However, this very freedom to do what we wish is the pitfall of many an Independent Agent. We are entirely on our own; for better or worse, it is up to each agency to decide how to solve their sales problems and run their stores. Herein lies a massive opportunity to become either rich or broke. I have hopefully written this book to help more of you achieve the former.

I have kept notes and thoughts about this industry for years in a diary of sorts. Throughout the book I shall put them in whenever I think they make sense. One thought I had which I feel is so appropriate for being in business for yourself, which I wrote down years ago, is this: *Please understand: the very instant, the second you finally decide to go into business for yourself, you are committed to playing the Business Game. This game has the highest stakes of virtually any game in the world except the War Game. The potential for profits, excitement, terror, and prestige are all there for you in this game. It will profoundly affect you for the rest of your life. It will change you and your family, your friends, and the families and friends of your employees. It can kill you. It can also be the best and greatest thing that ever happened to you. Enjoy; the stakes are high.*

In North Dakota we have many small struggling Independent Agencies. As chairman of the North Dakota PIA Education Committee, I was involved in putting on several seminars and schools titled "Survival of the Small Agent." This book has grown out of those schools. Others seem to think these ideas have helped them; I hope they will help you, too. For that matter, if you are in any business, there should be many ideas here that you can use. After 27 years as an Independent Agent, growing Western Agency, Inc., from nothing to $11,700,000 in premium, I think I have learned a huge amount about survival economics. As I said before, I've been broke in this business, and I've become a multimillionaire in this business. Of the two I like having money better. Here are the ways I did it:

• CHAPTER ONE •

OFF TO THE ROUNDUP:
Getting Into the Insurance Business

I started in the insurance business at age 23 in 1973, when I was hired to sell insurance for Nodak Mutual, a small captive company in North Dakota. Before that I had worked construction in the summer and attended college in the winter. I went into the insurance business because someone asked me. I had never actually been asked to go to work for anyone before; when I was offered the job, I was so flattered that I took it without hesitation. I did not know at the time that many people go into this business but few stick around to learn and understand it. I was just a 23-year-old guy with a new wife, and it seemed like the thing to do at the time. Not really an auspicious start, was it? Nodak Mutual is a small company owned by the North Dakota Farm Bureau. As a result of this, we sold mostly homeowners, auto, and farm insurance. Nodak was a very new company at the time I started working for them; I was one of the first nine full-time agents they hired. Also, at this time Nodak was so low in price that if you could get people to let you give them a quote, the sale was almost automatic. In retrospect it was a salesman's dream! However, I was new at the business and did not realize this for many years. I actually thought my sales effectiveness was due to my super salesmanship. This thought would get me into trouble later.

I was hired to work for Nodak by the then-division head, Tom Wold. Tom was a family friend, and I did not realize until years latter just how excellent a salesman and what a wonderful teacher he was. To this day many of the techniques and sales skills I teach my staff are a result of his mentoring. In addition, the head adjustor for our territory at that time was Bill Cresap, who had an incredible knowledge of insurance and was another tremendous teacher. Tom showed me the mechanics and basics of selling; Bill set me firmly on the path of always trying to sell customers policies that would take care of them when the claims came. Bill told me over and over to read my rate books. He was right: they are a wealth of information about how a company wants to rate and write a particular risk, along with the various coverages available to insure your client adequately. It is tragic how few agents sit down and really read them. Bill's teaching regarding always trying to sell the customer the best possible policy (coverage always trumps price), gave me a solid business practice that continues to this day.

At this time North Dakota Farm Bureau, the owner of Nodak Mutual, was having Iowa Farm Bureau do their training for them. This meant that we new agents traveled to Des Moines, Iowa, for training, several times a year. One of our instructors was Chuck Underwood, and I can still hear his big, booming voice as he told us the story about the $10,000 refrigerator. Chuck was an old life insurance salesman whose primary responsibility was to persuade us to sell life insurance. The $10,000 refrigerator story was about a client he supposedly had whose wife persuaded him to purchase a new refrigerator rather than buying a $10,000 life insurance policy. As Chuck told the story he sounded as if he was going to break down and cry; I can still hear the emotion in his voice as he related how, after the husband had died unexpectedly and Chuck was in the widow's home explaining there was not much life insurance in force, "The widow looked at me, and with tears in her eyes she pointed to a new refrigerator and in a shaking voice said, 'Mr. Underwood, I want you to see my new $10,000 refrigerator!' " I never found out whether or not the story was true, but its drama did give us new agents a sense of urgency to get out there and be sure we never had to leave our clients poorly covered.

It seemed at that time in the early 1970s that alcohol and being an insurance agent kind of went hand-in-hand. Most of our meetings, conventions, and training schools ended the day with a trip to the bar. Some people had a few drinks and then stopped, but not me. Several of us would always end up closing up the place, and the next day there we would sit in Underwood's class, massively hung over. Although I don't know if it was an accident or not, invariably we would be put in the front row so we could be asked questions and could better hear Chuck's booming voice. I would always have Alka-Seltzers with me and every few hours drop one into my glass of water. Not only did they really help my hangovers; I also think they were instrumental in keeping me in the insurance business.

I had the usual call reluctance--not making enough calls, not selling the whole package, not asking for enough referred leads, not asking for enough life sales--problems that most young agents have. In addition, like most new salespeople, I was having a hard time handling all of the free time. It is so easy to do nothing and say you are busy when you are an outside salesperson, is it not? Drinking coffee with your usual coffee group and telling each other how hard you are all working is a poor substitute for a good, hard selling interview. Yet how many times and how many days have we all wasted shooting the breeze over a cup of coffee, while telling ourselves we are hard at work? Since I had very little idea of what I was doing, I thought I was really hitting it. Nothing, however, could have been further from the truth. My saving grace was that I was, even then, trying to learn this trade. Though I was spending way too much time in the coffee shop, I was having plenty of sales interviews.

You see, I had one big advantage over most people in my situation: I could follow orders. I had a father who taught me well that you did what you were told, no questions asked. Since I was told to have at least three evening calls per week and have at least one life insurance sale per week, I made a major effort to do this. It did give me a track to run on, and to this day I constantly monitor the sales activity of my staff as well as myself to be sure enough sales interviews are being conducted. If you are in this business and you do not have a prospect list you are working effectively, ultimately your sales effort will fail. Furthermore, do not expect your star sales staff to work their lists, either, if you are not keeping track of them. I have copies of the main prospects of all my salespeople, including the managers, and we review them once a week. It is necessary and keeps the sales process moving.

Nodak Mutual in those years was way ahead of their competitors in many ways. First of all, they demanded that the agent make every attempt to write the entire account: the auto, the home, the farm, the crop hail insurance, the life insurance, the disability insurance, and the health insurance. Even now, after all these years, how many times do we as Independent Agents not get all of a person's coverage? And then what happens? We leave the door open to another agent. It is essential that we try to cover more of these bases by writing the entire account. I was talking to one of my agents the other day about his lagging sales and told him that whenever he finds himself in a rut for new sales, he should go over his existing client list and do some account development. Remember, these existing clients have already bought from you once; they will buy from you again.

Another thing Nodak Mutual had going for them was niche marketing. It wasn't called that at the time, but that is what it was. Maybe it happened because Nodak was owned by the Farm Bureau, which focused exclusively on farms. For whatever reason, they were primarily interested in farm and homeowner business and, of course, the life and health products that went along with them. As a result, we agents were not bogged down with having to know too many of the other commercial and brokerage products. I have tried in my Independent Agency to make sure that each person who works for me specializes in one area of insurance. I want everyone to be well versed in the insurance business as a whole, but I want each to be especially comfortable in one or two lines.

Probably the greatest thing Nodak had going for them, though, was the head of the company, Harold Gromesh. I am not really sure what background Harold had in the insurance business before he became the President of Nodak Mutual; whatever it was, he totally understood how to get the insurance product sold. He would tell us over and over again, "You go out to the client's home, you sit down with the husband and the wife at their kitchen table over a cup of coffee, and you take care of their insurance needs and questions." He was right: if you are selling farm insurance, it is now, as it was then, the only way to do it. Furthermore, whatever it is--whether it is homeowners or business insurance--meet the clients where they are comfortable, at a time when they can be relaxed, and take the time to go over their coverage and accounts thoroughly. It is the way the business ought to be done, and it is the only way a good, complete, and accurate application can be prepared. I wrote up a 17,000-acre grain farm many years ago. It took me three separate meetings and many hours sitting down with these people to get a complete package put together on all of their various farms, homes, and operations. I did sell the account, and after we finally got done, the client said, "Chuck, you know, in over 30 years of paying insurance premiums,

11

this is the first time I realize what we are spending all the money for." It was a nice compliment, and we still have their insurance after all of these years. What Harold had told us about how to sell the product is just as valid today as it was 30 years ago; in spite of all the computers, polished proposals, and bells and whistles, someone still has to sit down with clients and go over their insurance needs and questions. It is the way the insurance product should be sold.

When I was first hired by Nodak Mutual, they gave me 15 active files to service and a territory to work. This territory was the eastern half of Ward County and the western half of adjoining McHenry County. I worked for two years in the area. Then, just when I was starting to get the territory built up and beginning to make some money, they told me they were cutting my area in half and giving part of it to another agent. I was still a new agent; and when you are a new agent, it seems that your renewals never seem to build up fast enough anyway. Financially, new agents are always living hand-to-mouth. This is one of the big drawbacks of commission sales: more on that later. However, at the time I was really incensed at their cutting my territory in half and not giving me anything for the renewals and new policies I had written. Also, it was about this time that I was taken off the salary draw system and put on straight commission. This would have been no big deal except that a mistake had been made on my draw account. Instead of having a cushion of a few thousand dollars of commission ahead, I ended up owing Nodak a few thousand commission dollars. This seems like a small deal now when I think about it, but back then Nodak did not cut me any slack and stretch the payments out to help me. They simply quit sending me any paychecks until all of the money due on the draw was paid back. As you can imagine, this created a really tough time for me and my family financially. I had a new wife and a young daughter, and getting the bills paid was a nightmare for awhile. I really hated Nodak Mutual for leaving me out there twisting in the wind. This, plus cutting my territory in half, really started me thinking that maybe I was in the wrong career.

So there I was in 1976, not liking the insurance business very much. Since I had worked for a contractor driving a truck for a few years before I was employed by Nodak Mutual, and it occurred to me that it would be great to go back to a business in which you didn't have to keep persuading people to buy insurance from you. I was remembering only the good times about truck driving--having a cup of coffee whenever I wanted to, no sales quotas, no schools to attend--a nice simple life, right? I was feeling sorry for myself for having to meet sales goals, get more new prospects, work my prospect list, and have a company dump on me whenever they pleased. In addition, I had not had enough claims happen yet and hadn't seen what a wonderful thing a well-written insurance policy can be. Therefore, in early 1976, like so many new agents before me, I started looking for a way to get out of the insurance business. Luckily, I did not. It would have been the worst mistake of my life.

In those few months, however, I was casually looking around for another job. My family had a small irrigated farm; and since my father was also in the real estate business, I asked him if there was some way I could take over the farm. He answered that the farm was too small for a person to make a living on that amount of acreage, so that option was out. As luck would have it, the second thing that happened in 1976 has left me totally committed to the insurance business ever since.

Throughout the late 1960s and 1970s, North Dakota had lots of snow. Since the town of Minot where I lived is located in the Souris (French for mouse) River Valley and no flood control work had up to then been done, Minot was faced with several devastating floods in those years when the snow melted in the spring. Finally, in the spring of 1976, the mother of all floods came roaring down what had come to be known as the Mighty Mouse River. Having been a construction worker while I was going to college and having driven dump truck a good part of that time, I was asked by my former employer if I wanted to help out during the flood, driving truck on the night shift. Desperately in need of additional cash, I thought why not and started driving truck from six p.m. to six a.m. seven days a week. Twenty-eight exhausting days later, the flood threat was over, the town had been saved, and I got out of the truck that last day having decided that if I never saw another dump truck in my life, it would be way too soon for me.

In my short career in the insurance business, I had forgotten that truck drivers have problems, too. I had forgotten about old folks who pull out in front of you when you are loaded at 70,000 pounds gross. I had forgotten about the difficulty of backing up a narrow dirt dike in the middle of the night, in slippery mud with poor lights. I had forgotten about the guy who drives your truck on the day shift and leaves your truck box half full of dirt and mud. My hat is off to you truck drivers!

It was the spring of 1976. I was beginning to realize that I could make it in the insurance business and after driving truck in the 1976 flood, I was no longer looking to find a new career. I have been irrevocably committed to the insurance business ever since.

• **Coverage always trumps price.**

• **Good mentors help make good agents.**

• Follow orders: they will tell you how to succeed; listen to them.

• Too much freedom kills lots of agents; don't spend all day drinking coffee, telling everyone how hard you are working.

• Most of all, sit down and talk with your clients about their insurance needs and questions; do not just pitch them.

• Selling insurance sure beats driving a dump truck.

• CHAPTER TWO •

GIDDY UP:
An Agency is Born

Shortly after going back for those few days to drive truck in the flood of 1976, I found another way to move on in this wonderful business. By this time I had been working for Nodak Mutual for about three years as a captive agent. I was just starting to realize that there was such a thing as an Independent Agent out there who did not have to sell for just one company, but could sell insurance for many companies. The way I found out about this was that Nodak Mutual had such a narrow list of things they would write that many deals came our way that we could not put together. Therefore, necessity being the mother of invention, Tom Wold, my boss at the time, started a little Independent Agency in his desk drawer to write up these orphan deals. He called his little pocket operation Tom Wold and Associates. He had a contract with a little company called Sunshine Mutual and an even smaller little mutual called, of all things, Walle Mutual. To round out his stable of carriers he got lined up with a broker called Blackburn Nickels and Smith for our truck insureds and another broker called Insurance Facilities for our mobile homes and other contracts.

If a piece of business came along that Nodak Mutual did not want to write, we would simply write it with Tom Wold and Associates. This worked fine--lo and behold, by late 1976 we had quite a bit of premium in the little "desk-drawer" agency! There was trouble in paradise, however, as we had been putting so much premium into Sunshine Mutual that occasionally Tom Wold and Associates was listed in the top 10 producer list that little Sunshine Mutual published every month. Although we were writing things that Nodak didn't even want, they started asking some very pointed questions of Tom. Knowing I was not overly happy with Nodak anyway, he came to me with the proposition that I buy into Tom Wold and Associates and run it full-time. I would quit Nodak Mutual; we could rent an office, commit ourselves completely to our new agency, and go into business for real. This seemed like the best idea in the world to me, so away we went.

Neither of us knew much of anything about being an Independent Agent. Nevertheless, we headed out on the project. We had no clue that we were about to make a few errors that years later would cost the agency a huge amount of money and almost put me out of business. But in the meantime we rented an office and proceeded on. Tom decided he would sell me one-half interest in the business we already had in place for $10,000. In retrospect I realize I could have probably called up both of the little companies we represented and just gotten my own contract, but I was reluctant to do that since I knew absolutely nothing at all about being in business and figured Tom knew everything there was to know. In fact, it seemed like a heck of a deal to me. I went down to my bank and talked to my banker, Eldon Seelig, an old friend of the family. Eldon and his financial institution loaned me the $10,000 to get going. The next thing Tom and I did was to see a lawyer who set us up a sub S corporation. This was the event that precipitated the future problems. We had no idea at the time that this would happen, however, so we spent the $1,000 to get incorporated, made an attorney happy, and went into business together.

On the day we were supposed to have the incorporation put together, we still had not come up with a catchy name for our new company. Consequently, when the attorney asked us what we wanted to call it, we had no answer. After a few moments of silence, he said, "Why not call it Western Agency, Inc.?" The name sounded good to us. We gave it the nickname "Westy," and here we are today, $11,700,000 of premium later. Lots of water has gone over the dam and the name remains. The name works fine, but looking back with 20-20 hindsight, it is beyond me as to why we felt we needed to be incorporated in the first place. Being a sub S corporation turned out to trigger a financial catastrophe for me far ahead in 1990. Back then, though, we were incorporated, up and running and off into the wild world of business we went.

Next on our agenda was a trip to an office supply store to purchase $2,000 of office equipment. I picked out my own desk and chair, one four-drawer file, and a couple of customer's chairs. I still have the desk and a couple of the original chairs; maybe someday Westy should have a museum. Years down the line, after I found out how much premium it really takes to make a net dollar of profit, I began to buy my office equipment at Air Force surplus auctions, garage sales, or used furniture stores: wherever I could pick it up cheaply. You may not believe it, but years ago I liberated from a garbage dumpster an old coffee table we used for years--no kidding! In those early days, though, I assumed that when you needed office supplies, you just went to an office supply store for them. Was I brain-dead or what? At least we didn't waste money on an opulent office suite. Our first place of business, a 12X15 single room, was in the back of the old City Plumbing and Heating Building.

The third thing we did was hire a CPA to do our books. He asked us a very critical question, "When do you want your financial year to end?" Again, not knowing what to say, we asked him what he suggested. He said, "Well, I'm not very busy in the fall--what about 10/31?" Since this seemed fine, that was the year-end we chose. Picking this date was to be another huge error. Having a 10/31 year-end became one of the biggest mistakes of my life.

- **You do not have to be incorporated to be in business.**

- **What is in a name?**

- **You do not have to buy office equipment new.**

- **Get a CPA, a good one, one that will TALK with you.**

WESTY HITS THE TRAIL:
Cranking up the New Agency

Well, there it was: 12/15/76. I had a new desk and chair in my own office--now what? Making my prospect list was easy. I was still mad at Nodak Mutual for cutting my territory in half and leaving me twisting in the wind after their commission screw-up. Since I had no non-compete clause in my contract with them to keep me from writing up my old Nodak Mutual clients in our new agency, I started writing up my former clients into my new store. I guess I was something of a good talker after all, because there I was taking my clients from Nodak Mutual, a well-established North Dakota company, and writing them up with a couple of companies called--don't laugh--Walle Mutual and Sunshine Mutual: crazy. I always had to explain that Walle Mutual got their name from Walle County. It seems that they had started out as Township Mutual, located in--you guessed it--Walle County, North Dakota: hence the name. I cannot for the life of me figure out how I explained Sunshine Mutual. Who came up with that company name I shall never know. What were the A.M. Best Ratings on these two companies, you may ask? I believe Sunshine held a C-rating, and Walle didn't even have one. In those years, however, I did not even know what a company rating was. Sometimes ignorance is bliss.

One lucky break that did not occur to me until years later was that like Nodak Mutual a few years before them, neither Walle Mutual nor Sunshine Mutual had taken a rate hike in over five years. Therefore, they were offering rates that were downright excellent. I became a super salesman once again because I had super rates about which I was oblivious at the time; I'm sure I must have figured I was a sales genius. Whatever the reason, my faithful clients believed in me and signed up en masse with the fledgling Western Agency, Inc. In those days you could insure a new car for less than a $100 a year, and in my first year I wrote up over $150,000 in premium for the new agency. Also, in those years I had no secretary, so I was selling, billing, sending out the policies, filing the claims, and doing all the paperwork myself. I became a very busy fellow, I had never worked harder in my life, I was having fun, and, without even noticing it, I was not sitting in the coffee shop telling everyone how busy I was anymore.

I seem to have good instincts most of the time for what works in business. Two things I did right from the start with Western Agency, Inc., were publishing a newsletter and taking aerial photos of clients' farms and businesses. The newsletter was supposed to look something like the Kiplinger Letter, and I have been putting one out now for almost 30 years. The clients apparently love it. Over the years it has been one of the main ways we stay in touch with our people. We constantly receive feedback on it, so I have to say it has been a huge part of our success.

In one issue of the newsletter I ran a little contest

promising a $50 prize to the person who found the most grammatical and spelling errors in it. My God--this was before we had computers with Spell Correct and Grammar Correct! Little did I know that I had insured almost every current and retired English teacher in the state. The morning after the newsletter went out, our switchboard was jammed, and in the next three days 145 people called in mistakes. Evidently there were 32 grammar, punctuation, and spelling errors in the thing. Stupid me, I thought there were only two; I felt as if I were back in high school. Some of the clients took the time to send in copies of the newsletter with the errors corrected in red ink, the whole nine yards. Actually, I was elated. If that many people took the time to read the newsletter that carefully, we absolutely had to keep writing it. Yet a review of past copies reveals that many of our messages in each issue are largely the same. We continually stress the importance of calling our agents with problems and coverage questions. We constantly offer to come out and see clients in person to explain the various policies. We emphasize higher deductibles to keep premiums in line, and we usually try to highlight a coverage that needs further elaboration.

In addition, we try to feature individual clients or have various contests. One competition we have carried on for years is the Wear Your Westy Hat Contest. Over the years we have given thousands, of hats away. We put together a newsletter roughly every three months, and we select one client per newsletter we have seen wearing a Western Agency, Inc., hat for a prize. The reward normally consists of a $50 gift certificate to Perkins Restaurant in Minot, a new hat, and a new Western Agency, Inc., jackknife. Whoever chooses the winners is referred to as "The Unknown, All-Seeing, and Unnamed Judge." You cannot believe how hard some folks work to be chosen. We have pictures of people wearing our hats all over the world. It is a ton of fun.

In the beginning I typed the newsletter, got a bunch of copies made, and hand-addressed each one. It took forever. Now that we are sending out several thousand, that way would take too much time. So I simply type the newsletter in a Word document and e-mail it to the printer, who sets it up, sends me a proof to read, and then uses our mailing list to send it out. The cost to do this is very minimal, not to mention a major savings in time to us. I am probably getting ahead of myself here; my point is that the newsletter has been a very worthwhile part of our advertising program.

The second thing I did that turned out very well was taking aerial photos of my clients' farms and places of business. This is not as expensive as you may think. I figure the pictures cost me less than $5 each, including plane rental, developing, and postage. I take them, have two copies made, and send one copy plus the negative to the client. The other copy we put on a bulletin board in the office. People absolutely love it. Isn't it only natural that they would far rather have a picture of their farm, home, or business than a nice photo of my office? If you want to do this yourself, just hire a small plane and pilot and give it a go. Tell the pilot you want to be 350 to 400 feet in the air and a quarter of a mile or a little farther from the farmstead. Any closer, and all you get are pictures of the roof. Use a 35mm camera and a 75mm to 200mm zoom lens with 100 speed film. Set the F stop at 8, or use your light meter, and always remember to take the picture up the client's driveway. When I first started doing this, I took a few shots from the backsides of the farmsteads, and often the farmers could not recognize their own properties. People orient themselves the way they drive up to their home or business. Try to take the pictures on a clear day at about noon to minimize shadows. Finally, don't worry about opening the window of the plane. It just gets too windy, and taking the picture through the Plexiglas gives you a fine photo.

My clients have many pictures of their farms taken by us over the years, and they really appreciate our doing it. We also use these photos for prospecting. We print the picture, frame and mat it, and put a copy on the front page of a proposal for the sale. In addition, we frequently enlarge photos to 11X14 and have them framed and matted for our larger clients and prospects. As I said before, it seems that clients love the pictures and they would far rather have a picture of their places than ours.

But back to the beginnings: that first year was a madhouse. I was learning about: paying monthly statements; getting bills typed up and sent out; keeping an accounts-receivable log; taking claim forms, change forms, phone calls, and all of the day-to-day things that are done every day in an agency, the only problem being I was a staff of one. Tom was still working for Nodak Mutual. It soon became apparent to both of us that he was getting paid too much money there for him to leave and come to work full-time at Western Agency, Inc. So I started thinking about owning the business all by myself. In late 1977 I asked Tom if he would sell the rest of the company to me.

Tom said I could have his half of the agency for $14,000. I had no idea where I was going to get the money, but without hesitation I agreed to do it. Once more, I am aware in retrospect that I was buying something I already owned and could have simply gotten my own contracts for free. Tom and I were friends, though; it was still a good deal at the time; and it was the right way to do it. Since the company is now worth around five million dollars, I suppose this could qualify as one of those good deals a person makes in life. I financed the purchase by taking out a second mortgage on our house. I used the $25,000 this came up with to pay Tom off and keep myself afloat financially for the next year. The best news was that I was learning how to run an agency and the renewals were starting to build up. That second year I was again able to put $150,000 of new premium on the books. The fledgling agency was starting to take off, and the angle of my learning curve was increasing.

• **You do not have to deal with only A++ rated national carriers to be successful.**

• **Good clients stick with good agents.**

• **Regarding aerial photos, remember that your clients would rather have pictures of their places than yours.**

• **Newsletters can be fun and keep you close to your clients.**

THE FIRST ROUND UP:
Getting Some Good Field Reps and Good Companies

As the owner of an Independent Agency, I got to meet my field representatives. Each company had a field rep that came out to see their agents from time to time. These folks helped me enormously in getting integrated into the Independent Agency business, and I shall always be grateful to them for it. Field reps then and now perform a valuable service. Furthermore, I don't think we Independent Agents give these people enough respect. It is so easy to say that all they are good for is stopping by, drinking your coffee, and wasting your time. Yet over the years, when I look back, field reps have been absolutely essential to my success. Sure, some of them probably drink too much coffee and waste my time. But who taught them to do that? The agents who drink a great deal of coffee and waste too much time themselves, right? Remember, if someone is wasting your time, you are the one allowing it. I have found that if you tell field reps you are on short time, they will keep their talk with you brief. Also, I have found that if you want information about the business, a field rep is a very good source for it. Some of my best agency acquisitions have come from tips from a field rep telling me so-and-so was thinking about selling their store. Good field reps are like spices in food. You sometimes do not really know exactly what they are doing, but you sure miss them when they are gone. I know the current trend is for companies to get rid of the field reps. Possibly that will happen, but I believe it would be a mistake.

It was in that second year after starting Western Agency, Inc., that a field man named Bruce Meyer stopped by the office. He and I sat shooting the breeze for an hour or so, and we really hit it off. He was impressed that I had a bulletin board with aerial photos of some of the farms I insured and seemed to think I ran an OK operation. Bruce represented a little company named Prairie States that was looking for agents in North Dakota. I was in need of more contracts because all I had was Sunshine Mutual and Walle Mutual at the time, so I took the contract he offered. Giving a kid with a tiny agency a contract was a big leap of faith for a company, and I shall always be thankful to Bruce for helping me get it. It was a large favor. Luckily, the contract worked out very well for both of us.

Also, as you may recall, we had started Western Agency, Inc., from scratch. The well-established agencies in town all had what were considered good contracts: you know, the USF&Gs, the Crum and Forsters, the St. Paul Companies, the Hartford, all those so-called "good" companies. The funny thing is that all these

25

years later virtually every one of them has now left the state of North Dakota. Lucky me, I was forced from the very beginning to rely on the little regionals: those small companies with limited markets; the ones the "well-established" agencies avoided; also the ones who do not need a million-dollar commitment to give a contract. And, finally, gee whiz, you know, they are the only ones still writing in North Dakota. I have often thought that one of the reasons that Western Agency, Inc., was able to survive was that I was lucky to have to rely on these little companies. They helped me and nurtured me and were a huge factor in the agency's becoming a success. That is why I protect them as much as I can. Without them my agency would not have made it.

To this day I do everything I can to be sure that all of my employees and I try very hard to put good, solid, profitable business on the books. We do this by pre-qualifying accounts and doing a complete job of field underwriting. My little companies have taken care of me, and I would like to take care of them. An agency has a tough time surviving without keeping fairly low loss ratios, and our loss ratios have traditionally been low because of this good field underwriting. Field underwriting is not just a phrase; it works for both the company and the agent. Even in the worst times Western Agency, Inc., had, when we were desperate for every dollar of premium we could get, I was always trying to write quality business. I think the reason was that at Nodak Mutual writing quality business had always been stressed. Later, when I went into business for myself, companies were also telling me that, so I just got in the habit of trying to write up good business from the very start of my career. This quality business was to be one of the golden keys to my agency's survival. Good business will invariably over time produce better loss ratios. The companies love low loss ratios, and of course pay extra commissions for it in the form of contingency checks. By consistently having low loss ratios my agency was able to earn extra money many years in the form of these contingency checks. In the early years of the agency I was earning this extra money from most of my companies every year. Many times I think the only real profit we had from a year of selling insurance came from the contingency checks. They kept us alive through some pretty tough times.

What is 'field underwriting?' Just the other day a client stopped into one of our offices and was "going to give us a chance to write his insurance." The person running the store, fairly new to the insurance business, thought the deal sounded a little too good to be true, so she called me to ask my opinion before she wrote or bound coverage on the account. I said she should tell the client we needed a loss run before we could give him a quote. With his permission, we sent in a loss run request to his prior company to see what his losses had been, and guess what? It just happened to turn out that this good ol' boy had forgotten to tell us he was getting cancelled from his current carrier. Not only that, his loss run took up three full pages: lots of "accidental" fires etc. His loss ratio was over 600% for five years. My only question was why in hell his current company waited that long to get rid of him. Needless to say, we were "unable to find him a company," and I don't know or care where he went for coverage. At Western Agency, Inc., we do no phone quotes. If individuals drop by to give us a chance at their business, I want to find out who sent them to us, or go out to look at their property, or get a loss run, or maybe all of these things, BEFORE we do the quote. I call this pre-qualifying process our mini Dunn and Bradstreet's, and it has helped us avoid writing a bunch of bad business over the years. I do not mean to say here that we only write perfect people. I am just saying that before we write an account, we want to know what we are writing and what kind of a person we are doing business with.

When it comes to talking about company size, you may want to remember this: your clients will buy from the company you tell them to buy from. In 99.9% of the cases they will not ask for the Best's Rating; they will only want to know if you trust the company and recommend it. In the early days it never occurred to me to ask what the company had for a Best's Rating or if in fact they even had a Best's Rating. It was probably unimportant, anyway. I remember Sunshine's rating as a C-. Incredible, right? Your clients trust you, my friends. Furthermore, we have seen companies with A+ Best's Ratings go out of business anyway. Actually, I have seen as many A rated or better companies go out of business as C+ rated companies. Finally, we do have the State Guarantee Fund in place to pitch in if a company goes out of business. It is not the best solution, but it exists for the exact reason that sometimes companies do fail. What I am pointing out is that we are insurance agents and not company analysts. I am not advocating here that you go and get contracts with shaky companies. What I am telling you is that as an agent, and especially in these crazy times, it is not the end of the world if you use a less-than-perfect company to get your client a policy. You get the business, they get covered, you grow your store, they get their claims paid, you stay in business, they get a good agent. The system works. Sometimes as agents, and even as clients, we can analyze the system to death. You still have to have money to buy whiskey. In this business if you are not selling, you are dying.

Picking up the Prairie States contract proved to be a very good deal for many years. This little company specialized in package policies; in other words, you had to write the farm and the auto or the home and the auto if it was a city deal. This played right into my prior training with Nodak Mutual, for they, too, were always trying to get you to do the entire account. Here was a little company doing packages way back in the '70s. Writing the entire account will increase your retention, not to mention your profitability. It was then and is now the way to go. I began using Prairie States a bunch. Furthermore, being a little company, as my book of business with them got up around $100,000 within a few years, I was appreciated and noticed. It was the first time I started to realize it is a good idea to place fair amounts of volume with a company. I guess we started trying to do it before it was a fad.

In the late 1970s and early 1980s I was really busy but having lots of fun also. I was out in the country trying to sell insurance to farmers, and along the way it seemed as if more than once I took an hour or so to stop and do a little hunting. I still do not mind if my agents take a few hours out of a day once in awhile to do a little hunting or fishing. I especially do not mind if they take a good client or a good prospective client along. Since I had a mobile phone and an answering service, my clients could always get in touch with me. Of course, now everyone has a cell phone, but back in 1976 I already had a mobile phone. It was, then as now, a tremendous time multiplier.

Probably the biggest idea that got driven into my head in 1977 - 1978 was that you don't have to drink a bunch of booze to be a standup guy. This novel idea came to me several ways, but one incident stands out. One night in late October I had gotten drunk and rolled my pickup. Soon after, a close friend of mine, John Simonson, stopped to see me. John was quite a bit older than me (we raced snowmobiles together) and I had a tremendous amount of respect for him. When he was in town, he took me aside and said "Chuck, you're are going to have to decide if your are going to be a successful business man or just another good time drunk." No big speech, simple and direct, just the way John is. But it had a tremendous impact on me. Thank God he had the guts to say what needed to be said and I had the brains to follow his advice.

In the course of doing business with Prairie States, I got to know its president, Bud Becker. He and his head of claims, Dick Bukins, took an interest in me and really helped me in these times. I respected what they said, and they gave me advice and counsel on how to better run my store. One of the things Bud suggested was that I come visit their office in Sioux Falls. So in the late fall of 1979, I drove the 500 miles down to see them in person. This also happened to be when the state of South Dakota was having their Big I insurance convention at the Ramkota Inn there. Bud took me to the convention one night, and in the course of meeting a few people he introduced me to Cliff Hanson, president of North Star Mutual, from Cottonwood, Minnesota. Bud told me since I wrote so many farms I should get a contract with North Star, for they were a major farm underwriter in Minnesota and considering expanding into North Dakota. I ended up having a long talk with the North Star guys; and when they came into North Dakota, they gave me one of their first contracts. It was to be one of the best company marriages I would ever put together. Western Agency, Inc., is now the third largest agency North Star has company-wide, and we are by far the largest agency they have in North Dakota. This year the check they wrote us for our contingency earnings was just a little over $29,000.

Over the years I got to be personal friends with Cliff Hanson and his outstanding team. North Star, with their fantastic staff and solid contracts, has taken very good care of my clients and my agency. They have been instrumental in our success. I shall always owe a debt to Bud for taking the time to introduce a kid to such excellent people. One of my good friends, LaVerne Mikkelson, is always saying it is your connections that help you in life. I have sure found this to be true.

It was also in the late 1979 and early 1980 time frame that yet another field man stopped into the office. He represented a fair-sized regional company called Auto Owners. They too were just coming into North Dakota and needed agents. Of course, all the big agencies were not interested in wasting time talking to him because most of them only used large national contracts. Of course I took the contract and it, too, has been one of the luckiest hits I have ever made. Auto Owners is an absolutely fantastic company, one of the most loyal in the nation to both clients and agents. You play ball with them; they will play ball with you. My relationship with them now spans over 23 years, and we are just getting started. How lucky could a dumb kid have been? My lesson list was growing along with my business.

• **A good field representative can be a big asset to you.**

• **Good companies tend to look for good, innovative agents.**

• **Protect your companies by writing quality business.**

• **Your clients buy from you, not a company.**

CHEAP HELP AND SNOWMOBILE RACING DON'T MIX

In late 1978 I was still in the office Tom and I had rented. The renewals were not yet large, and between paying rent and trying to support my family I was having a hard time making ends meet. In a conversation with a carpenter friend, he said he could remodel the basement of my house for a few hundred dollars and change, so that was my next move. I believe we did this in the fall of 1979. When I think of it, I cannot thank my loyal clients enough for taking all of this in stride. None of them seemed to look at it as unusual that my office was now located below my house, and they stayed right with me. It supports the point that in the insurance business it is not terribly important where your office is. Your long-term success will depend on the quality of the service you deliver. My move to an in-home office saved me thousands of dollars. The negative side of this, though, was that people would stop in at all hours of the night and day, which probably was one of the things that contributed to the eventual breakup of my first marriage.

Soon after moving into the house it was becoming increasingly apparent that I could not stay ahead of the paperwork and still be out selling. I had hired a secretary, but she was a young person who was more interested in chasing cowboys than doing secretarial work. I finally had to lay her off. I could not afford expensive help, however, so somehow I needed to find some assistance I could afford. Some days I was up typing bills at 2:00am and going to work only a few hours later just to stay ahead. As a solution to this problem, my wife went to work with me in the office in the spring of 1979. An excellent secretary, she was every bit as hard a worker as I was. For the first year we made a pretty good team and got a bunch done. But the strain of working so many hours together and the fact that we had never gotten along that well anyway soon began to take its toll.

One day in the spring of 1980, we had a huge argument that culminated in her taking the kids and leaving for several days. When I finally heard from her, she called to tell me she had seen a lawyer--wow! In shock,

I begged her to come home. A few weeks later she and I took a vacation we could not afford but certainly needed. After that things were OK for a while, although our marriage still had difficulties which definitely were not helped by our working long hours together. We also had two young children and that in itself was a big job for her. If any of you are in a similar situation, I recommend finding another way to get cheap help.

When I reflect on it now, it seems absolutely crazy, but all through these times I was maintaining my cross country snowmobile racing career. I had been racing snowmobiles since the early 1970s, and in 1980 I turned professional. I was running Polaris machines then and starting to have some success as the 1980s progressed. The main race I entered was the Regina-to-Minot International 250, a 250-mile, two-day event from Regina, Saskatchewan, Canada, to Minot, North Dakota. In those days it was second in size only to the Winnipeg-to-St. Paul cross country snowmobile race. People from all over Canada and the United States competed in it. Because it was a big local event, I really wanted to win it. I had won the Family Stock Class two years in a row, but what I wanted was the Pro Class overall victory.

To stay in shape for racing and be able to compete at the professional level, I started on an intense fitness program. In spite of the time it took, this probably helped the agency more than it hurt it because I could work unbelievable hours when I was in that kind of shape, and of course it made me a far better racer. Also, I know it sounds funny, but many times you make sales because of something totally unrelated to the transaction. Sometimes it seems as if outside activities can be a great third-party influence. I know even now when I fly into a town to do a deal, it seems to help make sales when the client knows that I came in my twin-engine airplane and that I am flying myself. It seemed the snowmobiles were that way as well. Somehow some people respected me for the racing, or perhaps they wanted to say I was their agent. Whatever the reason, it helped us sell quite a few policies. In addition, in the late '70s I had pretty much stopped drinking; by late 1981 I found myself running 50 miles per week, doing weight training plus thousands of pushups, resulting in my being in better shape physically than I had ever been in my life. I am sure my wife thought I must have been crazy to take on racing concurrently with building the company. She was probably right, but I did it anyway. In my own mind I think the racing helped me to stay sane and gave me an outlet other than business to help me clear my head. Nevertheless, it did not help a sick marriage.

I eventually won the Pro Class of the Regina-to-Minot cross country snowmobile race and ended up being the Pro Class Champion for the Can Am Cross Country Racing Circuit for North Dakota, South Dakota, Saskatchewan, and Manitoba for the years 1982 and 1983. It was quite an adventure, and I really hated for that part of my life to end.

In the early 1980s another great thing happened that had a very positive impact on the agency: my brother Casey stopped selling real estate and came to work for me. In addition to being very smart, he is also an excellent snowmobile mechanic; so we worked in the insurance business together during the day and spent lots of hours at night on the sleds. Casey is a tireless worker, and it was definitely due to his mechanical aptitude that I was able to win the number of races I did. He literally blueprinted our race machines; therefore, they seldom broke. Business-wise, he was extremely interested in commercial insurance. Since I knew little about this type of coverage, even then he began building our commercial insurance department.

• If your marriage is shaky, probably having your wife help you in business for no wages is a bad idea.

• Good clients will find the office of a good agent, even if it is in a bad neighborhood.

• Snowmobile racing can be hazardous to your marriage.

• Fitness is a huge part of being able to keep up the pace.

• CHAPTER THREE •

NEW LOCATION, NEWLY SINGLE AND
SINGING "CRACKLIN' ROSIE"

Strange as it may seem, even with all that racing, we were steadily acquiring lots of new accounts, by 1982 writing over $450,000 in premiums. I actually started to think I knew something about the insurance business. I also knew it would help if I got the office out of the house, and about this time I was able to locate a little building a couple of blocks from home that I could buy cheap. By taking over an existing loan, and putting the down payment on a contract for deed, I was able to finagle my way into the little house at 1728 Burdick Expressway East, with virtually no cash outlay. I expected that it would be OK for us for quite a few years, and we ended up using it as our office until 1991.

I was just starting to set up the new office when my marriage really began going downhill. My wife had previously quit working for me because we thought that would help, and I had hired a secretary who was doing a very good job. Although my wife and I were not fighting anymore, we were not communicating much, either. I sensed us drifting apart, and I honestly believe it was my fault for being so involved in the agency and the snowmobile racing. Finally, in the fall of 1981, my wife returned to her attorney to have me ordered out of the house. I remember that one of her remarks was that I was married to my business: she was probably right. I did not blame her; both of us felt it was the sensible thing to do. I found out later she was just trying to teach me a lesson by having the lawyer send me that letter. I guess she taught me a good one. The day I left that house I never intended to return. I took my clothes, gave her the house and left.

Getting abruptly ordered out of the house was a surprise to me. I had nowhere to go. Yet I had two wonderful kids to take care of part of the time and very little money, so I required a cheap place to stay. I remedied that by remodeling the basement of the old house I had just bought at 1728 Burdick Expressway East for my new office, moving in there. This put me only a couple of blocks from my old house. Oddly enough, the kids and I were able to be in touch much better; the crazy thing about being separated was I really started to be a better father to Coiya and Matthew, probably because I was terrified that the separation would hurt or traumatize them. They came over for supper two days a week and every other weekend, and we had some fun times. One thing for which I have been eternally grateful to my ex-wife was that we never used the kids to get at one another; both of us took great pains to see to it that our bad marriage affected them as little as possible. And again, proving that, in spite of what you hear, insurance customers are probably the most loyal people in the world. My clientele stayed with me, and the agency continued to prosper.

A bachelor for the first time in 11 years, I was forced to start cooking for myself, and the kids when they were there. Actually, it was not too big a challenge as I like to cook. But one night while I had some hamburgers on the stove, the phone rang with a client who had a claim. By the time I had it recorded, smoke was coming out of the kitchen--the entire office smelled of it for a couple of days! Nevertheless, I was learning to be Mr. Mom, and the kids and I had a big laugh over it: hell, things were not so bad. A few days later I decided to make spaghetti, figuring that once I bought the sauce, all I had to do was boil the pasta. Someone should have told me how spaghetti grows. When it was done cooking, it took my roaster and both of my saucepans to hold all the spaghetti. The kids and I ate spaghetti for days to use it up. Luckily, we liked the taste.

Also, since the house was built shortly after World War I, it had very poor wiring and few electrical outlets. In order to operate my electric shaver, I had to unplug the fridge. That is right, you guessed it: after going on a ski trip for a week and leaving in a hurry following a fresh shave, when I came home, I could smell things spoiled in the fridge from clear upstairs. At first I was afraid the fridge was ruined, but, short for money to replace it, I found out that if you keep putting old newspapers and cat litter in it and changing them every day, they eventually take the smell away. Once I had cleaned up that old fridge, I had it for a few more years until I sold it used for $50.

At periods like this, work can be an anesthetic for the pain. It was in this time after my divorce that I truly threw myself into my business. In addition, I was running up to 50 miles a week and staying in shape for the racing year-round. It was just as well. Being in excellent shape enabled me to work long hours, thinking nothing of it. This capability was to serve me very well in the next couple of years.

The year 1982 was developing into a doozy. Living in the basement of my office and getting a divorce, I finally won the Pro Class of the Regina-to-Minot International 250 after eight years of trying. It just seemed that all the hard work and the training came together in the ditch that cold February day. I won the race by the largest margin of time ever, at a record pace that still stands. It was an exhilarating, incredible ride. I was in shape, I was focused and the adrenaline was pumping. I was singing "Cracklin' Rosie" in my helmet at the top of my lungs. It seemed as if I was suspended above my machine and I could watch myself sail by the other sleds. I was reaching speeds over 85 miles miles per hour. "Cracklin' rosie, get on board. We're gonna ride till there ain't no more to go…"

If someone offered me a million dollars to do that ride over, I simply could not repeat it. I have pictures someone took of a jump I did in that race that was well over 100 feet long. The guy who hit the snowdrift behind me, Gerry Devisher from Winnipeg, broke his back in three places. That day was just my day to ride.

When I think about all of the time and energy I invested in achieving that win, it is truly unbelievable. Casey and I were on top of the world. After the trophy presentation we took several other race teams out for drinks, setting a few records for champagne consumption at a nice restaurant in Regina. When the management told us we had to leave the restaurant at about three a.m., I asked the waiter why we had to go so soon. He answered, "Sir, we were supposed to close two hours ago." We left him a nice tip and wobbled back to the hotel.

- **Old houses make good offices.**

- **Basements make good bachelor quarters.**

- **Cooking and working can burn your house down.**

- **You can get the smell of spoiled food out of an old fridge.**

- **Some days everything just goes right.**

THE PHANTOM AGENCY:
Buying Midwest Insurance

Shortly after the race season ended, I heard that one of the other insurance agencies in town was for sale. The one in question was a little store about the same size as mine that was run by a guy who was in money trouble. A big attraction of buying him out was that he had a company called Milbank Mutual that was good at farm insurance, and we were a farm-writing agency. I reasoned that buying the store would expand our list of companies and our market share as well. We started talking; and before I knew it, I was running full tilt trying to find a way to acquire the store. We had arrived at a figure of 1.5X gross annual commissions (Sound familiar?) and a sales price of $110,000. Part of the money was to be paid up front and part on contract for deed. I checked with my bank, but this time they were unable to come up with the money for me. In retrospect I suppose they were influenced by my recent divorce, and the fact that my great banker friend Eldon Selig had retired. Whatever the reason they would not give me the money. I thought the deal was dead.

Meanwhile, Casey was talking to his relatives, who agreed to loan him $12,500, which was all we needed to make the deal go together. That is how we purchased Midwest Insurance for $110,000 on June 1, 1982. It was the worst buy we ever made: not just because much of the business was junk, not entirely due to the former owner's being a far-from-ethical seller. The true problems were the soft market of 1983, the high interest charges of the middle 1980s, and my not trimming my staff and expenses down. Completely clueless, I was heading for disaster.

The deal I had made was to buy the agency and hire all of the staff, excluding the prior owner, although we agreed he would do a few deals for straight commission. He sold very little, soon drifting away, which was fine with me. The biggest mistake I made was hiring all of his employees: one full-time secretary, one part-time secretary, and one full-time agent. He had been way overstaffed; by keeping his people, now so was I.

Furthermore, I foolishly gave the full-time agent a 10% ownership in Western Agency, Inc., along with a 75% commission on all new sales and 50% on renewals. I had just hired a full-time agent myself; that plus Casey and my existing staff amounted to eight employees--was that insane, or what? Assuming we had an average commission of 17% and the agency we purchased was as good as advertised, we would have had commission earnings per employee of $25,000. But the Midwest Insurance book of business was far lower than we had been led to believe. Instead of producing $75,000 in revenues that first year, it only contributed about $39,000. That left us with critically low earnings per employee of about $18,500, not that I knew it at the time. It would be years before anyone ever told me what earnings per employee even were.

As I write this in 2004, your store should have an earning per employee of at least $75,000; and $110,000 is not at all out of sight. What you do to get the number is divide your agency revenue by your number of employees. I include myself in the employees, and I count the part-time people as half. Another thing to remember when you are figuring this equation is that agency revenue is commission earnings, not premium. Western Agency, Inc., currently has earnings per employee of $108,629. But back in 1982 we were sitting at an anemic $18,500 per employee, which was killing us. I knew we were in money trouble; I just did not know why. Furthermore, remember that I was paying the agents 75% of new premium and 50% renewal, simultaneously paying for Midwest Insurance. In retrospect, the only reason I did not go broke in a matter of months was that I had Western Agency, Inc., paid for before the purchase of Midwest Insurance, and I was not on the float. Nonetheless, I was losing a breathtaking amount of money. After giving the Midwest agent 10% ownership in the new entity and Casey buying 10% with his $12,500 contribution, I was left with only 80% ownership of Western Agency, Inc. Yet I was shouldering all of the responsibility for seeing that it did not fail.

As I already said, when we bought Midwest Insurance, it was supposed to have around $450,000 of premium and $75,000 in revenue. Since Western Agency, Inc., had revenues of $111,141 in 1981, the year before the purchase, Midwest was just a little smaller than we were. With the purchase of their book we should have had revenues of at least $191,000 in financial 1982, right? Wrong. Our 1982 combined year-end earnings were only $148,838; the next year our combined earnings dropped still further to $144,626. I should have cried, "Fraud!" and renegotiated the sale: nowadays I would have. True, we were beginning to get into the soft markets that would plague us for over 20 years, and this was causing insurance premiums to fall, but the root cause of the loss in premium was that the prior Midwest owner had misstated the numbers. By and large, most of the book was simply junk. In those days I had not yet heard of retention ratio so naturally had not checked to see what it was. Western Agency, Inc., had a terrific retention ratio, then and now; when we write something, it stays on the books. Midwest Insurance, on the other hand, had a terrible retention ratio. Business was literally running off the books like water. Maybe one of the reasons was that I always wanted premiums paid on time. If they were not, I cancelled the account. The only part of the Midwest book that was worth anything had been written by the full-time agent whom I had given 10% to stick around. He had a solid book of farm accounts, most of which we still insure to this day.

It was only years later when I was researching numbers

from these years that I realized how worthless the book was that I had bought. The addition of Midwest Insurance to Western Agency, Inc., should have increased our overall revenue to nearly $200,000, but the real number was an anemic $148,838, including my premium growth for the 1982 year. Apparently, I had purchased my first "phantom" insurance agency! The revenue dropped still further in 1983 to $144,626, including new production, barely crawling up to $171,562 in 1984 and $188,810 in 1985. Only in 1986 did we creep up to $203,444. Keep in mind that this income number was after four years and included any new premium we had written. The trouble was that I had more than doubled my expenses in this time frame that began in 1982. The stage was being set for a financial time bomb.

- **Try to purchase agencies that are morally compatible with yours.**

- **If you purchase a store, be careful about keeping all the staff.**

- **Watch expenses after a purchase, and trust your instincts.**

- **Keep a careful eye on earnings per employee, which should be $75,000 or more.**

- **If you find you have purchased a "phantom" book of business, consult your attorney.**

NIGHTMARES AND FALLING IN LOVE

It is so amazing now when I look at numbers like those above--they just scream at me about a huge prob-

43

lem! However, back in 1982 and '83 and the following years, I simply did not have the expertise and could not seem to find anyone to decipher the numbers for me. Yet I was paying a high-priced CPA to do my books. Rather than helping me, he was letting the stage get set for an impending disaster that could have been averted. Can I have my money back? A little side message here: it is not good enough to have a CPA; you must have one who can communicate with you. You need to sit down with him or her many times a year and talk about your agency. Your CPA does not merely do your taxes; your CPA is someone who will help you manage your store. Final note here: a good CPA does not come cheap, but do not worry if you are charged a significant amount of money for these services. Anyone who can keep you on a sound financial path will cost you far less than the consequences of making bad financial mistakes.

It was this over-expensing at Western Agency, Inc., and using up our accumulated cash flow that got us into such serious money trouble a few years later. People have asked me, "Are you sorry you ever purchased Midwest Insurance?" The answer is "Absolutely not!" If it hadn't been for that terrible buy, all of those mistakes I made, and the trouble they got me in, I would never have really learned how to run an Independent Agency. It was probably this buy that earned me my School-of-Hard-Knocks Doctorate in Agency Finance and Management. Furthermore, I really don't think the original owner was being crooked in the true sense of the word--hell, he was just as ignorant of how the business should have been run as I was at the time! In retrospect the only thing that really makes me mad about the deal was that years later, after I had paid him off on the contract for deed we owed him, we were looking at buying another little agency west of Minot. The owner of the agency said he was wary of selling to me on a contract. When I asked him why, he told me that the prior owner of Midwest Insurance had told him he was late on a bill because "Tompkins was not making his payments to me on time." It was a bald-faced lie; I never was one day late on a payment to this guy, or anyone else for that matter, and that statement of his has always angered me. It was bad enough to have purchased a pile-of-junk agency from him that was making half the income it was supposed to. It was bad enough that I stupidly sweat blood paying for it instead of rescinding the sale. But then he has the nerve to say I didn't pay on time? No wonder I have no time for the turkey!

My divorce became final a couple of weeks after the deal finalized on the purchase of Midwest Insurance. I walked out of my marriage with my personal belongings, a couple of used snowmobiles, and a used pickup, giving Joyce the house, everything in it, and an excellent settlement. I felt it was my fault the marriage had not worked, and I wanted her and the kids to be OK. For myself I had 100% ownership in a paid-for insurance agency. However two months later, after the purchase of Midwest Insurance in early 1982, all I had was a bunch of debt, a huge amount of energy, precious little knowledge, and 80% ownership of a dream. I was the richest guy in the world.

Within a very few months I made a critical error, which was this: before the purchase of Midwest Insurance, I always knew exactly where I was financially. I figured out the commissions each month and put that money in my operating account, leaving the rest sitting in a separate checking account. (Actually, at that time I had placed these funds in an interest-bearing Money Market Account.) I always paid my companies on due date, had the money in the bank in advance, and always knew exactly where I was, money-wise. My system wasn't rocket science, but it worked very well. In addition, I had no late pay accounts, as I had gotten rid of them. Within a few weeks of the purchase of Midwest, my own secretary quit; I never really knew if she simply did not like the new staff or disapproved of my recent divorce from Joyce. Anyway, she left, so I moved the main Midwest secretary into the bookkeeping role. In those days we would enter every transaction in a ledger and do a column for premium, a column for commission, then a split of commission for the agent and the agency.

A couple of months into the deal it became apparent that money was drying up. The secretary I had helping me with the books came to me one day and said we had lost $8,000 or more in the previous month. I simply dismissed it as a mistake. Luckily, we were selling quite a lot of new insurance, which for awhile forestalled the inevitable money shortfall. But it seemed we were gradually getting further and further behind, and I quit having a separate checking account for the companies. In other words, I had committed the fatal error. I was on the float. Although I never was a day late on a company statement, I was still on the float. It worked briefly, as most things like that do, but it was to have major ramifications in a couple of years. In the meantime, we were selling lots of new insurance accounts, and things seemed to be going OK. Like many agents before me, I was going down the road of over-expensing the store while blithely believing that we would sell a bunch more insurance to make everything all right.

There is one absolute business law here, and it is: if you are over-expensed, you must either sell more product or cut your expenses. Of the two options you MAY sell enough new product to bail yourself out. But it is a MAYBE thing, and possibly, if your cost of production is too high, this still will not solve the problem. By cutting costs the effect on expenses is immediate, it WILL happen, and the results are instantly verifiable. If you increase production at the same time, so much the better. At the time, however, I knew nothing of this. I simply figured we would sell enough new product to make things OK and did not cut expenses. Another instance of "ignorance being bliss," right?

Also around this time, another major life-changing thing was happening to me: For the first time in my life I was truly falling in love. And as things such as this do, it kind of snuck up on me. There was this couple I had met through snowmobile racing. I had written their insurance and gotten to know them fairly well over the years. The husband was doing quite a bit of drinking, and their marriage broke up in late 1981, about the same time as mine. I had kept in touch with Linda, and in the summer of 1982 we started dating. She was a snowmobile racer herself, so, instead of being mad at me for racing, she encouraged and supported it. I could not believe how captivated I was by her; before long we were inseparable. I suppose she felt she was getting involved with a hot rod snowmobile racer/business entrepreneur. In reality all she had fallen in love with was a short sled rider with a bunch of debt who had a dream.

Actually, Linda is no fool, and I should have known she was aware of what she was getting all along. I did not know it, but a few years before, the first time she had seen me had been on a club snowmobile ride to a little town west of Minot. I was wearing my brand-new, custom-fit Bates Leathers with Tompkins on the back, Chuck on the front, and my new Bell helmet: I figured I was looking good. As I came into the room and sat down with some other people, I guess Linda turned to her friend and said, "Hell, Mary, he's just a little shit."

Since this book is about the agency, I should not spend a huge amount of time on our courtship, suffice it to say that I am still enthralled by this wonderful woman. We have now been married for over 22 years; she is the love of my life. Judge Wallace Berning married us in a small civil ceremony on December 2, 1982, and we moved into Linda's 14X70 mobile home. (I was able to get us into a house a couple of months later.) When we were married on that cold, blizzardy day in December, 1982, we were the two happiest, richest, broke people in Minot. A day or so later Casey gave us a party in the basement of his house. A bunch of our racing friends came down from Canada, and we proceeded to have one of the best celebrations I can ever remember. I had just married the woman of my dreams. She gave my life direction and made all that followed possible (even if I was "just a little shit").

The years 1983 and '84 were somewhat better than 1982. Still, I was not doing a strong job of managing. Remember, I had made some big errors up to this time. I had paid too much for a junk book of business; and, to make matters worse, even when the book came apart, I did not renegotiate the contract-for-deed part of the purchase. I figured I had made the deal and would stick with it. Many of those accounts turned out to be slow-pay or no-pay, and much of the business was running off the books. Claims were up; contingency income was down. Nowadays, when I purchase a book of business, I make sure it is morally compatible with my store. In other words, is the agency being purchased similar to the one you have? Is its owner similar in temperament to you? I have found that if you purchase a book of business from an honorable person, the book will invariably be the same. Also, we were going into the great soft market that started in 1983, and I saw the $410,000 of premium I had purchased drop to $250,000 in little more than a couple of years. As if that were not enough, I was overstaffed, I was overpaying unproductive people who were sucking my cash flow dry, and I was paying retail for all of my office supplies. Although I am sure I was making more errors than those, they are the big ones that come to mind.

- **Again, get a good CPA.**

- **Do not over-expense your store; if you see it is happening, cut costs immediately.**

- **Never, never expect future sales to save you; if they do, so much the better, but do not count on it.**

- **Snowmobile racing may just help you fall in love.**

KERMIT, THE WIZARD OF OZ, AND THE ROYAL HANGOVER

In this time frame Royal Insurance Group bought Milbank Mutual; I believe the new company name was Royal Milbank. They were having a big meeting in Bismarck to make the announcement, and Linda and I went down to hear the new manager of the company speak. This man was to be my first contact with someone from one of those big companies. The great man got up and talked to us assembled agents as if we were a dumb bunch of country hicks. We probably were, but it was not nice to have it rubbed in our faces. He gave us a vision of what he thought he could do with Milbank. He may as well have been talking about launching the space shuttle: this was North Dakota, not New York City.

When we walked out of that meeting, I told Linda, "Well, that's the end of that contract." I was exactly right. Within a matter of months good old Kermit (That was the great man's name.) had reduced the staff of Milbank from over 475 people to, I believe, around 140.

Those were the days when computers were first coming in, when companies thought they could just get rid of people and use computers for everything. Of course, Milbank was overstaffed, but not that much. Good old Kermit totally blew away the infrastructure of that excellent organization. Then the underwriting procedures and what and how the company insured things went in a totally unworkable direction. One of the big problems Royal Milbank had after its new direction was in place was they were now convinced that buildings had to be insured for amounts that were far greater than the cost of putting them up. Hell, North Dakota was in the middle of a recession--building contractors were working for a fraction of what they were in New York City, but I guess nobody told the great Royal this! Furthermore, they saw us agents as nothing but stupid Neanderthals and would not believe that they were wrong on their cost estimators. The only way we could keep business on the books and prices in line was by saying farm buildings were smaller than they actually were so the cost estimates would come out. I called Glenn Watson, my field man at the time, who was a good friend as well, and told him I had just witnessed a miracle. He asked what it was. I told him I had just seen a 100-foot-long machine shed shrink to 80 feet right before my eyes. As long as we had the correct "real" replacement cost, I knew the claims would be paid anyway. Just like in the military, they had the Honor System. Right: they had the honor; we had the system. Before the great Royal got done with Milbank and finally sold it, they had reduced a statewide book of premium from $16,000,000 to less than $5,000,000. To this day I cannot figure out why they ever bought the company in the first place if they were just going to kill it.

One of Kermit's other visions was that Royal Milbank could write any account etc. It just so happened that

Casey and I had an excellent "in" on a huge commercial account which was extremely well-financed, well-managed and had been in business for several generations. Since their old agent was retiring, they were looking for a new one. Fortunately, we were good friends with one of their best managers; it was a perfect setup. We were in the right place at the right time with what we had been led to believe was the right company. Excitedly we called Royal Milbank and talked to our commercial underwriter. After listening to Kermit's speech, we were confident that Royal could write anything, right? Being young and naïve, I still believed that when people like that give speeches, they are actually telling the truth. To our surprise, our commercial underwriter was very pessimistic, saying he didn't think it sounded too good. But this was such a great account! I thought that if we went to all the various locations, got apps and pictures, and took the account in person to the underwriter, then maybe he would see what an outstanding piece of business this was and write it. After all, the great Kermit had said Royal wrote oil tankers on the high seas! So off Casey and I went to do the deal. We visited all the various offices of this client, took pictures, filled out apps, and drove the 400 miles to Milbank to present our account to the great Oz.

What a disappointment--they would hardly give us the time of day! At first, I did not think the underwriter was even going to grant us an interview. We were like Dorothy and Toto, and it soon became very clear we were not in Kansas anymore either. After a cursory glance at the deal, the underwriter simply said, "We are not interested in looking at accounts such as this at this time." With those few words he blew off a $250,000 premium outstanding account. Folks, this was in 1983. This was from a company we had been told insured super tankers on the high seas. What a crock of BS! We left.

Now I know I should have taken this super account to a competitor and tried to see to it that he got it, as long as I was paid a finder's fee. I was in such a good position to get the account that this angle probably would have worked. At least I would have gotten something out of the deal. But back then we just gave up and let the deal die. What a shame.

Within a couple of years, we just got rid of the contract with Royal Milbank. I had bought a high-priced, junk agency just to get this wonderful contract, and it was now worthless. Many years later, in 1995, I would buy two other agencies that had somehow managed to keep doing business with Royal Milbank. I was leery of doing business with them again, but reasoned that the two books must be perfect if they had kept them. In this I was right: both books were as clean as the wind-driven snow. By then the Royal Milbank book of business had been bought out by State Auto; however, some of the old Royal-educated underwriters were still there for a few years. Although State Auto was trying, and has successfully rehabilitated the book of business, these old underwriters were still hard to do business with. I told my field man the last insured some of these underwriters would take an app on died on the cross, referring to them as Milbank's "Royal Hangover." Luckily, these old 'Royal' people have been largely replaced, and we are now doing tons of business with Milbank State Auto. They are one again a great company.

- **When two insurance companies merge, you have at best a 50/50 chance it will benefit you.**

- **All of the BS you hear from company executives is not necessarily going to work out.**

• Just because you have a good account to market, do not expect a company to see it that way; consider taking it to a competitor and selling it for a finder's fee.

• CHAPTER FOUR •

IF YOU REMEMBER NOTHING ELSE, REMEMBER THIS:
Losing and Gaining Markets

In those years of '83 and '84, even though I was making many mistakes, the agency was selling enough new premium to offset lots of our financial problems. I was naively thinking that with all the new sales, things would be OK. It took a crash in the price of wheat to show me just how upside down I was. Although now we write a substantial book of commercial insurance and a good number of personal lines, Western Agency, Inc., at that time was focused primarily on farm insurance. Therefore, when the price of wheat totally tanked in 1985, even though a bumper crop was in the fields, hail insurance sales were virtually nil because of the low value of the crop. Not getting the hail sales we were expecting caused the cash shortage at Western Agency, Inc., to accelerate and worsen. I continued to cut expenses and increase production, but I was beginning to learn that you can trim expenses all you want and increase production a bunch, but if you are overpaying agents and staff, you are still going to get in trouble. However, as most people do when faced with bad news and the prospect of getting into bigger money difficulty, I kept thinking things would be OK. Little did I know that the only thing that was OK was my marriage to Linda. At least in that department I was living in pure bliss.

So, in addition to overspending my store, this problem of losing our hail insurance market was rearing its ugly head. I had always sold quite a bit of hail coverage. Now, due to the low price of wheat and low sales, I saw $50,000 of commission income that I was desperately counting on simply not happen. What did I do about it? Did I drastically cut expenses, get rid of unneeded payroll? No, other than the band-aid fix of cutting my agents' commission a little bit, I did nothing. Like a fool I went to the bank and borrowed $50,000 at sky-high interest rates. To make things even worse, the next year, 1986, we went into four years of drought. Since people do not buy much hail insurance in drought conditions, in 1986 I was short another $50,000. What did I do but borrow yet another $50,000 without cutting expenses any appreciable amount. When I look back on these years, it is clear to me that what I was doing was insane, but at the time I was totally ignorant of the peril I was placing my young company in.

If you remember nothing else from reading this book, remember this: when you lose income--be it a market, a commission cut, whatever it is--you absolutely must either get equal income back or cut expenses immediately. Furthermore, you must have a plan on how you intend to do it. The plan has to be workable, realistic, and achievable. The only time it makes sense to borrow money in this situation is if you really, truly have a way figured out to replace the income, and soon. Do not forget that if you have to borrow $100,000, it will have to be paid off in profit dollars. In other words, to pay off the debt, you will have to generate a profit. By the time you pay the loan back and pay interest on it, you may have to make $125,000 to do it. The time to solve the problem and plan how to recover the lost profit is before you trot down and get the loan. Borrowing money is like the Chinese Proverb: "Be careful what you wish for, as you may just get it." My trying to borrow my way out of trouble was the absolute worst way to solve my dilemma. All I was doing was setting the stage for a major financial disaster. When I look back on those times, I wish I could have gotten my hands on a book like this that would have told me what to do. Those crazy financial times and the lack of having anywhere to go to get advice on how to pull the agency back together was one of the major reasons I felt writing this book was so important.

- **Losing a market can quickly impact your bottom line.**

- **Borrowing money will not fix a problem; only fixing the problem will fix the problem.**

- **You have to pay loans off with profit dollars.**

MOVING MY CHEESE:
Getting into Multi-Peril Crop Insurance

Since the agency was so chronically cash-short, finally, in early 1986, I tried to cut my agents' commissions from the ridiculous 75% to a more livable figure. I sat them down and made a big effort to demonstrate how the company could not continue if we did not control our expenses. I showed them how the companies had been cutting commissions, and how the margin of the agency had gotten much thinner because of this. I told them we could sell twice as much premium and the agency still could not survive if I continued to pay 75% of the commission to the agents. The new commission schedule I gave them was 50% on new business and 35% on renewal on casualty lines. On crop insurance my new commission schedule was 65%. These commissions were still ridiculously high. I explained that we were rapidly running out of credit at the bank, how I had to go and borrow $32,000 at the bank Monday morning to keep the store afloat. I told them that since the Midwest buyout we had made payments of $198,000 and still owed

$87,000 on a purchase price of $110,000. I tried to show them that high interest and our lopsided cost of production were killing the store. I reminded them that Linda had worked for several years in the office now for free. Did it work? Of course not; it went over like a lead balloon. But it taught me a major lesson: you can always give raises, but do not ever try to take one away. You will lose the person in virtually all cases. Do not ever expect your staff to understand that the company is in trouble. They will only see the car you drive, the freedoms they perceive you to have. They will always see you as the owner. They will not, cannot understand why their wages have to be cut. Do not expect them to.

Instinctively, I knew that when my hail insurance market went away, I had to find a way to replace that lost premium. The book Who Moved My Cheese? by Spencer Johnson deals with this very problem: too bad it had not been written when I needed it. One market that was a natural to replace our hail insurance market was multiperil crop insurance. The government had released this product to the private sector in 1981 so that agents like me could sell it. Up to 1985 my staff and I had only been making a halfhearted attempt to market multi-peril crop insurance. Now, in 1985 and 1986, I really kicked my sales efforts on this product into high gear.

Even though I knew little or nothing about multiperil crop insurance, I got out there and really started selling it. I was worried about selling a product I knew little about, but I reasoned that if I immersed myself in this type of insurance, the knowledge would come. I was right. In short order I was an absolute expert on the multi-peril crop insurance product. It would become one of my greatest survival tools. Even though I could not afford it, I also shelled out $3,000 for a little old computer called the Panasonic Senior Partner. By today's standards it was a big heavy piece of junk. But in those days it was considered "portable," and it was cutting-edge technology. Although all it had in it was a rudimentary rating system, it mesmerized my clients. I set it up in restaurants, bars, machine sheds, farm homes: wherever someone would give me the time. I really started pushing some premium, even at the then-low prices of multi-peril crop insurance. It was premium and I reasoned when the prices of grain went up, so would the premium on this product. In other words, I knew eventually I would have a winner. I was like the little poor kid who was an incurable optimist. This little kid kept asking for a pony on his birthday, yet all he was given was a pile of horse manure. Just like him I was happy as hell and kept digging and digging in the horse manure. Like him I figured with all that horse manure there had to be a pony in there somewhere.

The problem was that I could not get my agents to sell multi-peril crop insurance. They were on commission and did not think there was enough premium in the product to justify "wasting" their time trying to learn about it and sell it. Wasting their time? The agency was dying for lack of any real new production, and they said they would be wasting their time? What they meant was they did not want to do the work of learning a new product. Since my management voice was still but a whisper, I was not yet getting my idea across that the product would be the salvation of our store and for them to get a move on. I can tell you this: these days if I want a product pushed or sold, you can ask any of my staff, and they will tell you they have no doubt what it is I want sold at any given time. In 1985, '86, and '87, however, I just could not get my sales staff to go out and push what needed to be pushed.

By 1986 I had several hundred farms insured. Even then that was probably more than just about any other agent in the state. In prior years we were experiencing lots of vertical growth from these farmers purchasing more equipment. After the price of grain collapsed in 1985, though, due to the extreme shortage of cash out in the country, the farmers stopped buying anything that was simply not essential; so, at least in this section of premium, the vertical growth came to a stop. Even insuring the number of farms I did, I only insured two new farm tractors during a four-year period in the middle 1980s. Not only that, but also, as the existing equipment the farmers owned became older and worth less money, we were out there lowering values of farm blanket coverage and dropping premium still more. Of course, we were doing the right thing for our clients, but it was killing us. Just holding our premium the same as it had been in the previous year was becoming a challenge. Luckily, premiums in the farm insurance sector had not been going down as they had in the great soft market that hit all other lines of insurance in those years. Probably due to its specialized nature, premiums in the farm market remained relatively stable and did not drop. Thank God, because if premiums had gone down in the farm markets like it did in commercial lines, the agency probably would not have made it. The only good viable new premium growth I could see available was multi-peril crop insurance, and I had a staff of agents who did not want to push it--I should have fired the whole bunch right there!

Linda and I had been going to PIA conventions off and on over the past couple of years; and since the PIA convention was in Medora that year, we decided to take a couple of days off and attend. Little did I know that this convention was to do me the most good of any I had yet attended. At the convention we went to the usual meetings and listed to the usual speakers. In those days Linda and I did not know too many people other than the field reps, adjustors, and various other company people. The last night of the convention after the big banquet, there were a few kegs of beer opened, a band was playing, and everyone was fairly relaxed. As the night wore on Linda went back to the room, and I found myself sitting with a guy from Fargo whom I had just met. We were talking about the insurance business, and it turned out that he had a very large store; actually, later I found out he had the largest agency in the state. We got to discussing agents and how much they should produce in new premium per year. At that time I was happy to get one to produce $25,000, but I did not say that; instead I asked him what he thought. He looked at me and said, "If they do not produce at least $100,000 in new premium a year, get the hell rid of them. Even a bad agent should be able to do $100,000." We had both had quite a few Coors Lights. I could tell he was telling the truth, however, and my sales goals went up a whole bunch, right then and there. Meeting Harry Hayer was the best thing that came out of that convention. He opened my eyes to how much production I could and should expect from agents.

The year of 1986 was really to be a pressure cooker. The agency was in serious money trouble, I was still overstaffed and overpaying the staff I had, and I was neglecting the one person, Casey, whom I should have been trying to save. In addition, I had told him what Harry Hayer had said about how much an agent should produce, and he had taken it to mean I thought he was not doing a good enough job. I did not mean that at all: all I was telling him was we had to raise our sights and go for bigger goals. I was beginning to see the vision, and he just thought I was being too hard on him. Also, Casey wanted to be a commercial insurance agent; and after the disaster with Royal Milbank, he realized I did not have any good commercial companies. I am sure he reasoned that he would have a tough time being a commercial agent with my weak stable of commercial companies. In this he was exactly correct. The final result was Casey quit and went to work for another agency in town. It was a crushing blow to me, and to this day I am disgusted that I ever let that happen. Furthermore, I had always told him if he ever wanted his investment back, I would return it to him, plus interest. That is what he wanted, so I went to the bank and got him his money, around $18,000 as I recall. Losing Casey really hurt: I lost my best supporter, I lost my commercial insurance agent, and having to borrow the $18,000 to pay him off made my tight financial situation nearly intolerable. The day he left was a sad one indeed for me. In that year Linda was about all that kept me sane.

- **If you lose a market, immediately look for a new one.**

- **If you cut wages you will lose staff.**

- **Networking with successful agents can give you a whole new perspective on the business.**

- **In tough times lay off two weak employees, if necessary, if it allows you to keep one strong one.**

MANAGEMENT 101:
Learning the Ropes

At this time I was also going to management schools, reading books on agency management, and doing everything I could to make my shop perform better. I was thinking if I could just pay people more, they would want to work harder and somehow the store would do better. Again, I was painfully wrong. Also, I was still paying way too much commission, and just keeping the books straight on the commission salespeople was in itself almost a full-time job for one secretary. In addition, the salesman who had come with the purchase of Midwest Insurance was one of those folks who always thought he should get credit for every account. Commission does that to people. No matter whom we wrote up, this guy would try and say he had brought the account into the office. It got to the point every month when I figured out commission statements I knew it would be a battle. More on this later, but suffice it to say I do not pay commission anymore. Now all of my employees and salespeople are salaried. Guess what? It works great!

It was due to this problem of more than one salesperson claiming accounts that I no longer have any salespeople on commission. All of them are now on a salary, and we track the size of their book of business. Of course, if the book of business grows, we owe the individual a raise. If it does not, we do not. In addition, if the salesperson is doing other work not related to sales, which they often have to do, I make sure they are compensated for it. Also, by being on a salary, the salesperson is not reluctant to sell a product that "does not produce enough premium," like my situation in the middle 1980s with multi-peril crop insurance. Furthermore, by having the salespeople on salary, they are not nearly so protective of each and every sale. What I do is if a salesperson helps one of the other guys put a deal together, I give them both credit for it. Why not? The issue is for the account to be sold, is it not? I do not care if I have three people working on a given deal. I want the account sold. Moreover, if I feel a salesperson has done a particularly excellent job, occasionally I bonus out a particular agent or situation. Agents who are on salary and not commission know from month to month how much they are going to make, so they can keep their own finances in order. It really helps keep your sales staff solid. I know you can get in many arguments on this issue; but after escaping from the mess I had in the 1980s with commission and now with all my sales staff on salary, I can tell you salary is better, and I have about zero turnover on sales staff while still maintaining excellent sales growth. Try it: it works.

While we are on this little sidetrack about salary vs. commission, there is another benefit. What about if a product gets hot, and you are selling it like crazy, not because of how great a sales organization you have but just because of the situation? What if the price of a product goes way up just because of the economic situation? I have seen this happen many times. A good example is how the price of both commercial and personal insurance is going way up right now. Also, a few years ago we had a big price increase in multi-peril crop insurance. In both cases there is substantially more premium being written, but it is not due to any big effort or expertise on the part of your sales staff. Yet if you have them on commission, lots of the extra earnings that the agency can use to get solvent, get things paid off, and thus survive in the years when things are not so great goes to the sales staff. They buy a few new cars or whatever, and the agency does not get more solvent and solid.

However, back in 1986 and '87, after my cutting their commissions and Casey's leaving, pretty soon my other two salespeople left the agency. One went off to become a minister, and the other one went to work for his family. It became obvious that the one who had gone to work for his family had been "borrowing" money from some of his clients. A few months after he was gone, one of his clients came in and wanted to know why his life insurance policy was in danger of canceling. I checked and found out it was because there was no money in it. He said he had given my agent a check for $3,000 or some such a figure. I called the ex-agent, and he and I had a little chat. Yes, the agent had taken the money; he would try to pay me back. Meanwhile, I cut a check for the amount to get the client's policy cranked back up. Luckily, the client let it go and did not sue the agency. I never went after the agent, either. What was I going to do, anyway--call all this turkey's clients, tell them he was a crook, and lose some more business? No, I just hoped it was the only one. It turned out to be the only one that ever showed up. After 15 years I still worry about it. If it ever happens again, I do not know if I would handle it any differently.

When these two left I am sure they felt I would panic over losing their stellar sales ability. They probably thought it would be only a matter of time until I went broke anyway. You know how I really felt? Huge relief! I had decided by then I absolutely had to cut costs and expenses, and I was finally starting to stand up for myself and learn how to be a manager. More changes were soon to come. I had found part of my management voice. Though louder than a whisper, it still had a long way to go.

Also about this time I made the first of a series of other erors that would ultimately come within a hair of costing me the store. At the end of 1986 we had lots of customers' money in our checking account. Rather, it was in a Money Market Account, earning good interest. The money was from hail insurance premiums that had been paid and did not need to be sent to the companies until later in the year. The problem was--remember, all those years ago, when my accountant asked me when I wanted my financial year to end? And when I did not know, he suggested, "Why not use October 31 since I'm not busy then?" Well, I had taken his advice, and that had been the Western Agency, Inc., year end ever since. So there I was on October 31, 1987, with $140,000 of customers' money in my account, earning interest: nice.

But wait, did I also tell you I was on a cash accounting system? You know, the kind where any money in your account is "your" money, even if it is not really "your" money?

There I sat, fat, dumb, and happy, with this $140,000 of my customers' money earning me interest, thinking things were going really good. My secretary even asked me if I wanted to have all that money in my account at year end. I said not to worry about it. So we left it there, earning interest, making us money until I had to pay it to the companies on the due date, 12/1/87. We made a few hundred dollars' extra interest, and things were fine until tax time. Then they came to a quick head. I wound up paying around $10,000 in extra taxes because I had that extra "income" in my account at the wrong time. It was a very bitter pill to swallow. I should have done less partying and more studying for Accounting 101 when I was a college student. When they were talking about this kind of stuff, I think I was having way too much fun to pay attention. This $10,000 in extra taxes really hit me hard at a time I could ill afford it. Furthermore, it set the chain of events moving that would literally take me to the brink of having to sell the store.

- **Paying agents commission creates dissension on your staff**

- **Paying agents wages instead of commission makes the "that's-MY-account" problem go away.**

- **Paying agents wages instead of commission provides steady paychecks and helps retain agents.**

- **Paying agents wages instead of commission makes an agency solvent faster in good times.**

- Paying agents wages instead of commission is a better way to go--any questions?

- If you are on a cash accounting system, make sure at year end that the money in your checkbook is really your money.

- Too much fun in college can have bad consequences later.

YOU WILL WIN NO WARS WITH WEAK SOLDIERS:
Developing New Staff

Meanwhile, in 1986 while I was struggling to keep the store afloat, I was making a few good decisions. I hired a wonderful young man named Marlen Lenton, who would assume a pivotal role in the agency for many years. How this happened was I had insured his parents almost from the time I started in the business. One day out at their farm, while I was doing some work on their policies, I asked what Marlen was going to do for a career. Since he was about to graduate from high school, I suggested he look into insurance. I should probably say that Marlen is confined to a wheelchair and has been since the age of nine. After the conversation I thought little about it, going on my merry way. Then a few years later, in the fall of 1986 I got a phone call: "Chuck, this is Marlen." We exchanged pleasantries, and then in the totally honest and direct way he has, Marlen said, "I took a real estate and insurance curriculum in college, and now I've graduated and need a job." I was flabbergasted. I really could not afford to hire someone at this time, yet I knew I could use some more staff. How could I say no to such a request, anyway? We agreed that Marlen would stop by the office at 10 a.m. the next day.

Keep in mind that it was late October in North Dakota, and it was cold. Also, I had no handicapped access to my little office at 1728 Burdick Expressway East. I suppose it was around 10:15 a.m. when I remembered Marlen was supposed to be there at 10. I looked outside; and there he was, in his wheelchair, sitting outside the door, in the cold, waiting for someone to help him in. I could not believe his determination; even after all of these years, I still cannot believe the determination of this man. It has been a pleasure and an inspiration to work with him, and everyone on my staff feels the same way. Marlen was to work with us for many years. We only lost him because he became further disabled by a massive brain hemorrhage years later.

Marlen was what I call the first of "my new employees." What I mean is that from the time I hired Marlen, I tried to hire people whom I could get along with, who would do what I wanted done, who would not argue with me about how to do things, and who wanted to learn the insurance business. It was about time after 13 years in the business--I was finally starting to realize that I did know how in the hell to sell insurance! All I needed was a staff that would work with me to help me multiply my time. I realized if I could put the right staff together, we would build a big agency.

As I said before, also early in 1987 one of my full-time agents came to me and told me he was quitting to go to work for his family's business. This was good news to me as he was drinking too much and not making it in the insurance business. I could see that this would help me cut expenses. Perhaps if the store had been bigger and I could have given him more leads, it would have worked out; but at the time each of us was digging out their own leads, and he was starving to death, even on the 75%-of-new-business commission. If I had known then what

I know now, I would have eased him out of the insurance business earlier. But we had been to high school together; he was a friend of mine. At the time I remember feeling glad his family would now be taking care of him, not me. It seems that in those years many times I tried to keep people around who should have been in another career. Also, in those years I still was finding my management voice. And it was still not much more than a squeak.

The year 1987 continued to be a tough time financially for the store. When I had bought out that other agency in Minot in the spring of 1982, I had given their full-time agent 10% ownership in Western Agency, Inc.; that was about to jump up and bite me. When he left to become a minister, naturally he wanted me to buy him out. If one of the criteria for being a good minister is getting the congregation to support the church, this guy must be one of the best! How he talked me into giving him the amount I did for that little book of business he had is beyond me, but once again I coughed up. Nevertheless, I was just glad he was leaving, and I knew his departure would cut my expenses. More than anything, I was glad I would not have to fight over who was really the agent on every new account we sold. Whatever: it was good he was gone. Even with the buyout I was better off. I had now cut my expenses substantially since all three of my full-time salesmen were history.

So there I was in late 1987, still in bad money trouble. However, I had, without really knowing it at the time, begun the recovery process. I had substantially cut costs, largely keeping the book of business together, thus keeping my income stream intact. The remaining problem was that the office was running horribly. It just seemed as if I was getting nothing done: orders I was giving my two secretaries were not getting carried out; and I was going home every day angry, upset, and frustrated. In retrospect, I suppose both of those ladies resented the two agents' leaving. I suppose they resented the store's being in money trouble and figured it was my fault. In that they were absolutely correct. It was my lack of will in not setting things straight sooner that had the store in the shape it was in. It was my lack of will that left commissions, wages, and expenses too high for too long. When I look back over the years, so many times it has been lack of will on my part that let a situation get out of hand. As a manager, when you find you have a problem, for God's sake fix it--I can guarantee you it will not fix itself! A final thought on this is: do not expect your staff to fix the agency's problems, either. It is not up to them, and they do not know how to do it, anyway. By and large, employees will do what they are told and shown what to do. They will not create a company and show you how to run it. So many of us have this romantic little idea that "We shall just go into business, and we shall all work together, solving all of our problems and living happily ever after." Sorry: you started the business, you are in charge, and the business will win or lose mostly on the decisions you make and the systems you put in place. Deal with it. Do not expect the staff to solve your problems.

Another problem with the remaining staff members was that one of them was a secretary I had inherited from the agency I had purchased in 1982. At her former agency she had done pretty much what she wanted. However, that was not working in my store at all. This wonderful lady was very talkative, loving to tell everyone every detail about her family and how the kids were doing and yadda, yadda, yadda. I really do not mind a relaxed office setting that allows some chitchat, but she would take up a huge amount of time with her constant chatter. As a manager you must remember that when an employee is talking to another, neither of them can get much of anything done. You are losing not only the productivity of the one talking but also that of all the listeners. In addition, while the talking is going on, the odds on having an Errors and Omissions loss go up dramatically. But have you ever known anyone who wanted to give you back the wages lost while they were having a good old gab session? Or pay the deductible on an E&O loss? Not.

The second woman began coming to work late repeatedly, and it seemed she really thought that the only reason Western Agency, Inc., was even alive at all was because of her vast expertise. Many years later I purchased an agency where she was employed. Needless to say, she was not offered a position again with Western Agency, Inc. A funny sequel occurred several years after that, when we were looking for another CSR and ran a blind ad in the local paper saying a major farm agency was looking for a full-time Customer Service Rep. This was the job this same lady had held, and sure enough, she sent in her resume. On this resume she said she had worked for several agencies in town, helping a large local agency "achieve several major awards." It totally broke me up! I couldn't decide if she was "reminding" me of what a great CSR she was or if she was not even sharp enough to realize who was running the Help Wanted ad. However, to continue the story, back in 1987, we were just getting to the point that all the office chitchat sessions were seriously cutting into our productivity. Since I was finally waking up to this fact and trying to become manager of my own store, I began to think it was time for both of these women to go. What was making me hesitant to fire them was that my management voice, now louder than a squeak, was still far from a roar.

Two factors at last forced me to saddle up and head on down the trail to becoming an agency manager. The first was that my accountant, Iver Eliason, was literally screaming at me to cut expenses even more and get profitable. He sat me down in the fall of 1987 and told me that I either had to cut expenses further or face going under. The second factor was my continuing dissatisfaction with those two secretaries. I was going home and complaining to Linda constantly, and it was in the course of one of these bitching sessions that she had finally had enough. She turned to me and said, "Why don't you just fire those two ------'s and I will go back to work for you?" It was as if a very bright light had been turned on.

When Linda had worked in the office full-time from 1982 until 1985, we had gotten along extremely well together. In 1985 she went home to be a full-time mom for the kids. They were now about ready to graduate from high school, however, and we both felt Linda's returning to the agency for a short time would not hurt anything. We both knew it was the right thing to do. So Monday morning, when the chatty woman got to the office, I told her I simply could not afford to keep her and she was laid off as of then. There had been some bad weather over the weekend, and the second woman breezily called in to say she had been snowed in and could not come to work until the next day. Her increasing absenteeism and tardiness had been irritating me, but not this time. When she showed up at the office Tuesday morning, I laid her off before she could hang up her coat. I gave them each a couple of weeks' severance pay. Even after all these years, I can still feel the relief of getting rid of them: the pressure of their presence was instantly gone. For the first time in years I was back in control of the store; finally I was finding my management voice, and it was getting loud.

We now had none of the leftover staff from the purchase of the other agency. Actually, other than Linda and Marlen, I had no one working for me. From buying quite a few other insurance agencies over the years I have found that it can be very difficult to keep the existing staff. I have gotten to the point where I am very specific in explaining to the staff of a purchased agency what their new jobs and positions will be with my store. I tell them what I expect, and we follow up to ensure that they comply. You see, the cultures of another store and yours are likely to be different. There is probably a reason we purchased them: probably it was bad management. Part of bad management is not getting rid of bad staff. I am not saying here that we just fire everyone in the agencies we purchase because we do not, but we surely do make it clear what we expect of everyone. You know what? It works.

- **If good employees show up on your doorstep, hire them, even if you do not know if you can afford them.**

- **If people leave your employ, you do not have to give them too big a dowry.**

- **Do not expect your staff to solve your problems.**

- **Chatty Cathy has to go.**

- **As a rule, being chronically late for work is fatal to employment at Western Agency, Inc.**

- **If you have to fire your entire staff to get back on track, do it. What have you got to lose? If you do not get back on track, you are going to lose the agency, anyway.**

SEPARATING THE WHEAT FROM THE STAFF

I hope it does not seem that I had it in for this staff, and I hope it does not seem as if I am saying they were bad people. They were and are not. In fact, I was able to get the lady who was always talking with the other employees a job with one of the banks in town only a few days after I had laid her off. I was in there seeing my loan officer, and he said the bank was desperately trying to find someone who could answer the phones correctly and meet the customers. I told him I knew just the person, and they hired her. She still works for them to this day. I do not think she ever knew who got her the job, and I do not care. She is a very nice lady. She just was not the person I needed for the job at the time. I guess that best describes all of them. I could not let them cost me a company I had worked 12 years to put together. Furthermore, for what they were doing they were overpaid. I now pay wages commensurate with the work being done.

This brings up a point that seems to plague many new businesses. It seems that we who start these operations often think you go into business and hire a staff, and they "run the store" or "do their jobs" or whatever it is that employees do. Nothing could be further from the truth. You have to manage these people, telling them what to do and how to do it, give them the tools to accomplish their missions, and tell them what is expected of them. You must check to see what they are doing. In other words, validate the money you are investing in them. It is not up to these people to invent how to do their jobs. That is your task. If you do not have an employee manual, get one. A basic template is available from Virginia Bates, who does excellent work on this type of thing and has a manual on a disk. You can purchase the disk and insert your own information to make a manual for your employees to follow. I guess my point here is it is your job as manager to get these things set up. Way back in

1988 I simply did not know this. I think I probably was just like many people who find themselves managing a company. I had a whole bunch to learn, but I was so busy running the store that I could not see it at the time.

Another big problem that plagued me throughout the 1980s was that when I interviewed people for positions, if I liked them I would put them to work. I made many bad hires with this method. Bad hires cost your company money, they are disruptive to the rest of your staff, and they confuse your clients. I now do a personality test on everyone I hire to try and determine if the person even has an aptitude for the insurance business. The test I use is from Personnel Survey and Research Group out of Princeton, New Jersey. I suppose I most likely heard of them at some convention, or in some seminar I attended, or in some book I read. Late in 1989 I took their test myself; I wanted to see if it came back and described the real me. I was stunned--it hit the nail right on the head, showing up a couple of things even my wife did not know! One was that I have a pretty short fuse, something I keep hidden so well that most people would describe me as very mellow. The test showed otherwise; it was absolutely correct. The second thing has to do with my being known as a detail person. Anyone acquainted with me will say Chuck is a detail kind of guy, yet, in my heart of hearts, I absolutely loathe details. I want to see the big picture and leave the details to someone else. I have to deal with details to stay alive, but it is not what I want to do. The test showed this loud and clear. These tests cost me $150 each. I just hired two new people at Western Agency, Inc., and before hiring anyone, I tested 12 people at a cost of $1,800. Maybe you think this is a bunch of money just to hire a couple of CSRs; I vehemently disagree. Since starting to use this test on all my prospective employees, I have made far fewer bad hires in the past 13 years. Just think about it. What if you train a person for a couple of years, struggling to make a silk purse out of a sow's ear? Guess what--this individual is going to leave anyway! You have just wasted a couple of years' salary, angered and confused your clients and staff, and still you are starting over. Testing works: try it.

One other little benefit of testing all of your employees is that you can match them up to your personality. After getting rid of my entire original staff by late 1988, I decided that, by and large, the employees were going to have to get along with me, not the other way around. By using testing I was able to hire people who would not have any trouble getting along with me. An aside: I have been told that, to keep out of trouble with the equal employment people, if you are going to test anyone, you must test everyone. Also, you must tell new people that a condition of their being hired is that they must take the test and show an aptitude for the job for which they are applying. Gee what a concept.

Getting rid of the entire staff, except for him, was, of course, a huge shock to Marlen. After the last secretary had gone and the two of us sat alone in the office that cold, blizzardy North Dakota day, he said with tears in his eyes, "Chuck, what are we going to do? There's only the two of us left." I assured him I had started the agency alone, I had run it alone, and, by God, if I had to I would do it again. And I meant it. My management voice was becoming quite audible. I cannot believe that I was not more scared. Maybe I was reassured by the prospect of having Linda back in the office with her confidence that all would be OK. Maybe it was the fact that she and I owned 100% of our company again. Whatever the reason, I felt as if I could take on the world. It was a pivotal time for me and for the store. For the first time in years I once again actually owned Western Agency, Inc. Now the work was really going to start, but things would be better because as the TV evangelists say..."My clouded fog of ignorance was being replaced by the shining light of knowledge."

• Again, do not expect your employees to fix your management problems.

• Bad employees are not bad people; they are just people who have made bad career choices.

• Test your staff.

• Hire people who get along with you, not the other way around—it is your store, is it not?

• Be clear on what it is each person on your staff is supposed to do. Have an employee manual. If you do not now have one, get one. Use mine and put your name on it. But get one.

PAYING THE PIPER:
Getting Claims Paid

In spite of the trauma it causes, I think all of us should be very nearly broke at least once in our lives. It is then that we really find out how to manage our money. I know living through those tough years was certainly a tremendous education for Linda and me. We had trimmed the staff costs down, and now, in our search for still more places to trim, we turned our attention to office supplies. Up to this time we had been buying all of our supplies from a local office supply store--duh! I so distinctly remember the first time I went into a Sam's Club. My God--they had supplies for pennies on the dollar compared to prices I had been paying! When you realize that it takes thousands of dollars of premium to generate a net dollar of commission and you realize how much more you pay for things at the local office supply store, you will be headed for a Staples or Office Max very quickly. In those days we had no Staples, Office Max, or Sam's Club in our town, so I would drive 300 miles one way to Fargo to go to Sam's. However, it was well worth it since the first year we started buying our supplies from the discount supply store we saved over $5,000 net. Saving that much money was like writing a $200,000 account. Although it seems like very little now, back then it was a huge amount of money. Furthermore, those savings multiplied over a period of years are enough to buy a few new cars, are they not? Even when we thought we were being efficient and careful with our spending in those early years, we were hemorrhaging cash. At last we were finally starting to learn about getting costs in line. I guess there is a silver lining to every cloud. Even now we consider cost containment and check prices before spending money.

Early in 1988 I had, other than Marlen and a lady I had just hired, gotten rid of my entire staff. Our expenses were in line, we were beginning to develop a good management style, and after being in business 12 years, we were beginning to learn how to run the agency. Linda had taken over the bookkeeping functions, and I was working up to 80 hours per week, very much as I had when I first started the store. We were both determined to get the agency back on track, but my past financial sins were really ganging up on me. Although the store was doing far better, we were very cash-short. Not only that, even though we were putting in a ton of hours, we knew we were losing money every day due to my over-expensing the store in prior years. One of the hardest things about being in business for yourself is that sometimes it can be difficult to work many hours for months on end, knowing the whole time you are losing money.

I distinctly remember having a conversation with some other businesspeople one day when one of them brought up net income. I wondered to myself if I would ever be solvent enough to actually have one. Nevertheless, the important thing was we had finally done what was necessary to get our financial house in order. The ship was righting itself. Now I needed to convince my banker to see it that way.

In 1988 the major thing that was wrong with my farm insurance market was that we were in the middle of the biggest drought in North Dakota history. Crops were simply burning up and not growing. Making it even worse, the price per bushel of grain was simply horrible. The farmers were really suffering; and since I was a farm insurance agent, I was right in there with them. The only good news about the drought was I was selling a ton of multi-peril crop insurance; of course, the farmers were collecting literally millions of claim dollars on the drought coverage in their policies, which were helping keep them going. I appreciated the business, and they surely appreciated the claim checks I was bringing them. I was trying to be everywhere at once: getting the claims paid, going out with the adjustors to keep the claims proceeding smoothly, keeping the store moving forward. I am really proud of the job we did in those years. I remember hearing a complaint from one of my staff about all the extra work we were doing, and I distinctly remember responding, "We can put all this extra claim cost down to prepaid advertising expense." I was convinced all the good work we were doing would come back to help us with new sales in years ahead. As things turned out that is exactly what occurred. Word was getting out in the Minot area that if you wanted your multi-peril crop insurance taken care of properly, you would do business with Western Agency, Inc. The farm market is like a glacier: it takes years for it to start moving your way. But once it does, it is very slow, very sure, and very steady. We finally had that market coming our way; our farm and crop insurance sales continued to rise.

In those same years many of my competitors in the farm insurance market were doing an absolutely horrible job of getting their claims paid, which I was sure would help us and hurt them in the future. As time would tell, this presumption was right on target. We now cover over 500,000 acres with multi-peril crop insurance, and in our home county we insure 38% of the entire tillable acres of seeded crop. Probably the pace I was keeping up in those years was the hardest I have ever worked, yet I was probably doing the best job of my life. I was finally running the store the way it was supposed to be run. Borrowing from Dickens, I can say it was the best of times and the worst of times.

During the huge droughts of 1986, '87, '88, and '89, I learned exactly how to handle the multi-peril crop insurance product. Also, during these times Linda and I coordinated teams of adjustors to see to it that the claims got paid promptly. The dozens of losses going at any given moment were excellent training for the years ahead. In addition, we were writing enough premium by then with one company that they were trying to give our claims and problems first priority. That was when I realized it is a good idea to place sufficient volume with a carrier to make them aware of who you are.

What made it difficult in 1988 was that the crop product and the companies selling it were not yet up to speed and there were not enough knowledgeable, trained adjustors out there. I remember in the fall of 1989 as we were starting to get going on losses, the first adjustor they sent out did not know squat about what the product was or how to adequately settle a claim; I sent him home by noon. The second guy was one of those abrasive-type adjustors who can lose you an account, even if he overpays the loss; I sent him packing right in the middle of the first loss he was in the process of screwing up. Then I called Ray Schmitz, my field man for the insurance company we were using. Ray is just an excellent guy: by now we had done lots of deals together, we trusted each other, and he knew I needed to have a top-notch, competent adjustor or else. He said he had just the right one, Mark Brakel from Carrington. A fantastic fellow, Mark turned out to be Ray's son-in-law. He plowed into our losses, getting us caught up on our claims in short order. He ended up staying at our agency for over six months. We were lucky to have his help, and I still consider him one of the best adjustors I have ever had the pleasure to work with.

Having some say in the adjusting process is one of the huge powers of the independent agent and one of the very reasons we are so effective in the insurance business. By getting rid of those two poor adjustors I was providing far better service for my clients--for heaven's sake, refusing to let your client be saddled with bad adjusting is in no way being crooked or dishonest! As an agent all you are doing is seeing to it that your client is going to get a good, solid loss settlement. I am not saying here the agent should be the adjustor. I am not saying the agent should try and influence the adjustor. What I am saying is if you see your client is not being correctly served, it is up to you to do something about it. Remember, your clients are not idiots. Many times they are damn well aware if they are receiving poor settlements. They can and will hold you responsible if you let it happen. If you are an Independent Agent and you find yourself working with a poor adjustor, for God's sake send him down the road. Use this tremendous difference between you and the captive agent or the telemarketer agent to your client's advantage and yours.

While we are on the subject of adjusters: good ones

are worth their weight in gold; bad ones cannot possibly be gotten rid of soon enough. As the agency owner or manager, you must be sure you are working with a competent adjusting staff. If you find you are being forced to work with poor adjusting staff, you must find someone to right the situation for you. If you do not rectify the situation, it can and will cost you clients, especially in the crop lines. Finally, please understand me here, I do not mean you have to have adjustors who give away claims; I do not mean the adjustor has to come out to the field dressed as Santa Claus. What I am saying is you have to have a person who has the guts to make the calls, who can relate to people, and who can gain their trust. As I said before, good adjustors are worth their weight in gold: to the company, to you, and most importantly to the clients.

- **Being broke once in your life is not necessarily a bad deal.**

- **Cutting and containing costs is a work in progress; it should follow your entire career**

- **Do pay attention to the claims process.**

- **Do not tolerate poor adjustors.**

- **Doing quality work is one of the golden keys to success in business.**

- **Remember, one of the differences between the Independent Agent, direct writers, and telemarketing agents is that the Independent Agent CAN do something about poor adjusting.**

• CHAPTER FIVE •

DON'T BANK ON IT:
Moving Ahead When Your Banker Won't

During the middle of this crazy summer of 1988, an attorney friend of mine called to say he had an insurance agency for sale. I thought, why not look into it and Linda and I went up to his office to check it out. One thing led to another; though we had virtually no money, we decided to try and buy the store. Of course, the elephant in the room was our huge scarcity of cash. This small store had a very good book of business. Its owner had been Tony Swedlund, an excellent guy who had suddenly died; his widow Iris was selling the agency for the ridiculously low price of 50% of commission income. It would take $15,000 to acquire the store, lock, stock, and barrel--people, if you ever get a chance to buy a store this good, this cheap, it is better than an inheritance! Linda and I looked at each other and said, "We'll take it." The attorney said, "Well, I suppose we'll need some earnest money. Will $500 be OK?" We nodded, numbly knowing we did not have that much cash to our name. I ended up writing a cash advance MasterCard check for $500 to the attorney. We had just bought one of the best little agencies we were ever to purchase, on our Gold Card yet; now all we had to figure out was where to get the money to complete the deal. I went to the bank and told them about it. I showed them the type of book it was, how we could easily integrate it into our book, how we could not lose on the deal. Guess what: the bank thought it was a bad move. This was the first time I was to see just how damn ignorant bankers can be. If it is not bricks and mortar, then they really have a hard time visualizing the loan. I have many banker friends who are fine people;

but when they get involved in running your business, you are in big trouble.

Now I was in quite a quandary. I figured I could round up $10,000 of the money, but that still left me $5,000 short. About that time Marlen said he would like to purchase some of the store if I needed any partners. The deal we made was I sold him 20% ownership in the Swedlund Agency book of business for $5,000. I also guaranteed he would never get less than a 10% return on investment paid annually. Furthermore, if he ever wanted out, I would give him his $5,000 back. So we had our cash. We finalized the transaction, called the new store The Swedlund-Tompkins Agency, and cranked it up. The only bad thing about this was that it totally angered my banker. Rather than being glad we had been able to negotiate such a good buy, financing it ourselves, he was furious that we had not walked away from it. Too bad--faced with the same deal and the same circumstances today, I would do the exact same thing! It was the first really creative financing I had ever done and just the beginning of that kind of activity for me. Plus the little store made us money from the first day we purchased it. Over the years I don't know how many times this little agency has paid for itself, but it has been many, many times.

After we acquired the Swedlund Agency, our banker really started to drag his feet when we needed money. Here we had just found an absolute steal of an insurance agency, it was up and running and making us money every day, and he was mad. The new book of business fit right into our operation, helped us grow, gave us a new client base to expand on: and he thought it was a stupid idea. He was trying to run our business and he didn't have a clue how the Independent Agency system operated. If we had taken advice like his, not to grow by acquisition but only by writing new policies, it would have killed us. Luckily, we let our instincts lead us and made the purchase over his objections. I could never understand why this man was always so hard to deal with; it was not until years later that I found out he was big buddies with one of my greatest competitors in town. Moreover, this competing agent was a poor insurance person whom I had little time for professionally. Often I have talked when I should have listened, and I suppose I spoke poorly of this other agent from time to time when talking to my banker. Who knows? Possibly this loan officer was making things difficult for me to help his pal; if he was I shall never know. For the five years we did business with his bank, however, the guy made our lives miserable.

We sailed into 1989 running at a breakneck pace, inventing things as we were going along. I was finally finding my management voice, and I was really loving it. The pace soon picked up even more. In the spring I received a call from Anna Kerstan, a very good person who had been a CSR for a small agency we had purchased; years later I helped her get a job as a field person for one of my companies. She called that day to say that there was a fine little agency for sale in Garrison, a town 50 miles south of Minot. It was in money trouble, so the local bank had it for sale. When you are running hard you go on instinct. I drove to Garrison.

By this time I had a definite idea of what a quality store Western Agency, Inc., was becoming. I knew I was in money trouble, but I was proud of the steps we had taken to get back on track. I knew my store was poised to take off like a rocket and the plan to do it was sound. I was finally knowing and believing in my business. We had by now pushed the earnings per employee up to over $50,000, and we had a clear vision of exactly what we needed to do to run our agency and stay out of trouble. Furthermore, the necessary steps to get back on track had been taken. My problem was that, for whatever reason, my banker simply could not or would not see it. Nonetheless, I found myself in Garrison, talking to Dick Johnson and Ted Livesay about purchasing yet another agency.

Dick and Ted were both bankers who worked for the Garrison State Bank. The owner of the agency they had for sale owed the bank lots of money, and they were ready to foreclose on him. However, the bank did not want to be the bad guy in this small community. The solution was for someone to buy the store so the sale could be billed as a buyout and not a foreclosure. In retrospect I suppose they figured if I purchased the agency and failed they could foreclose on me, an outsider, without a bunch of local bad press. In this they were probably right.

The numbers they showed me on the store clearly indicated it was in trouble. Although at one time it had been the biggest agency in town, writing $1,000,000 of premium in 1976, by 1989 it was down to $400,000 of premium and was coming apart. The owner's wife was hospitalized with Alzheimer's, so running an agency was the last thing on his mind. Meanwhile, all the other agents in town were having a field day cannibalizing his book of business. The store needed help and it needed it soon. The agency had a basically solid book of business; all it needed was management and attention. The bank was willing to sell the book of business, the brick building that housed the store, all its supplies--the entire ball of wax--for $75,000: it was an absolute steal. The problem was again (Gee, what a surprise!) how in hell I was going to come up with the cash. I talked to my banker, who, without really even considering it, said no.

The only hope I had to get the deal done was convincing Dick and Ted to loan me the money. In a few days I went back to Garrison to show them the numbers on my store. I told them I knew I could handle the deal. I knew

I could save the agency and make the store prosper, I could keep the two secretaries employed, I could keep another storefront in small-town America from closing down. The bankers would not have to be the bad guys and shut down a local business. The only problem I had was I simply could not come up with any cash. They said they would think about it. A little later they called me up with the following deal: $10,000 down for the store and no other payments for one year. The $65,000 balance was to be on a loan over five years. My God, what a deal-- it was undoubtedly one of the best I was ever to get a chance to make! But I had no $10,000.

What I did was take the $10,000 out of Western Agency, Inc. It was July and I reasoned that I had enough crop commission dollars coming in to pay the $10,000 off before I had to pay companies at the end of October. With our hearts in our mouths, Linda and I did the deal. Marlen wanted to buy into it, too, so I told him he could have 15% of the store for $15,000; I would make him the same deal as before: guarantee him 10% return on investment paid annually, and if he ever wanted out, I would give him his money back. Was that a sweet deal or what? He went and borrowed the $15,000. I took that money and immediately put it right into Western Agency, Inc., to help with our critical cash shortage. Incidentally, the Garrison book of business is now far greater than its former size. One of the best books we ever bought, it continues to grow. At the time we purchased it, though, my genius banker in Minot thought I was totally crazy. It made him even madder that I had gone ahead and done yet another deal without his blessing or help. Unbeknownst to me, the noose he had around my neck was tightening.

Now things were really starting to roll. I had purchased two stores in two years; I had my payroll, my staff costs, my office supply expense--the whole package--in excellent order. The single problem I had was with only having 24 hours in each day. I was putting over 75,000 miles a year on my vehicle, and Linda and I were definitely running in the red line. One of the ways I multiplied my time was with the use of a mobile phone. Even then, and for that matter ever since the inception of Western Agency, Inc., I had a mobile phone. Since the Swedlund Agency was 20 miles east of Minot and the Rasch Agency was 50 miles south of Minot, I was doing a bunch of windshield time. I would take a stack of files when I left the office in Minot and talk to underwriters all the way to my destination and back. In those years I did literally hundreds of deals while driving between towns. If I were driving during the lunch hour, I would get a hamburger, fries, and coffee and eat on the way. I was absolutely on top of my game at that time; I have never been busier, and I really do not know if I have ever done better work. To this day I am intolerant of people who are always telling me how busy they are. They are probably busy, all right: drinking coffee and telling their buddies at the coffee house how busy they are or writing junk business that needs twice as much attention as good business. I find these people are clueless about how to manage their time. I was, too, until I had no choice but to learn how to get efficient and careful with my limited hours.

- **Plastic can be very useful at times.**

- **Bankers love loaning money on bricks and mortar more than loaning money on paper agencies.**

- **If the purchase looks good, instinct tells you it is good, and you can figure out how to do the deal, do it.**

- If you have to, it is perfectly all right to use more than one bank at a time.

- Although not smart, driving, eating, and talking to underwriters can be done simultaneously.

CREATIVE HOME BUYING 101

Next on the agenda was a better house for Linda and me. I suppose perhaps you wonder why I put this in a book about agency management but it helps tell how the bank and I parted ways. In the summer and late fall of 1989, the economy in North Dakota was really taking a beating. Houses were selling at an all-time low, the house we had was not much of a house, and I knew it was probably the perfect time to be buying a better one. It seems that my drive and instinct were accurate again. I just did not have enough sense to realize I was too broke to think the way I was thinking. Maybe I was reading too many books. It was around this time I encountered a self-help book entitled Wealth Without Risk by Charles Givins that elaborated on how to do deals with minimal finance. What else could I do? Taking a page from the Givins book, I called up my realtor buddy and told him, "I want to buy a house that is worth $120,000, but I only want to pay $80,000 for it. Furthermore, I want to find one with an assumable loan." He said he would start searching. Linda and I looked at a bunch of places and put ours up for sale. Although we only got one lonely offer on our house, we could live with it, so we closed the sale of our home. Suddenly we had 30 days to come up with a place to live.

We went through house after house without finding one that fit our tight financial parameters. Since I was determined to get a steal on a house or not buy one, and it looked as if I was out of luck, I started to search for a place to rent. We finally located something and called the moving company. Trouble was, this house was not even as good as the one we were living in at the time. The day before we were to move I could tell Linda was really tense; she tossed and turned all night, and neither of us got much sleep. Finally, at five a.m. I asked her what the problem was: she blurted out, "I'm not moving into that house!" "It's worse than the one we have now!" Although that was the last thing I wanted to hear, when Linda uses that tone of voice, the thought of arguing with her never even crosses my mind. I called my realtor buddy up to tell him we needed to find a different place to rent. He said he would call me back. Meanwhile, the movers showed up at 7:00 AM, right on time. They assured me they could leave the goods on the truck a few days if necessary while we found another place to live. My realtor buddy called me back about 10 a.m. and said he had found a house that was for sale and also available to rent. Leaving the movers at the old house busily packing up our stuff, Linda and I met the agent at 11a.m. out at the new location. The place he showed us was just perfect--we couldn't believe our good fortune! Furthermore, the rent was very affordable. I called the mover at two p.m.; he was just finishing loading the truck when I gave him the address for delivery of our goods. I know it sounds crazy, but given the way I was operating in those years, it seemed perfectly normal. How in hell Linda put up with it I shall never know.

The day after we moved in, the owner came to give us the rest of the keys and show us how everything worked. The house was a nice tri-level four-bedroom on five acres with a small barn. It was just what we needed. He told me the house had been built new in 1976 for $120,000. I asked him what he wanted for it. His answer was that the place had a $62,000 assumable 9 1/2% loan, he wanted $10,000 of walking-around money, and the realtor commission was $8,000: total price tag $80,000. Can you believe it--do I have a financial angel on my shoulder or what? I called my realtor buddy, gave him the numbers, and told him to write it up. Somehow I scraped the $18,000 together for the down payment, again with no help or approval from my bank. I had just figured out how to buy a $120,000 home for $80,000 with very little down, yet they were becoming increasingly unhappy with my moving ahead in life without their stamp of approval. We lived in that house for 10 years, then sold it for $165,000 cash--what a deal it was! Thank God we had, on still another occasion, not taken the advice of my genius banker.

- **If you are going to rent a house, probably you should get your wife's approval first.**

- **Good deals are out there, you just have to look.**

IRS vs SBA

We cruised into 1990 with things looking better. We had purchased a nice home, we had bought two nice little agencies at great prices that were making money, and Western Agency, Inc., was rolling down a sound management track. I was finally running the store the way it needed to be run. Cash flow was still terrible, though. Here I was thinking what a great job I was doing and I hadn't even started to get efficient yet. Nonetheless, I was momentarily starting to take a deep breath and relax: Then the bottom fell out.

Remember that year so long ago when the CPA asked me when I wanted my financial year to end and when

I didn't know what date to use, he suggested October 31? Remember when I ended up 1987 with a whole lot of money in my customers' trust account happily earning interest, but it cost me a bunch of extra taxes? Well, after I ended up paying a bunch of extra taxes because of this, it became readily apparent that October 31 was the absolute worst time for my financial year to end. At that time of the year, my trust account was flush with crop monies I had collected that did not need to be paid to the companies for 45 to 60 days. I could legally leave those monies in an interest-bearing account. This I did, earning some good investment income. However, after getting whacked on taxes, it became very obvious that the end of my financial year needed to be December 31, so I went ahead and made that switch. But wait: don't forget Western Agency, Inc., was a Sub S corporation. Remember, we had decided for no good reason to incorporate, when a partnership would have worked just as well. It just so happens that when you have a corporation, you cannot change your financial year without some strings attached. If you want to move from an October 31 to a December 31 year end, you have to have a mini-year of two months. We did this but guess what? In our little ol' mini-year we also had money left in the company. You can check with your CPA, but I am told it is an absolute certainty that if you have money in a Sub S corporation at year end and if you have minority shareholders who are considered to be self-employed, and if you take any money out and do not declare a dividend, you will be audited by the IRS. They will challenge the self-employment status of the shareholders. That is exactly what they did in the summer of 1990. The CPA I had hired the day we went into business clear back in 1976 had never told me this. Not only that: the IRS challenged the self-employment status for the years 1987, '88, and '89, coming after me with a bill of $36,000 and change; $36,000 represented the extra Social Security taxes due plus interest and penalties. My knees went weak, and I was aghast--I had just gotten full ownership of my company back, but these guys had the power to kill it!

After this disastrous financial year end advice, and having taken this sledgehammer hit, I got an aggressive new accountant: Iver Eliason, CPA. To this day Iver continues to be my accountant, and it is a rare month that he and I do not discuss something to do with my finances or taxes. He helped me get those $36,000 taxes and penalties reduced to $30,000. Then on his advice I hired a tax attorney who got the number reduced still further to $26,000. The tax attorney told me that if we fought the ruling it would probably take two to three years, with but a 50/50 chance of winning. Further, if we lost it would cost me even more interest and taxes plus probably $12,000 in wages for him.

The joke of the month was that this whole tax debacle was over minority shareholders. At least Casey had paid for his 10% share. I had given the other agent his 10%, for heaven's sake, because he was a part owner in that worthless agency I had bought in 1982. Man, was I paying for my ignorance! I was mad because I had hired supposedly good CPAs from day one and they had let this happen to me. This simply emphasizes that you have to hire extremely good support people, but you, and you alone, are going to be held responsible for the acts of your business. Still want to be self-employed? It does have a few strings attached, does it not? Anyway, even though I wanted to, I just could not risk trying to fight the IRS. With my hat in my hand, I went back one more time to my banker, who grudgingly gave me the money to pay Uncle Sam paid off. I even got in touch with the prior agent who was now the preacher and got a few dollars of concession from him since part of the $26,000 penalty and taxes were on his wages. Nonetheless, that $26,000 I had to borrow was to be the final nail in my coffin with my good-time banker.

Shortly after I borrowed money to pay the IRS, my loan officer introduced me to one of his associates, explaining that this new loan officer knew more about business loans, so would be a better fit for me. I should mention here that many times I had asked if I could bring my CPA to the bank with me, to better explain how Western Agency, Inc., was doing. Since I did not speak banking lingo that well, I wanted Iver along for assistance. Neither my old loan officer nor the new one was at all interested in talking to him. I did not like the new guy from the get-go. I did not relate to this cold SOB, he was even worse than his predecessor, and even now after all these years, when I see him out at the country club, it gives me great joy to know I am worth several million dollars and none of it is in his bank. However, that was surely not the case in 1990.

All the things that were happening in those years were not bad. One fine day in the spring of 1990 I got a call from an old friend whom we had insured for years. He and his brother had gotten into money trouble in the 1980s, losing most of their farm. Although he was living in California at the time, he phoned to ask me if I was aware that the federal Small Business Administration was giving out loans to businesses that had suffered financial loss due to the drought that had been going on in North Dakota. I had not heard about it before, but you can bet I looked into it in a hurry. Since I had lost close to $100,000 when my hail insurance market went away, I got together with Iver; and he and I put the package together to send to the SBA. The upshot of it was we were able to secure a $43,000 loan at 4% interest. It was wonderful, and was one of the lucky things that enabled us to survive the struggle just ahead of us.

• When you set up your financial year end, be sure it coincides with your company cash flows.

• If you hand out shares in your company, be sure you understand the long term-consequences.

• Thank God for friends who remember to call you when they get a line on something good.

YOU THOUGHT I WAS EFFICIENT BEFORE:
Cutting More Expenses

As any of you reading this book will know if you are a farm insurance agent, you sell the crop insurance products in the spring, but you do not get paid until the fall. This creates a huge gap in your cash flow. Therefore, even though we were selling lots of product, in the spring of 1990 the agency was strangling for cash. Furthermore, I was still paying the price for overspending the store in the 1980s. Even though we were now on a sound, solid management track, the old loans were still there to be paid off, at sky-high interest rates. My main bank was charging me 13.5% interest, and they were supposed to be my friends. Management-wise, we had done all the right things to get back in the game. Financially, we were living day-to-day.

I so distinctly remember driving to Garrison one summer day early in 1990. A favorite rich uncle was riding along with me to look at my store and spend some time with me. I was rambling on about the agency and how it was slowly coming out of the red but I needed to get some better long-term financing with a better interest rate so I could get my cash flow back. In a shocked voice he said, "Well, we sure don't have any money to loan out!" Maybe he had thought I was hitting him up for a loan. The rest of the trip was pretty quiet. I was embarrassed that it sounded as if I was begging for money; maybe I was. He went back to Seattle and died a few years later, leaving me nothing, which was fine. I jokingly told Linda by the time we ever got an inheritance, all it would do is screw up our tax bracket. Probably I was right.

In March 1990 as I staggered back into the ring for what would be a pivotal round in the fight to save Western Agency, Inc., there was little to be happy about except the fact that the IRS ordeal was over. I had sold quite a bit of multi-peril crop insurance that spring. Thanks to this the agency had $90,000 in earned income coming in the late fall when the farmers paid their crop insurance bills. A positive note: I had hired my good friend, crop adjustor Mark Brakel, to run the Garrison store. He was proving he could be just as good at running an agency as he was at adjusting, and he was in the process of getting the store going strong. Eternal optimist that I was, I thought things were looking better; I should have known. Since the $90,000 income on the crop insurance would not be in my pocket until November or December, the store was literally gasping for cash. Western Agency Inc. was living hand-to-mouth.

As I said earlier, since we were so heavy in the farm market in those days, even though we sold most of our insurance in the spring, we did not get paid until fall. Because of this sales cycle we would have been chronically short of cash, if not absolutely desperate, in the spring and summer even without the IRS sledgehammer. An additional reason for the cash shortage was that I had promised some severance money to both of the agents who had left the previous fall, paying the one $500 a month for his stock that I had given him in the first place when I bought the agency of which he was part owner. Getting rid of these two dead-weight agents wound up costing me $34,000. Obviously I was killing myself financially to be a nice guy.

I was also attempting to keep the Garrison agency's pair of overpaid, unproductive secretaries employed. This, however, was going to end very soon. Being broke can be so wonderful! At least I did not wait for years to do something; I went to Garrison and laid both of them off. Then I hired someone else to assist Mark at a far more realistic salary figure: this excellent woman worked for us many years. I had now replaced two useless secretaries with a full-time, hard-driving agent and another secretary at virtually the same cost, a terrific trade. I simultaneously laid off a part-time person in the Minot office who had turned out to be a weak hire. These maneuvers saved us some more cash and really made the agency run better, but we still needed more funds for our day-to-day operations. We continued to be cash-starved.

I re-examined every cost facet of the agency that could be trimmed: staff, office supplies, long distance charges, even the people who hauled our trash. The only thing we did not cut was service. I had really gotten it into my head that the fastest money we could make was the money we were not wasting. But I did not forget or ignore tools we could buy to make us more efficient. Broke as I was, I gathered enough money together to purchase two fax machines. In 1990 they were cutting-edge stuff. I could not believe how they helped us save time and move paper around. These Sharp units that cost me $1,400 each could be bought for $300 several years later. At the time, however, they really helped me multiply my time.

Since we needed one more secretary in Minot in this time frame, we hired an additional person. Initially I told her the first couple of days I was just going to have her file so we could catch up on that. I guess she felt that was beneath her because she quit after three hours. Maybe it was beneath her, but in those days we were all doing filing—I was, Linda was, and so were the rest of the staff. Whatever needed to be done, whoever had some time was doing it.

• **Just because you have a bunch of earned income on the way, do not count on it to keep you in business.**

• **Do not ignore good technology, even if you are hard up for money.**

• **If you have to fire a couple of weak employees to afford two good ones, for heaven's sake do it.**

DEATH GROUND

One other reason we were cash-short was that my wonderful banker had been harping on me to show more of a profit. So in the fall of 1989, I had left some money in the company to show we were doing better. Yeah, great--that cost us an additional $8,000 in taxes! Wonderful advice and help from a bank that was soon to shut us down anyway. Can you believe this stuff? I know $8,000 may not sound like a bunch of cash. But when you are already up against the wall, it seems like a very large amount.

As of March 20, 1990, the agency needed approximately $30,000 to pay off companies and wages. Like so many businessmen before me, I was sure the bank would come through one more time with one more loan. We had the $90,000 of crop insurance money coming in that fall, so I figured they would stay with me. I went ahead, wrote out the checks for payroll and company statements, and sent them out without prior approval for another loan. When I look back on this time, I cannot believe I did it.

Heavy-hearted, I scheduled an appointment with the "new" banker and went up to see him. I told him how I had gotten Western Agency, Inc., lean and mean: how our sales, income, and profitability were up; how we were writing more premium with fewer employees; and how we finally had the agency on a solid course for recovery. I showed him we had $90,000 in earned commissions coming in within a few months. Once more I offered to bring my CPA in to help explain my numbers if need be. With a face of granite he said, "But you still owe us the same amount of money you did six years ago." I replied that was true, but the agency had tripled in size since then. Dumb me, I felt that to grow that much in that amount of time with the same amount of debt was pretty good. I also wanted to scream at him that we would have had $8,000 more dollars in the bank if he had not insisted we show more money in the company at year end, thus incurring a bunch more taxes. His exact words will ring in my ears forever: "We don't look at it that way." Even though the agency was worth at least $500,000, had we sold it, and the total debt against it was only around $198,000, this ignorant banker, who had my financial life in the palm of his hand, denied the loan. To this day I am incredulous; this is why I find it almost impossible to trust bankers. With few exceptions they are making life-or-death financial decisions about business about which they know virtually nothing. To me in most cases they are like blind bus drivers careening down the financial highway of life. You, the borrower, are sitting behind them in the bus, shouting directions as to when and where to turn, knowing these idiots could kill you at any moment. No way, however, will they let you drive the bus. You know nothing about it, right? There we sat with a vibrant, excellently managed agency, moving ahead with strong sales, at a time when all other agencies in town were reeling and losing premium; and this stupid, cold-hearted fool was turning me down for a loan. During this time I was talking to a friend about bankers, and I told him, "It seems to me most of the bankers in this town are pathetically and dangerously incompetent." I felt as if I were in a fairy tale. But this was real, I was living it. I could not breathe.

I do not even remember leaving his office or the bank; I don't remember the drive across town. All I do recall is feeling like a wild, trapped, caged animal. Faint, clammy, sweaty, nauseated, I headed toward my little office at 1728 Burdick Expressway East; but when I got there, I could not turn into the parking lot. I had failed: I had written bad checks paying company statements and wages, adding up to around $30,000. I had let my staff, my wife, my kids, and everyone else down. My entire horizon was too bleak to face anyone.

It surely would have been easy to give up that terrible afternoon, and I almost did. However, as I drove by the office that fateful day, a strange thing began to happen. A very strong and comforting feeling began to flow over me. It was as if a strange and wonderful strength started to seep into my very soul. I started to shout and pound the steering wheel. With tears streaming down my face, I screamed, "You sonofabitching bastards are not--going--to beat me!" I had been an independent agent for 14 years by this time, but it was only on that cold, terrifying, spring day in 1990, that I really, truly launched myself into the Independent Agency Business. I made up my mind then and there that I would win this lopsided game and I was not going to be beaten. I just did not know how I was going to do it. I drove many miles that day before going home. I think more clearly when I am driving.

Coincidentally, I had three contingency checks that

were due from companies about that time and one of those checks came into the office that very day. It plus the $8,000 final cash advance available on my Master Card got us past the first 24 hours. Next day I received two other contingency checks that enabled us to keep the overdrafts covered--thank God for low loss ratios and plastic! They were instrumental in keeping the company alive through those crazy times. Hell, MasterCard was only charging me 4% more than my bank to borrow money, anyway.

Meanwhile, we were still $10,000 short of operating. I had already talked to my dad, who was unable to loan me any money. The rich uncle was out. My next best bet was Linda's parents, Don and Darleen Ballantyne. Don, who passed away this past fall, was not just my father-in-law; he was a very good friend of mine. A tough, self-made millionaire oilman, he was one of the best people I have ever had the privilege to know. Also, contrary to all the jokes about mothers-in-law, Darleen and I did then and do now get along great. What super people! I got hold of Linda, and she and I went up to her folks' place. My voice was shaking as I told Don I needed to talk to him. He said, "Sure, let's go for a drive." I do not really remember what we talked about until finally I blurted out, "Don, I need some money." He did not ask me what for or for how long. He did not remind me about having too many toys. All he said was "How much do you need?" I told him $10,000. Without batting an eye he simply wrote me a check for $10,000. At least for the moment, he and Darleen had saved Western Agency, Inc. We paid them back 49 days later with interest.

After getting the $10,000 from Don to keep the company alive, Linda and I went to the PIA convention. Basically, we were both so exhausted mentally that we just had to escape the pressure for a couple of days. I honestly can never recall being more mentally exhausted than

I was during that early part of 1990. The PIA convention has always been an excellent place to network and get new ideas for running the store. Over the years being a member of the PIA has been one of the best moves I ever made. We came back from the convention refreshed, ready to dive back into the game.

• Do not count on a loan until you are certain you have one.

• Do not write and mail checks unless you have the money.

• Never, never give up the ship.

• Thank God for good relatives.

• No matter how out-of-control things get, take some time to attend a trade convention so you can network, recharge, and regroup.

THE HUNT FOR "GREEN" OCTOBER:
Finding New Financing

When we got back from the convention, I embarked on a cash search in earnest. Feeling hunted, I knew that I could no longer count on my current banker. Now we even owed money to Linda's dad. I sold our boat, got a few thousand out of the cash value of a life insurance policy I had on myself, and took my guns that had some value and sold them to collectors I knew. For the short run we were safe. By cutting expenses that spring and cashing in some unneeded toys, I had generated almost $50,000, still further lowering expenses in this early part of 1990. I was learning 'Real World' survival financing.

I went to the bank in Garrison where I had financed the purchase of the Garrison agency and borrowed an additional $8,000 for operating capitol. I went to Norwest Bank in Minot, where we had a house loan, and borrowed $20,000 on a personal note. I borrowed $7,000 from the Credit Union in Velva, where we had the Swedlund Agency. Unbelievable: we were now working with four banks, the SBA, and the Master Card people, owing about $198,000, this on assets of well over $500,000. I think at the time I had 18 individual loans, counting the ones at my main bank in town.

Looking internally for more money, we sat down with our accountant and decided that we could lower the tax payments we were making by $1,000 per month and not be in trouble. That gave us $1,000 per month more cash flow. My full-time agent in the Velva office was not doing a good sales job at all, so I went down to have a serious talk with him. Since his excuse was another line of BS about how he just could not seem to make any sales, he ended up unemployed that day, saving the agency $30,000 in wages. Quitting was probably his only positive contribution the entire time he worked for us.

Just a small note on this type of salesperson, or any employee of yours, for that matter, who is not getting the job done: why in the world do we keep these people around? It only forestalls the inevitable. Even if you do not let them go, they are likely to quit sooner or later, anyway. Meanwhile, you have wasted your time and their time, not to mention your money. If you have a bad employee, for heaven's sake cut the cord! It will save you money, it will clean up your operation, and the employee will be better off in the long run. If the 1980s did not teach me this, I sure as hell was learning it in the 1990s.

The day after we got rid of the bad agent, we got more good news. One of our lowest-echelon secretaries decided to move back to Washington to reunite with her abusive ex-husband. I never did know how it worked out with them, but it saved us another $10,000 in salary. Finally, for the $500,000 of premium I had previously sold in multi-peril crop insurance, the company agreed to give me a commission advance of $10,000. All of these things refreshed our cash flow. We were able to pay Linda's dad and mom back their $10,000; and as we rolled into the fall of 1990, we were solvent, at least for the moment.

Who knows? On the surface of things, it might have seemed as if the banker was right in turning us down for the loan; I was probably not worthy of another one. At the time here is how my debts stacked up. Western Agency, Inc., owed $105,000 to our main bank at 13.5% interest. I had bought part of the Swedlund Agency and the Rasch Agency by taking out cash advances on my MasterCard and had gotten over a couple more cash hurdles with additional cash advances. This left me with a balance to them of over $50,000. I owed $65,000 to the Garrison Bank on the Rasch Agency purchase, and I owed $43,000 to the SBA on the disaster loan. None of this included our personal debt: house, vehicles, toys, etc. Even though Western Agency, Inc., was now up to sales of $2.1 million with revenues of around $315,000, we had painted ourselves into a very, very tight financial corner. However, when Linda and I placed our debt against what the company was worth, there were far more assets than liabilities. Even back then the company was worth $500,000, any day.

So in the fall of 1990 we were alive financially, but only just barely. The trouble was that the bank would never give me enough money at low enough interest for long enough terms. They always kept me in a bind where it took every penny to make the monthly payments with absolutely no operating capital. That was why I had to use MasterCard and other banks, sell part of a book of business, and make every other creative financing move I could think of, just to stay alive. We had too many small loans with too soon a payback at too high an interest rate. I had to somehow, some way, find a bank that would give us one big loan, at a livable interest rate, spread over enough time to keep the payments workable. This is what would free up our cash flow, reviving the company. Not just an Independent Agency problem, this shortage of working cash is the universal complaint of anyone trying to bootstrap-finance a startup business.

Yet all through these hard times, I was absolutely convinced that when I could be buying good, solid little agencies for pennies on the dollar, the deals could not possibly be bad ones. Instinctively I knew we had to grow to stay alive; and to grow at the rate needed, we had to be buying volume as well as writing it. I had been going to agency management seminars like the Certified Insurance Counselor courses whenever I could since the late 1970s. As the years went on, the refrain was that to stay alive you had to grow your premium volume. Late in the '70s they were saying you had to grow your agency to $250,000 in premium to stay alive, then in the early '80s it was $500,000, then in the late '80s it was $750,000, then in the early '90s it was $1,000,000, late '90s $2,000,000. I was always able to hit these production targets, and now we are at $12,700,000 of premium. At last maybe we are ahead of the curve. Yet in those years of our biggest struggles, whenever I would try to talk to my banker about things like this that I had learned at an agency management seminar, he would just give me a bored look and go on to something else. It was as if he gave what I said no credence at all, he seemed to feel Linda and I had to be very poor managers to have to keep coming to him for money.

Maybe other than being an incurable optimist and being too damn stubborn to give up, the reason Linda and I kept at it was my overwhelming opinion that it would not be long before this company was going to turn around. I knew we were in the right place at the right time. I believed in myself, my staff, my clients, my chosen market, and the companies we were dealing with. I kept telling Linda, my banker, and anyone else who would listen that the farm situation was not going to stay in the pits forever. I kept saying that when it did recover, we would have a very big win on our hands, not just a cash-starved little farm insurance agency. You see, through all these crazy times, we were continuing to write more and more farm business. Not only that, we were writing up the good farms: the leader farms, the survivor farms. These folks were having just as hard a time as we were, yet all of us were convinced this thing had to right itself sooner or later. In addition, the drought years of '86, '87, '88, and '89 were now behind us. Crop yields were up and the price of cereal grains was starting to rise slightly. In my own cockeyed way, I could not help being hopeful; the dream was still alive for me. Financially, we were barely, barely sneaking by, figuring out what to do as we went along.

- **Who says you only should deal with one bank?**

- **Do not tolerate unproductive employees; they will cost you cash, and they make the good employees mad.**

- **Try not to let yourself get into a corner where you have too many small loans at too short a pay back term at too high an interest rate; if at all possible, try to get one big wraparound loan.**

• CHAPTER SIX •

BANKER "BUCK" RIDES INTO TOWN

By the fall of 1990, we had somehow survived the financing crises of the previous years, but I was wearing down. Even with the tremendous support and love of Linda, I came home one day late in the afternoon completely beat and discouraged. I was having a hard time mentally. I distinctly remember lying on the couch half asleep, trying to watch a TV show. At 10 p.m. the phone rang. It was a field man who had been trying to get me to sell some more crop insurance with his company. An OK guy, he wanted me to take a "free trip" to Kalispell, Montana. I was just too worn out, too broke, and too pissed at the world to get fired up for some "free trip." He was calling me because his company had been purchased by Norwest Bank and they wanted to put on a big party for a bunch of leading crop insurance agents to get more business and keep in place the business they already had. Since these free meetings customarily ended up costing people money and we were so damn broke, I told him we could not afford a "free trip" and I did not have the time to go anyway; I know I was rude because Linda has told me I was, but I could not help myself. I was really having a "bad hair day." He persisted, however, and after asking Linda what she thought about it, I said yes. This decision would change our lives: we were about to meet C. P. "Buck" Moore.

We showed up at the airport on the appointed day for the short flight to Minneapolis and from there to Kalispell, Montana. We had hardly been on an airliner up until then, so the trip was really a big deal to Linda and me. We ended up getting upgraded to first class: it was a fun ride. The meeting also was first class. We met some very nice agents from all over the country. There were banquets, golf, and whitewater rafting. The weather was beautiful and we had a simply wonderful time. Several meetings were held on various subjects. You had your choice of which ones to attend. In my situation, of course, the one on agency finance and acquisition attracted me the most. Taught by C. P. "Buck" Moore, it was about to change our financial lives forever.

Buck had been head of the Montana and South Dakota Territory for Norwest Bank. Although retired, he was still doing some work for Norwest, and one of his projects was putting on this agency financing and acquisition seminar. Buck was a big, imposing guy who kept himself in top physical shape. Born and raised in Two Dot, Montana, he had the ability to talk to people in language and in a manner they understood, despite having been the head banker for Norwest in those two states. That day he came rolling into that room like a fresh prairie breeze and talked for about an hour-and-a half. I was fascinated. The numbers he was discussing just dazzled me because he was saying I could leverage my crop insurance book to get agency financing; I never realized I could do that. Hell, the bankers in Minot who worked for Norwest had failed to tell me that! After the rest of the people in the room had left, Buck and I sat talking for quite some time. Since I badly wanted out of the bank where I was currently banking, I had talked to Norwest Bank in Minot about the possibility of getting better financing there a few months before. They had told me I could not qualify for even an SBA-guaranteed loan because my company had a "negative net worth." I never did understand that one, as even then the company would have been worth at least $500,000 if we had sold it. The loan officer in Minot was a friend of mine, but he had told me there was just nothing he could do. Now here was Buck, who was far up on the command ladder of the same bank, telling me the exact opposite. He was saying I could borrow twice the amount of money his bank had just turned me down for a few weeks back--how could that be? When I asked him about this, Buck said, "Chuck, send me your numbers and your business plan, and I'll take a look at them." With that the meeting broke up, and Linda and I went to the final banquet. We came home refreshed but exhausted, happy about getting together with some very nice people and finally hearing encouraging words about agency financing.

I had been most happy to meet Buck, and I got in touch with my accountant Iver as soon as we got home. I wanted his help to put some numbers together for the amount of the loan we needed. Buck had also asked for something I had never done (and had never had my banker ask for), my business plan. Honest to God, I do not know who told me how to prepare a business plan; but whoever it was, bless their souls for giving me good advice. In a nutshell your business plan should say where you came from, where you intend to go, and how you intend to get there. I sat down and feverishly wrote one up on a yellow legal pad. Then I hired a temporary secretary to type it up for me. It was nine pages long. I must have really written from the heart; for even now, all these years later, having expanded to 15 pages, it still has much of the original content in it. When you are on Death Ground financially, you can speak from a deep place. Within a couple of days of my return from Kalispell, I had my material ready to send down to Buck at his office in Sioux Falls, South Dakota. I was proud of having written the business plan and pleased we had prepared all the figures but I never really expected to hear from Buck anytime soon. I was still unable to believe that a banker could actually be expected to follow through on anything.

You can imagine my surprise when a week or so later

I got a call. The secretary buzzed me and said, "There is a Buck Moore on the phone." It was a pregnant moment. I took the call and Buck and I talked.

Buck said, "Chuck, this is an interesting story you sent me. I would like to come up and look at your agency. When would be a good time?" To my shock and amazement we agreed on his flying up to Minot on the following Thursday. Before we hung up he said something else that blew my mind. He told me to have my CPA at the meeting. Wow, a banker with a brain--what a concept!

Iver and I picked Buck up at the airport on the appointed day and drove over to the office. Iver and Buck went over the numbers while I just sat there answering questions. What impressed me was that at last I was talking to a banker and there was a total lack of bullshit. All we were discussing were the functions and finances of Western Agency, Inc. There was a total absence of telling me what to do. It was just business. Iver and I had decided we needed about $175,000 but had decided to ask for $200,000, which would give me a bit of a cushion. After a couple of hours Buck looked at me and said, "Chuck, I know you want a loan of $200,000, but it looks to me like you really need only $175,000." He was right on the money. I guess you do not get to the top of the banking game without knowing numbers.

After we had talked a bit more, Iver asked Buck if he thought the loan could be put together. Buck said, "Yeah, it's a done deal." Then he laughed and added, "No, you'd better wait to hear that from the people in Minneapolis." Once we had wrapped up a few more details and signed some paperwork, we headed back to the airport to put him on the plane back to Sioux Falls. It had been quite a day. Within a few weeks we had a loan set up for $175,000 at the then-unheard-of low interest rate of 9%. It consolidated most of our other loans, gave us back our operating capital, and saved us $17,000 in interest charges alone the first year.

The new Norwest loan not only gave me space to breathe for the first time in years; also, by saving the money in interest, we had a far lower monthly payment. We had finally escaped those deadly balloon payments at the end of the year, and I could see we were definitely headed up and out of being in money trouble. Even after all these years, I can still remember the sense of exhilaration and happiness it gave me. Perhaps most of all, I was proud that yes, there really were good, solid bankers out there who did have enough sense to see a good deal when one came up. Maybe by making us that loan Buck and his bank had validated the dream Linda and I had of creating our business, giving us our pride back. I was determined to prove to him he had made a wise choice, and he has our eternal thanks for believing in us way back then.

A few weeks later the money was in our account, and we were preparing to go down to our prior bank to pay them off. I had moved all of our accounts over to Norwest, and now came the fun part of totally cutting the ties with the people who had almost forced us to sell our business. It was as if a huge thunderstorm had just passed: the air seemed fresher, the birds were singing, and we were safe to take our agency to the next level. The sun had never shone more brightly, the wheat fields waved golden in the breeze, and I had forgotten what a pretty sound the song of a meadowlark was. We paid Norwest off a few years later; there has never been the need for another loan on our company. That day in the fall of 1990, Linda and I were simply on top of the world.

• **Incentive trips can be a super-good thing to go on.**

• Network, network, network: when you are done doing that, network some more.

• Good bankers plus good agencies add up to good loans.

• Write a business plan, which should say where you came from, where you intend to go, and how you intend to get there.

• Having good financing in place helps respiratory problems.

EPILOGUE FOR THE BAD BANKER

One of the happiest days in my life was being able to go down and pay off the entire amount I owed at my former bank. My original loan officer, who had handed me off to my "new" loan officer, just happened to be there when I was paying off the loans. I had called in earlier that morning for the exact loan payoffs, and I suppose he figured something was up. He wondered whether anything was wrong and why I was leaving his bank. He mentioned that he had been talking to the bank president. They had decided that he could be my loan officer again, after all. Gee, what a great deal, trade one turkey for another! This man continued to be completely clueless that in the six years he had handled Linda's and my account, we had expanded Western Agency, Inc., from a tiny little operation into a pretty solid store; we had grown up and taken control, cutting expenses and increasing production. We now had a statewide reputation for good work and excellent expertise. Our client list was starting to read like a Who's Who of the leading farmers in the area. I would then and will now put my client list up against any I have ever seen. Furthermore, our retention ratio was a fantastic 95%. The agency growth was terrific and was accelerating.

In those six years that this poor bank officer handled our account, we had almost quadrupled our size but kept our debt nearly the same. Our loss ratios were super-low, we had no overdue accounts receivable, and we had never been late to him on a payment. Furthermore, the drought was over, the price of grain was up, and the farmers were making money again. Western Agency, Inc., was writing more farmers than any insurance agency in the state. In the late fall of 1990 we were like a rocket ready to take off. If this man had known anything, anything at all, about an Independent Agency, or at least OUR Independent Agency (which he had been financing for six years), he would have thanked his lucky stars he had been fortunate enough to get us for a client. Yet he had thrown us away like a couple of drug addicts. All this guy could see was that we owed him money; I think many bankers are like this. All they can think about the borrower is that same tired line: "If you're so smart why are you coming to me for more money?" They are not at all knowledgeable about your given business. But instead of calling in someone who is, some of them cannot wait to flush you down the financial toilet. In a conversation with Linda while I was writing this book, she reminded me how this man would literally make us beg for loans, even when he knew damn well he was going to give them to us. After a few years of going to the bank with me, whenever I had to see this guy, she absolutely refused to accompany me anymore.

Standing there in the bank talking to him that day, I was so emotional and my throat so constricted that I could hardly speak. For the life of me, I do not remember what I said. I know what I wanted to say was that I considered him and the "new" loan officer they had

112

saddled us with to be two of the most dangerous and pathetically incompetent bankers we had ever had the misfortune to meet--they had literally come close to taking our financial life! I still feel this way. After meeting and doing business with a real banker, I wanted this other financial idiot back for a loan officer: right. Turning away, I walked out. The sun was shining brightly, and I was having no trouble breathing at all; it was simply too much fun to be imagined. Amazing, is it not, how in a few months you can see your life turn around? That day paying off all those high-interest, short-term loans, trading them for a beautiful low-interest, long-term wraparound loan, was one of the happiest I can ever remember.

Probably the reason meeting Buck was such an incredible breath of fresh air, was that he had really looked at our business. He had asked me for my business plan, five years of my production and growth data, and my loss ratios. He had talked to his people in Minneapolis who did insurance agency loans. He wanted my CPA to supply the financial data he needed to do the loan. Buck actually did the research and took the time to find out whether or not his bank wanted to do the deal. After deciding it was feasible, he helped design a loan that was good for both his bank and me. This was the way I thought the system was supposed to work. It had just taken me awhile to find the folks with the right know-how.

I do not want to give anyone the idea that Linda and I hate all bankers. For heaven's sake, even a bad one is better than none at all. These people fulfill a very important role, and they are indispensable to the conduct of business. However, there are good ones and bad ones. If you are saddled with a bad banker, try to find one you can run with. If you are reading this book and these banking problems sound familiar, do not hesitate; put your papers together and go looking for better banking expertise. Having a poor banker is like dragging the anchor on your boat: it really makes it hard to get going, and if you do not watch out, it will sink you.

• **If you discover you are saddled with a bad banker, search the world until you find a good one.**

• **It is possible to get a loan with terms good for both you and your banker.**

LOANS AND CARE PACKAGES

If you intend to go shopping for money, you need to have: a business plan; copies of your taxes, personal and business, for two to three years; a personal financial statement; a copy of all three of your current credit reports; and your last three to four years' production and income data by company and class of business. You also want to bring along any other pertinent data, such as your procedure manual, brochure, newsletter, and anything else to show that yours is not just an average agency. In addition, be prepared to discuss your plans and dreams with your bankers. Of course, your business plan will tell them where you came from, where you intend to go, and how you intend to get there. But your dreams demonstrate that you have a vision that goes beyond all that. You need to talk about your business, and the dreams you have for it at the same time.

Sounds like a lot of work and data, does it not? Well, I guess in some respects the bankers are right: if you do not know your business, who does? Furthermore, if all you know is that you need more money, that is the wrong answer. You have to know where you are, how you got there, where you intend to go, and how you intend to get there. Again, that is the content of your business plan. Then, to back up your data, you need the tax statements from the past few years. The production data is invaluable; you should have it at you fingertips, anyway.

When I finally got all these materials corralled as a result of going after the SBA loans in the late 1980s and the loan that Buck put together for me in the early 1990s, I called the assembled data my Care Package. The Care Package is a copy of my business plan, three years' taxes (business and personal), personal financial statement, and a spreadsheet showing the last four years' production, commission earnings, and loss ratios by company. Every year when I get all my statistics collected at year end, I take them to a local printing store and have them make 20 copies of each item. Then I rubber-band them together into 20 Care Packages. What is so fun about it is if a bank or a company wants my financial information, instead of giving them some half-baked numbers, I present them with one of my Care Packages. It is priceless to see the look on the face of a banker or a company field rep or some visiting company dignitary who asks for information on your agency or financial numbers when you are able to reach into a file drawer and pull this package out--it is a total joy when someone requests these materials from me! Of course, I am expected to take forever assembling them, but I am able to pull out pretty much every pertinent number on my store and hand it over. This is really impressive, not only to banks but also to companies. You are supposed to have control and knowledge of your agency numbers, anyway--you wanted to be in business for yourself, didn't you?

- **Care Packages consist of: business plan; taxes, personal and business; current credit reports; personal financial statement; and production** records. Have several made up, and keep them around to hand out.

• Companies love Care Packages.

SOLVENCY AND WOODEN DUCKS

Every day felt like Christmas after we finally got our cash flow back, and I can remember some very fun experiences that happened in quick succession during that time. One of the neatest was when Linda and I were in Norwest Bank doing a deposit and a loan officer that we had known for years came running over to talk to us. He exclaimed, "How do you happen to know Buck Moore?" How funny! Now we had finally gotten the loan we needed, we had gotten our cash flow back, we could move again financially; but it was sure in hell no thanks to him. A year prior to meeting Buck, when we had gone to talk to him to try to get a loan exactly like the one that Buck had put together, he told us Norwest was unable to help us at all. Suddenly, because we had been able to go way above his head to secure our needed financing through one of the gurus of his corporation, we were OK. I wondered to myself why in hell he had not suggested that I get in touch with the Norwest department that dealt specifically with agency acquisition and finance. Norwest is a pretty big company, so probably he did not even know such a department existed. The thing is, though, in the insurance business, given the same situation, in which we do not know either how to solve a problem or cannot find a product in our stable of carriers, we call a broker, or even another agent, to assist our clients. I guess you do not see that happen much in the banking community.

Somehow I found out that Buck Moore collected

116

carved wooden ducks. It just so happens that one of the better wooden duck carvers anywhere in the country has his studio located in a small town about 100 miles from Minot. At that time there was an event every spring in Minot called Art Fest. I had seen this artist's display at Art Fest before, and in the spring of 1991 I could not wait to see it again. On the appointed night Linda and I dressed up and headed over to the gala event. Rushing through the doors, checking our coats, hitting the line for a glass of cheap champagne, we took off to find the duck carver artist's booth. Sure enough, there it was, and he had an absolutely beautiful carving of a mallard drake. It was so exquisite and the carving and coloring so perfect it actually looked alive. I bet that in the history of this man's marketing his art he has never made a faster sale. I asked him how much the duck was worth, he answered $850. I said, "We'll take it." I could hardly wait to send it to the man who had literally given us our financial life back. The whole transaction took only a few minutes, but what made the moment so perfect and why I remember it so well was that here came the banker we had been talking to at Norwest a couple of days before who had wanted to know how we happened to know Buck Moore. He said, "Chuck, what are you going to do with that duck?" I suppose in his mind he was thinking now that his bank had loaned me money I was just out peeing it away. With a huge grin I turned to him and said, "I'm going to box it up and send it to Buck. He collects them." The look on that banker's face was absolutely priceless.

- **Once you have secured a good loan, it is as if you have gotten legitimacy.**

- **Do not forget to say thanks to those who helped you in your time of need.**

• CHAPTER SEVEN •

CASEY'S BACK AT BAT

It was during these first years when things started getting better that I jotted down a little analogy comparing an up-and-coming, struggling agency operation such as mine to an army at war. Probably I looked at it like that because I really felt Linda and I had been in one. The analogy goes like this: *A young growing agency like ours is like an army at war. During the war there are the highs and lows, the charges, the valiant deeds, the danger, the adrenaline rushes. The army is vital, healthy, energetic. In peacetime, even though it is then that the resources are gathered to sustain it, the army tends to atrophy.* I think what I had in mind when I wrote this was we were doing the best work in our business life when things were the worst financially. I knew we could not sustain that kind of energy forever; and I knew that when things are going well, you tend to slack off. Although we could not run ourselves in the red line as hard as we had been doing, when times got good again, I did not intend to let my staff and myself get complacent and lazy. Despite our getting out from under the rock we had been under, I did then and do now still keep my store as lean and mean as I can. I tend to run just a little bit understaffed, for I find we work better when we are all busy. If we are not, pretty soon people are standing around shooting the breeze, and the productivity of the entire store suffers.

Linda and I had been looking for a new office location for some time. By the late '80s and early '90s we had totally outgrown our little office at 1728 Burdick Expressway East but of course had not been able to locate anything we could afford. Late in the fall of 1990, while in the search for a cheap and affordable new office, I noticed a property on the south side of Minot that had been for sale for years. It was an old realty office and a smaller cement block building located on about two acres of land. Both of the buildings were junk, but they had one of the highest visibility locations in town. I reasoned that if any of my farmers came to town, they would invariably pass within a few blocks of this excellent location.

I visualized putting a small strip mall in the location or simply remodeling the old realty office and putting our agency there. The asking price was $50,000, and the property was owned by a bank. I had been reading another of my business self-help books, which had mentioned that many times banks will sell property cheaper at year end, just to get things off the books for a given year. I do not know whether this is true, but it was December. I discussed it with my good friend LaVerne Mikkelson. He and I decided to try to buy the property, so we went down to Bremer Bank, who owned it, and asked to talk to Duaine Espegard, the president. An excellent person, Duaine was a pretty good friend of mine, even though we had never done any business. We told him what property we were interested in, and he lined us up with the loan officer in charge of it. We had agreed that LaVerne would do the dickering; so when the guy asked us what we would pay for the property, LaVerne said we would pay them $20,000. The officer said no way the bank could sell it for that, and we went back and forth until he said he would let us have it for $30,000. LaVerne countered at $25,000. Just about that time Duaine stuck his head in the door and said, "How are you guys doing in here?" The loan officer said we were deadlocked at $30,000. Duaine asked how much we would be willing to pay and, when we said $25,000 he laughed, turned to the loan officer, and said, "Take it." The deal was done. Since Linda and I were still pretty strapped for cash, it was not easy to do; but we did manage to get our half

119

of the $25,000 together. But I would not be wasting your time telling this story if it had not played a big part in our getting the office we still have at 408 20th Avenue Southwest. Here is what happened.

Just a matter of weeks after we had bought this property, a real estate agent called me up and asked me if we wanted to sell it. Curious, I asked him how much, and he answered $50,000. I could not believe it, but said I would call him back. I called LaVerne and the two of us went for coffee to try to figure out what was going on. In a few days we had determined that a large grocery chain wanted to build a huge new store in the area, and we just happened to hold the key property to close the deal--whoa! We decided to sit tight and see what would happen. Within a few more days the realtor called back. I told him we had talked and decided we were going to build a strip mall, so we really didn't want to sell. He said, "Would you sell for $75,000?" I said no. He said, "Would you sell for $100,000?" I said I would get back to him. My fingers were shaking as I called LaVerne. I'll tell you this: LaVerne Mikkelson is one of the toughest negotiators I have ever known and he also has a brilliant business mind. We met for coffee again and decided to hold out for $135,000. For the life of me, I have no idea where we came up with that figure, but $135,000 it was. I called up the realtor and gave him the number. After a few days of haggling, we finally sold that property for $132,000--man, what a hit! Furthermore, I ended up buying a far better piece of property a few blocks away for $65,000 and by doing a tax-free exchange was able to get away with my half of the entire profit tax-free. I have to have a guardian financial angel on my shoulder, do I not? The structure Linda and I purchased was the old Ward County Government Farm Services building, which could not have been more perfect. In a few weeks we had moved our office to the new location. Since ev-

120

ery farmer has to talk to the Farm Services people at their office several times a year and we had just bought their old building, now every farmer within 50 miles of Minot knew exactly where our office was located.

In the spring of 1991, things continued on the roll that had started with the Norwest loan. Farm prices were up even more, so in addition to seeing plenty of new accounts being written, we were seeing tons of vertical growth. Whereas in the bleak years of the 1980s, I had once gone for four years and only insured two new tractors, now my client farmers were buying tractors, trucks, pickups, cars, and equipment. If it was for sale in North Dakota in the early 1990s, somebody was going to buy it; and if they bought it, we insured it. Interest rates were dropping for the first time in years and North Dakota's economy was really rolling. . Since by now we insured over 300 farms, as I had predicted to the bankers, Linda, and my staff, we were rolling right along with it.

To make things even better, my brother Casey came back to work in the agency. Although I was happy with how well the farm market was working for us, I was concerned that we had all of our eggs in the farm insurance basket. Since leaving the agency years before, Casey had been working as a commercial insurance agent for American Hardware, so it was logical that he come back and take over the commercial part of Western Agency, Inc. Since American Hardware Mutual at the time was beginning the slide that would end a few years later in their leaving the state, it was a good time for him to make a move. I could now afford to pay him enough to come back, and it made real sense for both of us. However, only after lots of discussion, during which we really tried to figure out how to prevent any problems from developing again, did we do the deal. After a bunch of soul-searching for both of us in the early part of 1991, he was back managing the commercial department of Western Agency, Inc. It was to be one of the best decisions either of us had made in years.

- **Keep your staffing and expenses lean and mean, even in good times.**

- **Three words regarding real estate: location, location, location; however, there is a lot to be said for just being lucky.**

- **If you are going to negotiate a deal, be sure you have a good negotiator along.**

- **Again, when good employees show up, hire them.**

GOING COMMERCIAL:
Getting Into the Commercial Markets

With Casey back we really started bringing in the commercial insurance. He had a good stable of clients from over the years, and I had many people who had told me, when I was ready, to come and give them a quote on their commercial business. Now was the time and we really hit it. After Casey's first year, when he had gotten his book rolled into Western Agency, Inc., we started working on my guys. One of the first people we went and talked to was Bill Burke. Bill and I have been very good friends for many years. We grew up together, cut firewood together, and partied together; and I had written his and his wife Elaine's personal insurance for years. Bill and Elaine owned a large construction company. Since he was one of those people who had said, when we were ready to quote their business insurance, to give him a call, in the spring of 1992 call him we did.

122

Bill's commercial account was with one of the oldest agencies in town, one that had been there forever when I started my store. Well-entrenched in the commercial insurance market, they did a pretty good job at it. The manager of this agency is a good guy, and I have lots of respect for the job he and his staff do; they run a quality store. The trouble was they were writing an account that I needed to have. Bill was really an up-and-coming contractor: just like me, he had been steadily growing his business. Just getting into larger performance bonds, he was beginning to be a power in the contracting business in our area. Casey and I were acutely aware that it would help us enormously if he would honor us by letting us be his insurance agents.

We went after his account with everything we had. I do not remember what company his then-agent had him with, but we came up with a solid quote by using Continental Western. Continental Western had been a good company for us, and our underwriter, Don Becker, came up with a fine quote. When we go after any account, we look for any mistakes on the existing contract the client has. I want to compete in the coverage arena, exiting the price arena as soon as I can. Of course, we have to be competitive to get the deal. I want businesses to be aware from the onset, however, that their insurance program will perform on coverage, not price. The only mistakes we found in the policy Bill had were a couple of semi-trailers that had not been described on the vehicle list: this was not too big an error. So whether or not we got the deal was simply going to hinge on Bill's and my friendship. We had to make him believe we would work harder on his account than his present agent. I do not know if it was our brilliant pitch, our sincerity, or that he knew me well enough to be sure I was not blowing smoke when I said we would exert extra effort and could handle his business insurance; but Bill agreed to give us

123

the deal. It was to be one of the most pivotal accounts we ever wrote. Bill and Elaine now have a very sizable construction business, and since 1992 we have been with them every step of the way. Also, sure enough, it was not long before one of their trucks pulled out in front of a car, resulting in one of the biggest liability losses my agency has ever sustained. Continental Western did a super job of handling the claim, helping us make good on our promise to Bill and Elaine of being able to take care of them when they needed us.

Nevertheless, in that first year Bill left his bonding business with his prior agent. I knew that agency would keep attempting every year to try to get the business back, so to solidify Bill's account I had to write his contract bond business in addition to the casualty business we had already written. I told him we could do a good job on his contract bonding and the following year he did me another huge favor, letting us take over his performance bonding. Sure enough, in that second year Burke did a $2,000,000 job, and we got him his performance bond without any trouble. The commercial agents in town were beginning to find out we were not just a farm agency anymore. They had no clue as to just how much commercial coverage we were soon going to be writing.

Once again, not having old, established companies was inadvertently going to provide us with an excellent company outlet. The agency writing most of the performance bonds in our town at this time was employing one of those old-line bond companies for their bond outlet. While we did not have very many outlets, we had begun to use EMC Company's bond department more and more. Not many other agents were doing so in our market. We put a very good relationship together with Liz Beck, our bond underwriter. We have since done dozens of deals with her and her company. Once more, by doing business with a mid-sized regional, we had discovered an excellent bond outlet that most of our competitors in town did not even know existed.

In the middle 1990s Casey and I wrote contractor after contractor. Even today we are still writing lots of contractors and commercial business. Our commercial book, now several million dollars strong, is a good, solid part of our insurance in force. Being the new kid on the block, we were not able to write many of the old, established accounts in town. Thus, then and now, we target the guys like us who are growing their companies. We spend lots of time showing them how to get their books in order so they can get appropriate performance bonding. We offer to sit down with their bankers and CPAs to be sure they are getting the best bond program possible. We make sure our clients have contracts that will pay their claims when the claims happen. And we sit down with them at least once a year, usually several times, to be sure they are correctly covered. We really do not do anything different from what we do for the farms. I do not make a big effort to hire hot rod salespeople. What I want my sales staff to do is get the account put together and keep it together. I want the agency's reputation to be one of taking care of things at claim time. Since we get the vast majority of our new premium on our referrals, it seems the idea of using our reputation and service to help us sell the account is doing OK.

One place in which the insurance industry could use a whole bunch of improvement is in the area of audits. Perhaps companies simply do not trust agents, maybe they just need to fill data banks with more information; for whatever reason, endless audits have now become a fact of life in this industry. It would not be right to discuss commercial insurance without them. For that matter, any type of insurance will occasionally incur an audit. It may come in the form of simply checking receipts, a new drivers list, the number of employees or a safety inspection, but count on it; sooner or later the policy will incur an audit. Sometimes I really wonder with all of the information that the companies expect the client to supply if the companies are not drowning in information. My brother Casey coined a phrase a few years ago when he said companies are becoming "information junkies." The fact remains that if a company wants to talk to your client, you should be involved. Not your job, you say? If it is not yours, whose is it, then? It sure as hell is not your client's job. Of course it is the job of the auditors, but do they know your client? Do they know anything about the insurance business, for that matter? Do they care? Of course not. Usually these auditors are kids fresh out of college, telemarketer types of people, maybe "road warriors" with drinking problems, or just a sheet of paper sent out from the company. I have seen them all, and they are all universally, unequivocally bad. If your clients are to be audited, educate them to get in touch with you so you can help them get things handled CORRECTLY the first time.

Leave it up to the auditor and your client to do the audit, and 99 times out of 100 it will be wrong. Why not? The auditors, as I just said, are probably fresh college graduates who know nothing about the business or telemarketing "experts" who know even less; and your clients never said they were insurance audit experts, did they? Naturally, without your help they will get it wrong. Then you will have disgruntled clients on your hands, and you will be spending countless hours straightening out the audits with the companies. Meanwhile, very possibly you or your clients will be slapped with a multi-thousand-dollar audit that you must try to get corrected after the fact. I suppose the reason I am putting a blurb on audits here is that Bill's company got an audit after a few years. The auditor was a man with little experience who totally messed it up. It took Casey and me several months to get the numbers back in the right places. In the meantime I paid the $12,000 audit myself until we got it corrected. It was a valuable lesson.

Educate your clients that if they get a letter from the company, or someone calls from the company and wants a bunch of financial data, or even if an auditor stops by their business: The only company person your client will deal with is you, the agent. I do not care if auditors are at your clients' offices at the time. Clients have every right to tell auditors to go drink some more coffee until they get in touch with you, their agent, so you can be with them when they are answering difficult audit questions. We have found over the years that by having our clients use this method, we have had far fewer screwed-up audits. I do not care if the auditors, or the companies, for that matter, think we are stepping on their toes. They are not our clients.

- **When you are trying to break into a new market, write up a key person in that market.**

- **Try to make every attempt to write all that client's business.**

- **Do get involved in audits; educate your clients to let you know if one has arrived, either by mail or in person, so you can help them get it done: being involved in audits IS your job.**

CAN SOMEBODY TELL ME WHY THE AGENT SHOULD'T BE INVOLVED IN THE CLAIM?

While we are talking about service and how it helps sales, it has to be time in this story to discuss the claims process. We need to talk about good adjustors, bad adjustors, inexperienced adjustors, and the approach to the claim process in general. I know I covered crop claims in prior chapters, but adjusting in all lines needs to be discussed.

First and foremost, we at Western Agency, Inc., do get involved in claims. I know that any of you company people who are reading this just let out a big gasp, right? Most companies think the agency should fill out a loss report and stay out of the way. I do agree that there is a big difference between helping the claim process go smoothly and meddling in the loss. At our agency we certainly want to keep the process moving and do not want to meddle; we are not adjustors and do not intend to be. My question to companies who do not want agents to be involved in the claim process is this: how do you think Western Agency, Inc., sustains the growth it does, consistently maintains a 95% or better retention ratio, and has traditionally low loss ratios if we do not get involved in losses? Are not numbers like those above the ones you like to see? Why should the agency not get involved in the claims process? It is no different from field underwriting. It is all part of the way to keep the flow of business moving.

I sincerely believe the agency must be involved in seeing to it that the loss is settled correctly. Agents who think they can just turn over the responsibility for settling their claims to the adjustors or their CSRs and forget about them will someday find their agencies for sale or will find their management careers over. You would not have a job as an agent if it were not for the fact that bad things happen. Claims and getting them settled correctly are a part of agency life. For heaven's sake, when you sold the policy, all you talked about were claims and how you would get them paid--now when they happen you are not going to get involved? Wake up! Claims are where the rubber meets the road in our business. They are what set agencies apart. They are the opportunity to shoot ahead of your competition. Yet every day I watch other agencies simply delegate this responsibility to the adjusting community. Time after time the claim gets bogged down, and the ill-served customer is justifiably angry. The agency that does not keep track of things and help the claims process keep moving is an agency that is missing the chance to excel and move ahead. I guarantee that ultimately the way you see to it that your clients' claims are settled, not your super advertising program, will be the major factor in the success or failure of your agency.

Several years ago we had a very severe hailstorm, which caused us lots of extra work and extra expense. My staff was tired and for a short time very overworked. However, I reminded them that we were doing a spectacular job of getting all the losses turned in and settled in a timely manner. Many of our competitors were not and did not do as well. I told my staff that all of our excellent work and extra effort would be simply prepaid advertising. Guess what? The next year we had absolutely outstanding sales! My agents and staff were selling much more product simply because of the reputation we had for getting the job done on the prior year's storm. The claim process does not end when you fill out a loss report and send it somewhere. It ends when you and your clients and the adjustors arrive at agreeable, understandable, equitable settlements and when your clients have claim checks in their hands. Do not relax until these things are accomplished.

If you have a claim that has gone to subrogation, keep track of it. I can never think of a time when a subrogation was settled favorably and the client got the deductible back. Possibly it happens and I just do not see it, but I really doubt it. When we find a loss is in subrogation, we keep track of it so if it is settled in our favor we first of all make sure our client gets the deductible back and secondly that the client is not being charged extra premium for an accident at fault that the company got reimbursed on. If you have a claim in which there is a holdback of money until the client gets the damage fixed, do not forget about it. Usually, the damage will not get fixed right away. If you do not keep your clients aware of the time consequences, when they do get the damage fixed, they may not get the rest of the money due them. For that matter, they will forget they even have any more money coming to them half the time. So you look like a hero when you get it for them. To me, though, it is all just part of doing a good job for your client.

While we are hot and heavy on the claims process trail, let us get another thing out of the way. Yes, Virginia, there are good adjusters and bad adjusters: deal with it. How do you get the good adjustors? Maybe another little story will help explain it.

I am here at the office: it is 6:30 a.m. on June 25, 2001. Several of my very large accounts have been hit with light hail on early crop in the past few days. To those of you who do not work in the crop insurance lines, this does not mean much, but those of you who do work in crop insurance know how difficult early losses on young grains are. Although there is usually no real big damage, what is there looks worse than it is. The problem is the clients are looking at large crop insurance premiums to pay in the fall, and they want to believe the damage is worse than it really may be; in many ways they are correct. The companies will tell you that no real damage is done on early hail to wheat. In actual fact, however, many times it stresses the crop and adversely affects your yield. Many factors combine to hobble a crop that gets early hail. Very seldom will a crop with hard early hail yield up with a non-hailed crop. The solution to this is to be very sure you have an experienced adjustor who

130

is an expert on crops and early hail. These types of adjustors will many times pay more on this type of loss if the damage is in fact actually there. If the damage is not there, they will be experienced enough to explain to the farmers why they are paying what they are paying, and both you and your clients can be assured that the adjustment was solid. I am using crop insurance here for the example, but in the day-to-day operation of claims in the agency, and in particularly difficult claims, what I am saying is you do not want a rookie on a tough loss.

So here I sit, waiting for one of those good adjustors. Why? Because the company head of claims and his area supervisor think I have stepped on their toes by requesting an adjustor who I know is very good on this type of loss. Thinking I have stepped out of the chain of command, they are mad. They would be happier sending an adjustor from my area who could go out and 'just do the loss': right. Some companies still do not get it, even after all these years. It happens that two of these clients who recently got hail damage have annual crop premiums of over $150,000, yet these company people want to treat them the same as if they had $1,000 of premium and send out a rookie. Furthermore, I am writing premiums of over $5,000,000 with this company, and I know the crop lines. I know how easy it is to anger a big account (any account, for that matter) and watch it go to a competitor because an inexperienced adjustor went out and "Just worked the loss." So what do I do? I'll start calling in about 15 minutes, get in touch with my field man, and start reminding him of all the promises he and his company made: you know, the promises about how I would get good, experienced adjustors when I need them, etc., when he was recruiting my agency to write with his company. I am not even mad. Yet. After all the years and all the claims, though, it would be nice to think that you would finally reach a place where the companies would simply do the correct thing. Nah, never happen. The message? When crap like this happens to you, get it fixed before you are out in the field with baby adjustors who need diaper changes, or ones who act as if the money they are spending is right out of their own pockets and you end up losing a big account.

Guess what? After a few calls the company finally agrees to send me the experienced adjuster, Duane Knutson, I had requested in the first place. Now here I am, out in the middle of a canola field. I have walked a few hundred thousand acres of crop over the years, so I have a pretty accurate idea of how bad a crop is hit myself. However, this is canola, a fairly new crop to me. Thus the adjustor and the farmer and I look over the many ruined plants, talk about the crop, and try to see what the damage is. Many of the counts, of course, have to be factored into a chart to see what percentage of loss we are at, but in my own mind I am thinking that the crop is at least half shot. Finally, after counting and looking at his charts, the adjustor says it looks to him as if the loss is around 70%. Wow--I am impressed! It turns out that both the farmer and I were thinking about 50%. It really pays to have someone out there who knows what is going on. We all walk off the field satisfied: me, the adjustor, and, most importantly, the farmer-client. Best of all, after a half-sleepless night worrying about whether or not I would get a good adjustor out there for my client, I realize it is an absolutely beautiful day: puffy clouds, 72 degrees, a light wind, and no mosquitoes. What a difference it makes when you work with the best! Good adjustors keep good accounts on the books. The message here is that you absolutely must see to it that you have secured an experienced adjustor for your client.

Now about the corollary to the above story: if you find yourself out in a field or, for that matter, in the middle of any claim, and your client and the adjustor are not getting along, it is perfectly OK to declare a timeout and call the claims manager for that company to see if

132

a change can be made. If you let the situation escalate, I virtually guarantee you this account will not stay with you long. You, the agent, and your client both have a perfect right to say you want another adjustor. However, many times clients do not say enough; they talk by moving their accounts somewhere else. It is up to you, if at all possible, to know when the adjustment is not an accurate one. Please understand that most of the time when I am talking about a bad adjustor, I am not talking about a crook or someone who wakes up every morning with the thought of shafting the consumer. Usually when we are talking about a bad adjustor, we are talking about someone who has poor people skills or is simply inexperienced. Remember, in most cases clients really do not know what they have coming anyway. They probably do have something of an idea, but in most cases they rely on the adjustors to guide them through the claim process. It takes an adjustor with good people skills to do this. Remember, if clients do not like adjustors, or do not trust them, or simply cannot get in sync with them, it can heavily impact how happy clients are with settlements, regardless if they are good or not. I have seen a bad adjustor actually overpay an account yet make a client so mad we lost the business. Bottom line; see to it that the claims get handled successfully and your clients will see to it that you are successful.

• **Do get involved in the claim process.**

• **Yes, there are good and bad adjustors; use the power you have as an Independent Agent to be sure your clients get the good ones.**

• **Ultimately, professional claims service, not a flashy advertising campaign, will determine the success of your store.**

- **The extra work you do on claims is just prepaid advertising.**

BIG DEDUCTIBLES, ANYONE?

It is impossible to talk about losses and not talk about deductibles. I have always been a believer in large deductibles. Nevertheless, I have learned over the years to be sure when we sell clients on larger deductibles to be equally sure they understand what they have purchased. Talk to your clients about the fact that the money they save on large deductibles, multiplies over years. In other words, if they save $1,000 a year by going to a larger deductible and save this money for 10 years, they have saved $10,000. So what if clients have a few claims? They will usually be thousands of dollars ahead anyway. With higher deductibles clients do not look at the insurance industry as a warranty on their lives; they look at the insurance industry for what it really is: protection against catastrophic loss. Furthermore, what companies and agents so many times fail to understand is that if you have clients who are buying large deductibles, they simply get out of the mindset of having or even looking for claims all the time. By selling larger deductibles you, your agency, and your companies can get back in the catastrophe recovery business and out of the warranty business. You have less work, the company has fewer claims, and the clients save lots of money. No one loses with this equation. Take your clients to higher deductibles. Use the money they save to purchase better policies. How many times have you seen a poorly written policy that has only minimal coverage, yet has a low deductible? By using higher deductibles you will be able to save your clients money, get them better policies, and get them back in the proper mindset about insurance.

Linda, me, good friends Rick Anderson and Bill Burke. Bill and his wife, Elaine, let us write their contracting business and it opened up a whole new nitch market for us. Rick and his wife, Kathy, are good farm clients.

We do get snow in N.D.

Me and some snow mobile trophies.

Me and good friend, Ken Yuly with one of Ken's re-
stored Jeeps.

Casey left, and son, Matt, right. A perfect N.D. after-noon in the shade.

Linda, Gene and Ann Reiling on the docks in Vancou-ver, B.C. "Baby, baby, you know I love you, baby..."

Getting the N. D. PIA Agent of the Year Award from good friend, Darrel Rued of Auto Owners.

Brother Casey, son Matthew, me, Linda and her sister, Jackie. We had just tested and passed a new belt grade.

LaVerne Mikkelson, in hat, competing in a tractor pull. He is a super friend, a business genius and one of our biggest clients. He is the one who dickered the bank down on our South Broadway property buy.

The Glenburn office. We use part of the building. We rent the rest to the U.S. Postal Service and a two bedroom apartment. Result: we get a free office.

My residence where I had the offices of Western Agency, Inc. in the basement.

Western Agency, Inc. office in Minot.

Linda at Big Sky.

Banker C.P. "Buck" Moore. His loan saved our company. We went riding a few years later at Big Sky. First, he rode me into the ground. Then, he beat me at golf. Linda and I are eternally grateful to him.

Linda's folks, Don and Darleen Ballantyne.

"Ice on the wing", "Angels may sing".
Just before selling good old 7949Y.

Who says we don't have trees in North Dakota. Me after dropping a huge, dead cottonwood.

Casey, a field rep, Marlen and author. We had just moved into our new offices at 408 20th Avenue. Marlen was still feeling fine, I had less grey hair – times were good.

Linda on her rodeo horse, "Red".

The "Little Shit" at speed during a race.

The idea for the cover pose.

The truck I drove in the 1976 flood. "My hat's off to you, truck drivers". "Me, I've been committed to the insurance business ever since."

1980 - Skinny and no grey hair.

Me, John Simonson, Bob Richter, Dan Messnore. John is the one who told me to quit partying and go to work or I'd just be another drunk. Luckily, I took his advice.

The guy who hit this jump behind me broke his back in three places. 1982 Regina - Minot 250 Mile Cross Country Snowmobile Race.

North Dakota Govenor John Hoeven and me. I flew Gov. Hoeven to several campaign stops during the 2004 election.

The Problem:
Ice on the windshield of 7949Y. I couldn't see a thing straight ahead. I went home and told Linda that we needed a plane with de-iceing capabilities.

The Solution:
Casey and I the day we took delivery in 340 PP. It is a "known ice" plane with heated windshield, heated props and device boots.

Linda and I in front of the old office at 1728 Burdick Expressway. The basement is where I lived as a bachelor

Linda at the finish line of the 1980 Regina - Minot 250 Mile Cross Country Snowmobile Race. She took fourth that year.

Jesse Zwak, Chuck Barney, me, brother Casey and
Wayne Zwak. After a successful pheasant hunt, what a
perfect, beautiful day. Oh yes, the one who did all the
work and found the birds was Wayne's dog, Scout.

Me and Linda at fundraiser for North Dakota Gov. John
Hoeven. We flew Gov. Hoeven to several campaign
meetings in North Dakota and Minnesota in 340 PP
during Hoeven's 2004 Gubanatorial Campaign.

15

Bill and Elaine Burke and their partner Jeff Anderson, after a hard day of Marlin fishing off Kailua Kona, Hawaii.

Kilauea Caldera on the Big Island of Hawaii. The volcano has been active for over 20 years. I fly a few air tours when I'm on the Big Island.

Higher deductibles are a no-lose proposition: use them.

A final word on big deductibles: a few years ago I was reading a financial advice book with a section on insurance. The highfalutin financial advisor was preaching big deductibles as if he had just discovered the Holy Grail. Furthermore, he made it sound as if it was a big secret and we insurance people were kind of keeping this big secret on saving money from the public. Hell, I have been pitching big deductibles for 20 years; I am sure many of you have, also.

In the early 1990s I had an account that was pretty tough to deal with. The client was always complaining about premiums, and probably the only reason I had been able to insure him at all was I had his uncle insured. It was always a huge struggle to get him to insure things adequately so we would be able to get his claims paid. About this time the company where we had placed his coverage came out with an excellent discount for a higher deductible. I was out doing the renewal and explained this to the client. I told him we could go to the higher deductible, and with the money we saved double the coverage on his machine shed, and raise the coverage on his blanket equipment coverage. Without raising his premium. Grudgingly, he agreed to do it.

This would have been just one more customer policy review for me if a small tornado had not gone through this man's farm yard, destroying a machine shed about a year later. When the farmer called me after the storm to report the loss, he wanted to know when I would be out to inspect the damage. We agreed to meet at six a.m. the following morning at his farm, and I told him I would have an adjustor there by noon. When I arrived at the farm that next morning, it was a spectacular day; on a day like that, North Dakota is one of the most wonderful places in the world. It was hard to believe that less than 15 hours before a roaring tornado had gone through the very spot where we were standing. The birds were singing, the crops were growing lush green, and I was in a marvelous mood. Furthermore, there was absolutely nothing left of the machine shed except some bricks in one corner, a ruined furnace lying on its side, and a few piles of miscellaneous nuts and bolts. Everything else was scattered over the south side of Renville County, never to be recovered. It was hard to believe that the day before this had been a busy farm shop with literally thousands of nuts, bolts, tools, spare parts, chemicals, and dozens of other things that keep a busy wheat farm humming. But to make my point, I was glad the building was a total because it would be an easy loss to settle. However, from the very moment I got there, it was obvious my client did not feel the same way.

We walked around taking pictures of the damage to the other buildings, marveling at how the twister had missed the man's house by less than 100 feet. Still, my client was in a very glum mood; I could not get him cheered up. I said "Jim, don't worry about this loss. It will be easy to settle, and I'll have an adjustor out here in an hour or so, to get you taken care of." "Yeah," he responded dejectedly, "but I didn't have near enough insurance on the machine shed, did I?" It was then I reminded him when he had gone to a higher deductible the previous year, we had used the money saved to double the amount of coverage on both the tools and the equipment as well as the machine shed. After hearing this his face lit up, and the difference in his attitude was absolutely beautiful to see. I just wish I could have had my new agents (or, for that matter, the entire staff) with me that day so they could have seen first-hand the results good work can bring. Not only that: the adjustor did not have to fight about the adjustment with a client who was underinsured and wanted to create more coverage after the loss. Needless to say, we still have this man insured and most likely will have his insurance for the rest of his financial lifetime. Furthermore, he gave us his car insurance a few weeks later. Claims like this are what make me happy I chose the insurance field for a career. People do not want to pay a premium and buy an insurance policy. But when things hit the fan, that policy is the best friend they have. If all of us do our jobs, the system works.

We are now in a hard market and finally the companies are really clamping down on people who are career claimers, but we have always tried not to do business with these people. You know who they are: the ones who think they have to get their premium back every year by either having a loss or creating one. After having run into quite a few of these people, all I can say is why do business with them? I absolutely love to get my clients paid a fair settlement when they have losses. But you simply cannot win with someone who looks at an insurance contract as an income opportunity. Some of these folks are crooked; some are only excessively careless. They have the attitude "Who cares if I have a claim? I've got insurance." When we find we have an account like this, we do everything possible to send the person to GEICO or a direct writer or one of my competitors. Let the career claimer ruin your competitor's loss ratio, use up their time, give them ulcers. You can use the extra contingency money you earn and the extra time you have to go to Hawai'i and have a good Mai Tai.

Another thing I have found in people like this is that they are seldom very nice people. Invariably they are the ones who are constantly bitching to you about how much they pay for premiums. Am I right? Then why do you insure them? We try to get these people to go to another agency and usually can do it with a minimum of fuss, but once in awhile they get mad over it. Yes, we constantly hear statements like "You should never make a customer

137

mad because he will tell at least 10 other people how dissatisfied he was with your service." You know what my read is on this? Jerks run with jerks and good people run with good people. It would be my nightmare to make a good account angry and have him tell 10 other good people what poor work we did. However, when I find we are dealing with a jerk and need to send him on his way, I sincerely hope he goes and tells at least 10 of his jerk buddies what a horrible store we are. We do not need them either.

- **Big deductibles are a win for you, your client, and the companies.**

- **Good claims service sells you more policies**

- **Get rid of career claimers.**

LESS IS MORE: Learning to Delegate

In the early 1990s, after we had gotten our financing secured, I was also in the process of learning how to delegate more authority. The store was now writing $2,100,000 in premium, and I could not be involved in all the accounts directly. This delegation of authority is the hardest thing I have ever learned. Furthermore, to teach your staff how to delegate properly is a big task in itself. Delegation in its simplest terms is simply this: you decide whom you are going to delegate the task to, you tell them about the task, you make sure they know what it is they are to do, and you get them committed to doing the job. It is important that it is made clear they will do the work in the time frame you need to have it done. You then teach them how to do the work or see the client you have assigned them to take care of, or you assign them to do whatever task you have decided to delegate to them. Then comes the key part of delegation: after the person has been given the job, the person doing the delegating is responsible for checking back with this employee to see if the job is actually being done; I use my automation to do this. However you decide to do it, you absolutely must check back to see if the job is being correctly done. Depending on the complexity of the task, you may want to check back hourly, then daily, then weekly, then monthly, then every six months, then yearly. You get the idea. Whether it is you or your staff; whoever is doing the delegating must check back and validate that the job is in fact being done and done correctly.

Again, I go back to my notes I took so many years ago. *I am sitting in the carwash: wishing it would go faster, watching the soap drip down, drinking yet another cup of coffee I do not need. (I have had too damn much already.) I feel so busy today; it seems as if I am just not getting enough done. But wait: most of the big things are done; the staff is on top of everything. Maybe the game has changed again, and I am really getting a huge amount done, only in different ways...* *by delegating.* I wrote this at 9:10 a.m. on September 10, 1991.

Delegating is hard. Many times people do not delegate because they feel that the job will only be done right if they do it; anyone else will screw it up. If you are in business for yourself and you feel this way, I can tell you this: with rare exceptions it will most likely kill your business eventually if you cannot learn to delegate. If the people you have hired cannot learn, get rid of them and hire a staff that can. Is delegating hard to learn? Yes. Do you have to do it? Same answer.

• **Regarding delegation of authority, the more you give up, the more you can do.**

139

• Validate the delegation.

• If you cannot learn to delegate, you will eventually kill your store.

RETENTION: The Cinderella of Management

In the early 1990s, after taking tight control of my production numbers to help get my loans together, I was more and more paying attention to what the agency was doing. I could see we were growing at a good steady rate, yet our new sales were not spectacular. I would go to a sales meeting or seminar, and it would seem our sales numbers were anemic compared with many of the stars of the show. Aside from the fact that most agents lie about production the way people lie about gas mileage, it seemed to me, compared to many stores, we simply were not selling as much new premium. Yet when I looked at how many years these stores had been in business compared to how many years Western Agency, Inc., had been in business, we had super growth compared to theirs. I finally began to realize that it was our spectacular retention ratio that was making our "real" growth so good. It was just one of those things I had kind of been aware of but had not graphically seen until I got into analyzing our year-end numbers compared to prior years. Perhaps now is a good time to go over how we track and work on client retention.

Ever since Buck had made me write a business plan, I had started to be more and more focused on where we came from, where we intended to go, and how we intended to get there as an agency. I had begun to track written premium for each company we represented, the commission we earned each year, loss ratios, etc. I put this material on a spreadsheet and I have done this document for years. Four years' records fit on this spreadsheet. In addition, I can go back in prior years' files and see many more. I originally had the document typed out until I had it entered on Excel. No matter how you do it, it works either way.

In addition, every month I began keeping track of any accounts we lost and why we lost them. Many times I have the agent or one of the CSRs get in touch with a prior client whose insurance we have lost to find out why we lost their account if we do not already know. This information too is entered on an Excel spreadsheet so we can track our retention numbers all through the year. At any time during the year I can quickly see how many accounts we lost, how much premium, the average premium for account lost, which agency, which agent is losing them and so forth. This information, too, I put on the above production spreadsheet. It not only helps me see what my retention ratio really is; it also helps me know which clients, what type of premium, and the size of accounts we are losing. It really helps me stay focused and quickly see if we are having a retention-related problem.

Western Agency, Inc., has had a 95% or better retention ratio for as long as I have been keeping records. Maybe the reason for this good retention ratio goes way back to my Nodak Mutual training: we had to do a complete account review every year, or we simply did not get paid commission on that account. I have always tried to continue this close contact with our insureds. We are probably meeting with our large accounts almost monthly, but on all of our accounts we are still very high-touch. Even on the smaller accounts, my CSRs divide them up and make sure we call every one of our accounts at least once a year. We have dubbed these our "warm fuzzy" calls. Sure we are trying to account develop, but by and large the 'warm fuzzy' call is not a high pressure sales call. These calls are telling our clients we are there for them, and if they have any questions or problems, we want to get them fixed. As I said before, we do try to stay in touch on losses to be sure they are correctly settled. We do shop accounts if we feel they need it, but only if we feel they need it. Then we can tell our clients we have looked over the markets to see where they sit in them. I am not saying we move accounts for every little premium raise; we do not. But we do discuss where clients are in the marketplace and let them decide what to do. In most cases the difference is not that great and we are able to keep the account where it is. The bottom line is our clients know we are looking out for them.

However, I really think that this great retention ratio of ours stems from one main thing: we try to do the BEST job for the BEST people. In other words, we have, ever since the inception of the agency, made a steady, consistent effort to write the better accounts. By this I mean the agribusiness men and women: solid businesses, responsible homeowners. It seems to me if you concentrate on good people, you can work with them better. Solid accounts will take the time to let you set them up a good insurance program. They will better understand the need for extra coverages and the costs of such extra coverages. In short, these people will let you do the job you need to do. By doing a better job and selling a better product, you can be sure the claims will be paid. This even further cements the relationship, getting you out of a price arena and into a coverage arena. I guess a final point is that we do everything we can to be talking about coverages instead of price. Remember this: whatever the price is, it will be too high. Remember this old proverb also: " He who lives by the sword will die by the sword." If you only sell on price, you will eventually lose the account on price. How do you feel when you get your own premium notice? It is not as bad as a root canal, but still it is far from a fun thing. Yes, we have to be competitive. It sure pays, however, to discuss coverages with your clients and educate them to buying a better product. In the end you both win.

We are always looking for quality prospects, and the way we find better people is from our existing client base. We are always asking for referrals. Many times we have one of our clients call a prospect on our behalf. They seem happy to do it, and it really works. A couple of years ago we had a contest in which if someone gave us a referral and we wrote the account, we put that person's name referring the account to us in a hat for a year-end drawing. The drawing was for airfare and the use of my condo in Hawaii for one week. The first year we did this contest we wrote over $300,000 in new premium and sent a happy man and his wife to Hawai'i; I guess we can spring for some airfare and condo rent for that amount of new premium. To guard against the contest being called a rebate, we did not specify that the person giving us the name of a prospective client be one of our insureds. Nonetheless, one of my ever-zealous competitors called up the insurance commissioner to accuse me of rebating because we were giving away a trip. The commissioner called me up to tell me that even though it was a gray area, it would be a good idea if I did not do the contest anymore, so we stopped it. Maybe if my competitors were spending more time being out in the field doing a good job for their clients and less time checking to see what I am doing, they would not be losing market share to us. Poor babies!

Finally, in the attempt to write good business, we really screen our accounts. If someone walks into our office asking for an insurance quote, our first question is "Who sent you?" Remember what I said about good people running with good people? I strongly feel that if the person referring the prospect is a good account, the person being sent to us will be also. After we get a new prospect, we then try to determine who the person is. If the individual needs coverage for a farm, home, or business, we go out and inspect the premises before we get started quoting I call these pre-inspections our "mini Dunn and Bradstreets." We do no phone quotes of any kind: if you are doing phone quotes, you are just running a public rating service; and often you are wasting your time because you are not getting paid. All of these things seem to combine to get us some spectacular clients; I would put my book of business up against any I have ever seen. What we are doing to keep our good clients is working, and I intend to keep doing things this way in the future.

Of course, we do lots of very local advertising, but probably not the kind you would think. We sponsor after-prom parties, we sponsor after-graduation parties, we do scholarships in many small towns where we do business, we spend lots of money on 4H projects, and we help sponsor local rodeos. In short, we try to be a good neighbor in more ways than just an ad on TV. In addition, we send out a quarterly newsletter to our clients and do quite a few giveaways such as jackknives, hats, and specialty coffee. We do no radio or TV ads. I sincerely believe the methods of advertising we are using work because our clients send us a steady stream of new prospects and do everything they can to help us get more business. I always call the jackknives I give away "my business cards." I just love it when a client stops by the office and says he needs "a new business card"--how great! When you have your clients wanting to stop by your office, it is such a change in paradigm from the attitude most people have about stopping into their insurance agent's office, is it not?

- Stay high-touch with your clients to improve retention; retention is one of the golden keys to a successful store.

- Find out whom you lost and why you lost them.

- "Warm fuzzy" calls: try them.

- Know where your clients' policies are in relation to the market so that you can defend where you have their coverage placed.

- Retention goes up if you insure better people.

- Always being the cheapest is not the way to have good retention.

- Advertising can be fun and does not have to cost you an arm and a leg.

DON'T WAIT, AUTOMATE

By the mid 1990's I had been looking at automation for years, going to numerous seminars and demonstrations, and reading many books on the subject. It seemed in the early 1980s that automation in the agency was not really there yet and the cost was totally out of our league anyway. In the 1990s there were automation systems out there that were true agency management systems; thus we started looking into them in earnest. I had decided that I would probably use Agena because it seemed Applied Systems was too expensive at the time, but at a PIA convention in the early 1990s I ran across a vendor from Minnesota who had a small agency management system that was "much cheaper," so we ended up going with it. Going for a "cheaper" automation system turned out to be a short-term fix for a long-term problem. It was to prove a mistake for us to have gone this way a few years later. However, for the first few years, it worked very well, giving us a management system with a database that finally brought us into the automated agency age. Nevertheless, I was about to find out something that all the seminars and books and demonstrations had failed to mention, which is that all vendors do several things the same: they lie about how good the system is and what it will do; they lie about how simple it is to get it up and running; they lie about the total cost of the system; they lie, lie, lie. Over the years I have come to believe that if computer software people's lips are moving, they are probably not telling me the truth. Do we need automation? Of course! Just remember, there is no Santa Clause.

I am probably getting ahead of myself, but I may as well say right now that the problems with our first agency management system started as we got bigger, really coming to a head in 1998 when our vendor came out with their "new updated software." The new software was a nightmare; we installed it too soon after it was released, so it still had many bugs in it. As a result, we could not get the programs up and running reliably, which made a total mess of our system. Since we were not the only agency having trouble, the phone lines to the vendor were always busy, we could never get through, and nothing was working. As you know, once you are automated, it is really a nightmare if the system crashes. I begged the vendor to send someone out to our store to get us back up and running; I told the company I did not care what it cost. But the little vendor had nobody to send. In retrospect I realize that they simply did not have enough people on staff for someone to go out to our agency to get things going. For three months we struggled along, paperwork and files getting more and more screwed up. Finally, I began calling a bunch of agencies that had automation to find out whom they were using. The name Applied Systems kept coming up.

Early in July I called Applied Systems and was put through to a salesman whose name, I believe, was Jeff. I said, "Hi, Jeff, this is Chuck Tompkins with Western Agency, Inc., and this is your lucky day." When he asked me what I meant, I replied, "I want a different automation system, I want it now, and I want yours. How much is it?" He explained the cost and what we needed to do to get up and running. I said, "When can you start?" We agreed on August 1, 1998. Of course, as I said previously, the cost was more than they said it was, and not nearly as much information transferred automatically from our current management system to theirs as they said. Consequently, it took far more time to install than they initially told us. However, it was far superior to our first system. One of the big advantages of the Applied Systems software was they had people on staff who could come out to your agency and help train your staff. The woman who was to train us arrived right on time; furthermore, she did a spectacular job. When all was said and done, the cost was not that much more money than the junk system I had been trying to use, anyway. At last we had an automation system that worked. The only drawback was that we had to re-input our entire database. It was a bunch of extra work, but we had no choice: it had to be done.

This brings up a couple of points on automation. First of all, buy the absolutely best system that you can without bankrupting yourself. DO NOT, I repeat DO NOT buy a cheap system that is "just as good as the big guys." It is not and they are not. Remember what I said about their lips moving? Furthermore, after you have a junk system and have to convert it to a real system, you are going to end up re-inputting your entire database. This takes lots of time, costs you a bunch of money, and will be very disruptive to your staff: not as much as using a poor system, but disruptive nonetheless. If you are shopping for automation, try to talk to as many people as you can, particularly someone who has had a bad system and had to convert. I find many people will call someone with a cheap system up and end up buying the cheap system, unaware that the person with the cheap system does not even have a clue as to how much better a real system is. A good automation system will unquestionably help you run a better store. It will help you generate beautiful proposals. It will lessen your E&O exposure. It will add professionalism to your operation. Excellent automation can easily network people together if you have multiple locations. It is better when you are trying to find out information on automation, talk to someone who knows about it and is using it; not someone who is getting a commission for persuading you to buy it.

A final note on automation: go with a vendor who will send someone out to train your staff. It is virtually impossible to send a few folks from your staff to a far-away town, train them for a week, and then have them come back and get your entire staff up to speed on a complicated agency management system. It cost me $8,000 in 1998 to have Applied send someone out to train my staff, but it worked so well it was worth the money; the trainer came out for one week when we first went on the system, then came back for another week after a month had gone by to show us how to close out our month end. I am not saying Applied or any other vendor is perfect, but they sure as hell are better than what I had (probably enough said).

There is a funny footnote to this story, however. The company that sold the first system I had was constantly using me for advertising--having people call me and ask how the system worked etc.--and for the first few years it worked fine. Back then I probably helped them sell quite a few systems. After I had gone with someone else, though, they did not know it and were still having people call me. I told these people that they would be crazy to buy that system and that they ought to go with another vendor. It stands to reason that I recommended Applied because that is what I had and it was light years better than my old system. It was not too long before the sales guy with the original company called me to ask why I was badmouthing his product. I told him for heaven's sake because it WAS bad. He seemed to have totally forgotten how they had left me out twisting in the wind for three months a year ago; he apparently did not remember how I had begged him to help me when his junk product crashed and my agency was upside down. Once I had reminded him of this, he did not use me for referrals anymore.

- **If the lips of an automation salesman are moving, he is likely to be lying.**

- **There is no such thing as good cheap automation; buy the best system you possibly can without going broke.**

- **Automation will cost you more than they said it would, take more time and effort than they said it would, and will not be quite as good as they said it would; and their help line will put you on hold virtually all the time.**

- **Automation will save your store, increase your professionalism, skyrocket your reaction time, give you excellent proposals at the touch of a finger, and move you to the head of the class.**

• CHAPTER EIGHT •

HOLDING ONTO MY YOUTH

Western Agency, Inc., has always been a niche marketing organization, and the early '90s were very good growth years for us. We were really finding out how to run the store; now it was time to capitalize on the vertical growth of our main niche market, farms, and develop our new niche market, contractors. Being in the right market became obvious in 1992 when we posted solid growth of 20% in the casualty lines. The growth in casualty slowed to 10% for 1993, but still the store was moving steadily ahead. Again in 1994 we showed solid 10% growth for the entire store. We had gotten our earnings per employee up to $66,000; efficiency was starting to come into focus in our operation; in addition, we were now paying wages instead of commissions. Since the wages were commensurate with the job being done, we were finally showing a significant profit for the first time in the history of the agency. I was able to have a net income at last.

I started the year of 1995 by returning to snowmobile racing. Basically, I had been retired from the sport for quite a few years. Although I had done some racing in the late '80s and early '90s, I had not been very serious about it. In the early 1990s my son Matt had talked me into going to a karate class with him. Since I thought it would be good exercise and good father-son interaction, I enrolled in the class. It turned out that it was the best exercise program I have ever been on and I found myself in better shape than I had been for years. Since being in good shape is the main requirement for cross country snowmobile racing, I decided to see if the old guy could still do it. I bought a new Polaris XCR 600 cross country

150

race machine, called my old mechanic, and told him to set it up for me. I started practicing and riding, and he soon had the sled running like a rocket. The first race I entered was the Pro 600 Class of the 1995 Belcourt Lake Race. It was a Can Am Race Association sanctioned competition, so there were entrants from Alberta, Saskatchewan, Quebec, North Dakota, and Minnesota. I had been the Pro Class Champion on this circuit for two years, but that had been a long time ago.

It seemed like déjà vu as I found myself unloading the sled on a cold, crisp, beautiful winter morning at Belcourt Lake. The smell of the two-stroke exhaust was perfume in the air. The rasp and crackle of the engines being warmed up made a raucous symphony of sound. It was great to be back at an event, sitting in the pits, talking to many old friends, who were surprised to see me actually entered in a pro race since most of my contemporaries had long since retired. Many of them had kids who were now competing. I know most of them were wondering what the hell this old man was doing out there. What they did not know was that the old man was in killer shape and had come to race. The distance was a 90 mile cross country, 12 laps around Belcourt Lake. The day was perfect for racing, cold and clear. As I shook off the pre-race jitters and stared down the starting straight-away, it was as if the years melted away. They say when the green flag drops, the BS stops: so it was to be that day. The sled ran like a bullet, and I was physically and mentally ready for action; I was pulling over 100 m.p.h. down the back chutes, and the exhilaration was indescribable. When the snow dust finally settled, I had taken second place in the Pro 600 Class in an internationally sanctioned race--what a rush! Once the excitement died down, I told Linda, "To have a race that good that late in my career must be a sign." I sold the sled and have not raced since. It was a special day that I shall never forget.

Youth and fame are sweet but fleeting, are they not?

- **Know what your markets are and try to develop them: find your niche.**

- **Grab your youth and hold onto it like grim death for as long as you can.**

- **Even if you are busy in your job, do not forget to live.**

LET'S GO SHOPPING: Buying More Stores

The year 1995 was just getting started when I got a call from a small agent in town who told me he wanted to sell his insurance agency. I knew he had an aged book of business, but we went over to have a look at the store anyway, agreeing within a couple of days on a purchase price. Since the agency was quite small, the price was $26,000. The deal closed on January 1, 1995. Not only was the price cheap; but also, we had to pay merely half down and half on a contract for deed. We did not have to hire the prior owner or any of his staff, and I could see that the agency would be an excellent fit for us. I did not expect it to grow by a huge amount of premium, but it would be good, solid business; it turned out it did not grow much, but it has paid for itself many times and will continue to do so. Incidentally, this was the little store where one of my former secretaries was working. She was one of the women we had let go in our huge money crunch of the late 1980s, the individual who was chronically late and had been a pretty weak player, anyway. Needless to say, we were unable to offer her a job. Inputting the book of business was a snap. I got our

152

entire staff together one Saturday, taking care of the basic inputting in one day. Ain't automation grand?

We had just barely started work on this agency when another store I had been trying to buy for many years came up for sale. It was a slightly bigger store for which we agreed on a price of $36,000. Again, the purchase agreement was half down and half on a contract for deed. This owner, too, wanted to retire and had no staff for us to take over: another sweet deal. We got the staff together again on a Saturday to accomplish all of the basic inputting in eight hours once more. The big difference in this agency versus the other one we had just bought was this second agency was a younger book of nearly 100% farm business, on which the owner had never written multiperil crop insurance. Since the agency was located in a small town 30 miles from Minot, we purchased a small office building there to open up shop. You think I was crazy to purchase an office building for a small book of business? Probably so, but consider this: half of the office building was rented to the United States Postal Service, a two-bedroom apartment was rented out in the back, and I only needed the two little rooms up front. With the rent from Uncle Sam and the apartment, the building made us money from day one. I ended up with a personal presence in the town and some extra rent income to boot. How did we do on this buy? We developed that little store from $300,000 of premium to over $3,500,000 in the next six years--what a deal!

Naturally, neither of the stores was automated; and in both cases we did not keep any staff, for basically both former agents just wanted to retire from the business. This pair of excellent buys has paid for itself many times. The automation was easy to put in place, and often it is simpler if the prior owner does not stay on. You thus avoid the constant battle of trying to get them up to speed on learning automation, attempting to teach the proverbial old dog new tricks.

Both of these buys made us money. Over the years the aged book of business has, however, slowly died off; though, as I said, it has paid for itself many times, we have not been able to grow it much. I think the main reason is the average age of the clientele of this store was probably at least 60. These people were very resistant to change, we simply could not get many referrals from them, and they were dead-set against upgrading their policies. Furthermore, the policies this agent had been selling were basic fire and so forth on pretty poor buildings. Every time we tried to upgrade the coverage and get the clients to purchase better policies, they dug in their heels, constantly using the line that they already were "insurance poor." This prevented us from really developing the book. Yes, we have made money on this buy, but I still do not think I want any more aged books like this because you simply have too tough a time growing them.

It turned out one of the clients of this agency really was "insurance poor." He had a basic coverage on his farm outbuildings that one of my agents tried to get him to upgrade to a better contract, but he gave us the "insurance poor" line, telling us to leave the policy as it was. Two months later we had a terrible blizzard that totally destroyed his main barn, which collapsed from the weight of snow on its roof. Yep, he was right, he was insurance poor: his basic contract did not cover collapse. If he had purchased the broad form policy we had been trying to sell him, he would have been covered. He was typical of most of the people this little agency insured.

On the other hand, the agency with the younger, more vibrant book is, as I said, far bigger than when we bought it. It is possibly the best purchase we have ever made, continuing to grow and prosper. It has been a good model for us. We really like to look for agencies that are similar as we pursue other acquisitions.

During the purchase of these two stores, we again ran into a bit of a fun time at the bank. By now Buck Moore had retired and our big loan that had saved us a few short years ago was paid off. We were now using a local Norwest Bank where the officer was a friend of ours. He was the same one who was so amazed when I bought the $850 duck for Buck Moore. Since both agencies were half down and half on a contract for deed, I needed to borrow around $30,000. I stopped in at the bank one afternoon to talk to this officer about a short-term loan on the $30,000. Maybe I caught him in a sour mood. Anyway, I explained the terms of the deals and the fact they were both steals at the price we had been able to negotiate. Then I told him about the $30,000 I wanted for a couple of years on the required money down.

Right away, he asked how much of my own money I was putting into the deal. I told him none, reminding him I was giving him a personal guarantee on total assets of over a million for a lousy $30,000. He exclaimed, "Chuck, you never want to put your own money into a deal!" It was a pregnant moment. I looked at him, laughed, and said, "Piss on you, Kenny--I'll put it on my MasterCard!" He said, "You wouldn't." I said, "Just watch me," and left the bank. Neither of us was mad, and we were then and are now good friends; I guess he was not in the mood to deal that day and I was not in the mood to beg. So what did I do? Put the $30,000 down stroke on plastic. At that time MasterCard charged, I believe, only six or seven percent interest, while the bank wanted 11% on short-term money. I paid the credit card off eight months later. A month or so down the road I happened to see my banker buddy at some function, and he said, "You sonofabitch, you did put it on plastic, didn't you?" Banking was starting to be entertaining. Sales in 1995 were really cooking; and, with the addition of the two stores, we ended 1995 with growth of close to 20%. As you may recall, I was not paying commission anymore. Consequently, profits were actually beginning to skyrocket, along with our business acumen.

- **If a good little agency goes on the market, do not waste a bunch of time crunching numbers; do the deal.**

- **Often if the prior owner and staff do not go with the deal, it is a good thing.**

- **Pay attention to the age of the people insured.**

HAIL STORMS, LOST CONTINGENCIES AND JUAN VALDEZ

The year 1995 was shaping up to be another wild and crazy one. Early on, we had purchased those two insurance agencies, combining them with our book of business. Although we had hired some people along the way, I was still not happy with how my staff was functioning. Obviously, we were very busy and I knew I needed to hire more help, but we were just getting things paid off and I was really cautious about getting too heavy on overhead. Even now I tend to run the stores a little lean on employees. Once you have really been up against the wall for money, I guess you are never quite the same. You tend to try not to spend money quite as freely. In my case in those years, I was probably pushing my employees a bit too hard.

Another problem was starting to rear its ugly head; it seemed that Marlen, who had been such a solid, stable rock, whom everyone in the agency so admired for his excellent, steady manner and wonderful sense of humor, was not getting things done the way he had. Nothing I could put my finger on, it was just that he was not as infallible as usual. Apparently tired all the time, he was starting to make mistakes: he was not himself. Hoping it was merely a phase, I paid little attention to it at first. But it gradually began to worry me.

In addition, one of the new secretaries I had hired a few weeks earlier was looking like a bad hire. One of the few people whose test had come back false, the woman simply seemed untrainable. When I let her go a month later, I had come to the conclusion that we indeed could not teach her a thing. To date she is one of the few misfires I have had on the personality test I give all of my employees. I suppose nothing is perfect; in this lady's case the test turned out to be emphatically imperfect. Her one and only well-honed skill was drinking coffee.

By and large, though, the agency was thriving. The two new books of business had been integrated into our software, and we were going through a good, solid crop insurance year. There had been minimal claims and hail by early August, so Linda and I decided to take a short five-day trip to Philadelphia. While we were gone I called in every day or so to see how the office was doing. The new employee, with whom we were having some trouble, was answering the phone. Linda and I had been to the Gettysburg Battlefield for a couple of days when we got back to Philadelphia on August 17, 1995.

The next morning I phoned the office. The poor secretary, mentioned above, cheerfully told me I had no messages and everything was OK. For some reason I called back after lunch, and still she said I had no messages and everything was OK. I had been having Marlen work on something for me, so I asked to talk to him to see if he had gotten it done. When he came on the phone and I asked him about it, he said no, he had not gotten time to do it yet. A little disgusted the job was not done, I

157

told him so. All of a sudden he just blew up and yelled, "Goddamn it, we just had the biggest hailstorm we've had in 100 years! We've recorded over 150 losses so far today, and you're bitching about me not getting that other little job done?"   After a long pause I said I had heard nothing of the storm and asked him to tell me what had happened. It turned out that a colossal hailstorm that we later found out was 150 miles long and up to 15 miles wide had carved a path right through the middle of our territory. In the first two days afterward, our agency recorded 326 losses on this disaster.

Luckily, I had my computer and printer with me. After Marlen had plugged me into the problem, I sat down and typed up a letter to be sent out to all of our insureds who had claims, telling them what to do.   Then I went downtown and bought a little fax machine, hooked it up in my hotel room, and faxed the letter to the office so they could get it printed and sent out to each person who had filed a loss. The letter gave our phone numbers, the procedure for protecting their property from further loss, and the names of several reliable contractors I knew who would do good repair work. By four p.m. we had things pretty much back under control. I turned to Linda and said, "I really need to get rid of that secretary as soon as I get back to town." When I returned the next week, first thing Monday morning I called the lady into my office and gave her a sheet of paper with 20 things she needed to rectify if she was going to continue to work for Western Agency, Inc. I told her the items were non-negotiable; either she got up to speed immediately, or she could no longer work for us. She took her lunch break, and I have never seen her since. She was such a good coffee drinker that possibly she is now working for Juan Valdez at Folger's!

Getting rid of this one bad CSR was a good move, but I knew I had still more problems with my staff. This was to be a project I would not feel I had fixed until late 2004. By then I felt I had the best staff I could possible have. I really believe you never stop working on keeping your staff running smoothly. As I said, we do testing to try and match not only the staff to the management but also the staff to the job. I know it is working since our staff turnover rate is getting lower all the time. Nonetheless, keeping your staff operating smoothly with a common mission to do good work, keeping them in the mindset that, by and large, they enjoy coming to work, and having them all getting along is really a tall order.

The storm of 1995 was to have major consequences for the agency. We had never been hit with an event of this magnitude, and the end result was that we paid out over $8,000,000 in losses. Needless to say, our contingency income did not recover for over three years. Up to this time I was so used to getting $30,000 or more in contingency income every year that I kind of took it for granted. After the storm of 1995 I saw my contingency income drop to extremely low levels: 1995, $1,500; 1996, $3,400; and 1997, $4,183. It just seemed after that storm we were unable to get back in the contingency game like before. Figuring an average contingency income of $30,000 per year before the storm, I calculated that it cost me $90,000. Furthermore, afterward it just seemed as if every year something came up to kill our chances of getting a check. Finally, in 1998 we were able to get back in the game with a contingency income of $24,829. If that storm had hit in 1990, it would have been the end of the store.

Here are a couple of little notes while we are talking about contingencies. First one: it seems to me that companies have rewritten these contracts many times over the years, and I more and more notice that the contingencies are harder to hit and smaller when you do get them. I know when our field reps stop in with the "new" contingency contracts, they are always "better." But all I see is that our contingency income continues to be harder to achieve, even in the face of excellent low loss ratios. You will never convince me that the game has not changed. Further evidence of this is that we had hit a contingency with one of our main companies 11 years in a row. After the field rep came in with the new and improved contingency contract, I think it was five years until we got another one. Furthermore, we never have hit as high a number on a contingency check from this company as before, even though we are writing far more volume. People, someone is pulling a fast one. If it looks like horse manure, tastes like horse manure, and smells like horse manure, you can call it ice cream all you want, but it is still horse manure.

Second contingency note: if you companies or field reps are reading this, why is it that when the contingency check comes out, many of you insist the field rep has to deliver it in person? I tell you this: the contingency check is not some wonderful gift that you are going to bestow on the agent; no big presentation is necessary. In the early 1980s, when contingency systems first came into being, you companies were lowering commissions. You soft-sold it to us agents by telling us, "You 'good' agents with the low loss ratios will really be getting more money, due to being paid this wonderful contingency money." In my mind the contingency money is just commission dollars that were taken away years ago that each year I try to get back. Also, only by doing everything the company wants and having a low loss ratio do the dollars come back at all. Either way, I consider the contingency money to be a result of the good work of my staff and me; I don't consider it a gift. I need no big presentation--just send me the check! Often the field rep holds onto the check, supposedly waiting for a major moment; and by the time I get my money, all I am is mad. Message? Just send me the money.

Probably the only good thing to come out of the storm of August 18, 1995, was the spectacular job the agency did in getting losses settled and our people taken care of. Even though we had that dreadful agency management software system then, we were able to stay on top of and follow up on the claims. We got lots of good press for our work, and I knew that once again all the hard claim work would pay off as prepaid advertising. Evidently it did because again in 1995 we clocked over 20% net growth in the agency. Things were actually looking up, even if our loss ratio appeared pretty poor.

- **Big storms can kill your loss ratio for years.**

- **Contingencies are fleeting, not guaranteed, and they are not gifts since you earned them.**

- **Contingency checks should be sent out; they do not need to be hand-delivered.**

HOUSTON, WE HAVE LIFT-OFF:
Crop Prices Rise and Things Take Off

As year was drawing to a close, I had one more thing to accomplish. Years ago I had worked with a good friend of mine at Nodak Mutual. He, too, had quit after a few years and gone to work for Cass Clay Creameries as a deliveryman on a route for 14 years. The reason Craig had begun working for Cass Clay was that he got a steady paycheck; even though he loves to sell, he does not like the up-and-down income stream of commission sales. We had stayed in touch, and he and his family had been insured with me for many years. Since he was tired of getting up at three in the morning to go to work and

161

running in and out of coolers delivering dairy products all day, we had started talking about his going to work for Linda and me in the latter part of 1993. Finally, we were able to make a deal. What brought things to a head was that Craig also wanted to start farming part-time; since his dad was ready to turn the family farm over to him, it was a good time for him to make a job change. Of course, there was no way his present employer would allow him take off in the spring to plant his crop and in the fall to harvest it; so if he wanted to farm, he had to look at another form of employment. Our ability to offer flex-time hours was the perfect solution. In addition, he could continue to have a steady, predictable paycheck because we now paid salary, not commission. We also had a good benefit package. I agreed that Craig could take off up to 30 days in the spring to seed his crop and 30 days in the fall to harvest it. We set him up on a salary that he could live with, and away we went. It was the first time I used a flex-time package to get a quality employee, but it was surely not going to be the last.

The salary Craig needed to be paid to stay financially alive really pushed my budget to the limit. Linda and I talked long and hard to decide whether or not we could afford to put him to work at his price. I knew he would develop a good book of business which would eventually pay for his wages and even more, but in the beginning we were going to have to subsidize him for a few years until he was up and running. Just getting out of money trouble, we were very cautious in those years. Thank God we took a chance on this excellent person! Craig, after getting his insurance legs back under him, sprinted off with a string of sales that continues to this day. He is now manager of our entire farm insurance department, has five people working under him, and has probably been our best hire ever. Gee, come to think of it, maybe I should go out and recruit a bunch more deliverymen.

Since we had just purchased the two books of business and one was located in the area where Craig was born and raised, he took over both of them and got back in the insurance game. Furthermore, since he was a farmer himself, that line of insurance was a natural for him. Contrary to the agents I had gotten rid of, Craig took to multi-peril crop insurance like a duck to water. Still farming, he is now supervising over $6,500,000 in premium. Our getting back together has been a super deal for both of us.

At the end of 1995 we were up to earnings per employee of $68,000, and the store was really poised for a launch. Western Agency, Inc., was showing good, solid profits. Our debt had been reduced radically; we had been off the float now for years. The vision Linda and I had of being in the black was getting clearer by the day. What fun it was to own and manage a strong, healthy agency--it was a dream come true!

The prices farmers were being paid for their grain continued to rise so that 1996 turned out to be a very excellent year. Since we were now writing over 500 farms, we saw some of the best growth the store had ever experienced with final numbers of 18% growth. By not paying commission I was able to give my staff nice raises and still clock record profits for the store.

All through 1996 we were developing the two books of business we had purchased, seeing huge vertical growth as farmers replaced old, worn-out machinery with new farm equipment. There was a tremendous desire on the part of the farmers to purchase new equipment in those years. The growth I had foreseen and for which we had waited so long had finally arrived. I had gotten in the habit of sending Buck Moore our production numbers every year; even though the loan had been paid off long ago, it was getting more and more fun to send him the reports. Linda and I shall never be able to repay him for

163

believing in us and helping save Western Agency, Inc., in the late 1990s by giving us that loan.

In the fall of 1996, we went to see Buck in Montana. He and his wife Bobbi had a couple of condos at Big Sky resort, and he had invited us out many times to golf and go horseback riding with him. He was spending most of his summers at Big Sky, leading trail rides for one of the dude ranches in the area. He set up a trail ride for us, and away we went. On the first afternoon we headed up the Buck's Ridge Trail system on an excellent trip with lots of clear skies and beautiful Montana scenery. I was ready for a break when we dismounted, and so was Linda, while Buck looked as if he was not tired at all. The next day he took us on a long, all-day ride up into the Porcupine Trail system, where there was more spectacular scenery. This was one of the best trail rides we had ever been on. Although we were both totally pooped out when we returned, again Buck was not tired at all. When he suggested we do another ride the next day, we told him we were all ridden out. I could not believe the shape Buck was in for his age; he must have been in his late 60s at the time, yet he just rode us into the ground. We decided to golf the next day. Sure enough, he beat me at that, too.

In 1996 I was voted PIA Insurance Agent of the Year for North Dakota. A side note: I had been nominated for this award many times, each time dutifully doing a resume and sending it in to be voted on. When I got yet another nomination in 1996, I actually sent them a rather snotty note telling them I had submitted resumes for years and they could just use one of them. I mailed this missive off and forgot about it. You can imagine my surprise when my name was announced as the winner and I had to get up and give a little speech. All I can remember saying is that I could not have done it without my staff and if there had been an Olympics for Independent

Insurance Agencies, the staff of Western Agency, Inc., would take the gold. I still feel that way. We have had good staffs and better staffs; but, by and large, in the past 15 years we have had a bunch of good people working here. We came out of 1996 with earnings per employee of $79,000. This is a very good benchmark management number. When you start exceeding $75,000 earnings per employee, your Independent Agency is operating the way it ought to.

- **Use flex-time to get good employees.**

- **Old cowboys not only can ride you into the ground but also kick your butt at golf.**

- **Used award resumes work the best.**

CANCER AND REMOTE CONTROL:
Learning to Run the Store from 500 Miles Away

The final thing that happened in 1996 was that the price of wheat again took a nosedive. In early 1997 when I sat down and ran the numbers, I realized that we were going to lose at least $250,000 and possibly as much as $350,000 in premium the following year. This meant we would be $50-60,000 short on revenue. The lessons learned in 1985, '86, and '87 were remembered well. I sat the sales staff down and told them we somehow had to come up with $350,000 in brand-new, additional premium to replace what we were going to lose in the upcoming year. I was thinking this new premium would have to come primarily from multi-peril crop insurance and commercial insurance. We laid out a plan to replace that premium, and at the end of the 1997 year, it was amazing. The crop lines had indeed dropped $200,000.

However, due to advance preparation and good, solid sales work, my staff had been able to replace the lost premium and then some by adding new accounts and really pushing the commercial lines. At last I was running the store proactively instead of reactively. The system works if you know enough to use it. Things were looking up.

We started out 1997 like any other year. The future could not possibly have been brighter. Linda and I had gotten in the habit of going to the Big Island of Hawai'i for the past few years, and we had finally taken the plunge and bought a condo. We had begun by buying a time-share a few years prior but had gotten rid of it because we had no luck with it. We figured that the condo, a nice one on a golf course, could be rented out when we were not using it and by the time we retired it would be paid for. Life was looking pretty good. We should have known that we were about to get some bad news.

May of 1997 was going fine; we had super sales in both hail and multi-peril crop insurance, and the year was looking like another real home run. One busy day I was working in my office doing the usual things for that time of year when Linda came in and sat down across from me. She had just been to the doctor for her checkup. I did not look up until she started to speak, her voice shaking. Since Linda's voice never shakes, I really sat up in my chair as she said, "They told me I have cancer." She began to cry. A shiver ran through me as I ran around the desk and held her for some time. It was the most scared either of us had ever been in our lives on that early Wednesday morning, May 7, 1998. The reason the date is so easy to remember is that Linda's son Ryon was due to be married in Fargo exactly one month later. We did not know it, but a tough, long chapter was about to be written in our book of life.

Typical for a small-town medical operation such as we have in Minot, the solution Linda's doctor had suggested was to schedule her for surgery the following Monday "to go in and see what we find." I called my sister Cheri in Minneapolis, where she is in charge of prenatal care for United Hospitals in St. Paul. Needless to say, she is very well connected in the medical community. We had both gone to school with Victor Corbett; and since he was by now one of the best internal medicine doctors in the Minneapolis-St. Paul area, she recommended I get in touch with him. I got his home number and gave him a call that night. Luckily, he was home. I think the conversation went something like this. "Rick, this is Chuck Tompkins, can you talk a minute?" When he said yes I continued. "Rick, I've got big trouble, Linda has been diagnosed with colon cancer." We talked a few minutes, during which he said he had a friend who was a colon cancer specialist and he would call in a few days. We went to bed and tried to sleep.

The next day we got a call from Dr. David Rothenberger himself, who was then head of the American Colon Cancer Society and one of the foremost colon cancer doctors in the world. We agreed to meet him in St. Paul the coming Monday, so the next Monday morning, instead of Linda's being wheeled into surgery in Minot "to see what we find," we were sitting in David Rothenberger's office in St. Paul.

David told us that they would run tests for at least a week to determine exactly how big the tumor was, where it was, and how they intended to treat it. It was the first time in almost a week that we could tell we were talking to someone who really knew what he was doing. They say confidence in your treatment is half the battle in treating cancer, and we sincerely believe that is true because after meeting David we felt if there ever was a chance for Linda to survive, he would provide it.

Tuesday morning Linda started the regimen of tests that would consume every hour of every day for the next week. When she was not being tested, we rented a small apartment near the hospital and moved in. Linda says all she can remember of that first week is that she was X-rayed, prodded, probed, poked, and jabbed a thousand times. The following Monday we were again in David's office, where he showed us an ultrasound of the tumor. "Here is your tumor," he said. "It is a stage four, and here is how we are going to kill it." In a few more moments, he laid out the entire battle plan for Linda's life: he called it a protocol. According to him, Linda had a 60% or better chance of recovery; if we had waited even 30 days to come and see him, her chances would have been far less. As any of you know who have ever had much to do with cancer, if a tumor goes beyond stage four, you are in terrible trouble. David explained that Linda would be on chemo and radiation treatment for the next couple of months. Then and only then would the surgery be done to remove the tumor. We went home to get our affairs in order so we could spend the better part of the next six months in St. Paul. However, after hearing how they were going to treat Linda, both of us had a strange calm about us. We honestly felt we would be in the best place in the world and had the best doctor in the world to deal with her cancer. It turned out we were exactly right.

Since Linda had been the comptroller of the company, overseeing now almost four million in premium and over $600,000 in commission earnings, we needed to hire a replacement for her immediately. Luckily we had been trying to do just that anyway as we both felt it was time she should at least go to part-time at the office, so we had hired a gal who had an accounting degree only a month or so before. For years we had both been worried that since I managed the store and Linda did the books it was hard for us to both be away from the office. This sickness of hers just pointed up that nothing could have been closer to the truth. As I packed up my laptop

168

computer and we headed for St. Paul to begin the fight for Linda's life, I knew we would have to learn a bunch of new management procedures very quickly. We would not return home for more than a few days at a time for almost six months. We literally had to learn how to run a store from 500 miles away.

There is no sense in boring you with how the treatments went. All I can tell you is that it was incredible to watch the staff of United Hospitals in St. Paul and the team of Dr. David Rothenberger, working together in this most complicated, intense ballet of talent and caring. I had always known the woman I loved was one tough cookie, and the way she went through the ordeal with such strength and grace amazed me beyond words. Somehow, even though she was on chemo and radiation, she was still able to plan her part of Ryon's wedding, get a dress lined up, decide who would be invited and where we would have the rehearsal dinner. She was and is awesome--no wonder I am so mesmerized by her! By late fall of 1997, we were back home, trying to return to a normal life.

The agency came out of 1997 with written premium of $3,867,075, average commissions of 15.7%, and earnings per employee of a little less than $75,000. We had hired another woman, and the loss of our contingency income from the 1995 storm was really starting to tell, but still we were moving ahead. This loss of contingency income dropped our average commissions from 16.5% to 15.7%. Since our average commission had been 17.2% in 1995, it was the lowest our commission had been in three years. When I did my business plan for the upcoming year, I made it a priority for us to start looking at writing the higher- commission type of insurance. Furthermore, our premium growth from '96 to '97 had not been very good. It was one of our first years without strong growth. However, we were still up $200,000 in premium growth in casualty lines. The problem was that we were down almost an equal amount in the crop lines. We had by now expanded our multi-peril crop insurance writings to the point where they were 30% of our entire store, so the price of grain was still having a big impact on our financial numbers. The reason for the crop lines premium numbers decline was that grain prices were dropping a bit; all of the crop lines are price-sensitive, thus the premiums dropped with them. Since I knew it would be a temporary problem and our numbers were still good, I did not worry about it all that much. We still had earnings per employee up at a solid $75,000, and the store was running well. I resolved for the 1998 year to have the staff concentrate on writing more insurance lines that paid higher commissions. Now, contrary to the late 1980s, I had a staff that I had no doubt would do it.

I had read many good books while in Minneapolis, one of the best of which was The Goal. It talks about the constraints and bottlenecks that hobble many businesses and how to keep production moving forward. My step-son Ryon Boen, who was then working on his MBA, had read this as part of his course of study; it was and is excellent. Some other books I read in this timeframe were Wealth Without Risk, The Wedge, and The One-Minute Manager. While we are on the subject of books, I read many of them. I feel they have been a big part of my success; and although I tend to read many biographies, such as the ones on Donald Trump, Colin Powell, Norman Schwartzkopf, Jack Welch, etc., one of the best I have read in the last couple of years was It's Not the Big Who Eat the Small, It's the Fast Who Eat the Slow. Also, I just finished Good to Great and First, Break All the Rules. I know over the years reading books on business has helped direct me to be a better manager of my agency.

All in all, 1997 was not a bad year. Linda had been

through her cancer surgeries, chemo, and radiation; her doctors were telling us she had an excellent chance of a full recovery. One good thing that had come of her being in the hospital and in recovery all those days, weeks, and months was I had gotten our employee procedure manual typed up and printed after all these years. It was 44 pages long, and I was proud of it. Our agency numbers were solid and well within guidelines. My only big problem was that while we had been in St. Paul for Linda's cancer treatment, I had been trying to keep weight on her. To do this we ate in many of the great restaurants in Minneapolis and St. Paul. Linda still lost 12 pounds going through her treatments, but when I got on the scale at home, I was horrified to realize I had gained 42 pounds.

- **When you see a market getting into trouble, be proactive to prevent it from adversely impacting your store.**

- **Cancer will change your life.**

- **Keep a close eye on your average agency commission.**

- **Fighting cancer tends to put weight on the caregiver.**

• CHAPTER NINE •

BUMPER CROP:
CRC Means New Products and More Growth

On getting back to Minot in the fall of 1997, I realized we were still short on help. Since Linda was not returning to work, we started interviewing. One person who applied was the office manager of a major accounting firm in Minot. Although she was an excellent person who tested well, I felt she was overqualified for the job. When I told her this, she replied that she had two young kids and was tired of going to work before they got up and getting home after they did. She wanted to have a workday from 10:00 a.m. to 3:00 p.m. I had not really considered part-time help before, but we decided to give it a try. It was one of the best decisions we ever made. Brenda is still with us, and we now have two other part-time people. Flextime has really worked, helping us add some very talented people to our staff.

We started out 1998 by taking a trip to Hawa'i for three weeks. Actually, we had been going there since 1992 and are still visiting every year. We started looking at property in earnest in 1998, purchasing a nice two-bedroom condo. After the bout with cancer, both of us started to realize how short and uncertain life can be; since then both of us are trying to take time to smell the roses much more than before. Also, since spending all that time in Minneapolis, I realized if I just took my laptop along, I did not need to be in the office to get things done.

In 1998 a new multi-peril crop insurance product was for sale. It was called CRC for Crop Revenue Coverage. Although it was going to revolutionize the crop insurance business, CRC was one of the most complicated products that I had ever seen. It took me and my agents two or three schools before we finally were able to understand how the product worked and realize how tremendous this CRC was. Now, how was I going to get my clients to understand it?

People hate change. Your clients are inertia-driven. What I mean by this is they like to leave things the way they are. Here I was with a super new product for them, but it was a very BIG change. CRC was complicated and cost more money but it was a fantastic product that would pay far more on a claim than their basic multi-peril crop insurance. We put on seminars, wrote letters, and personally sat down with all of our clients to help them understand CRC. Many times my entire pitch would be "Bob, I know this is a complicated product. The staff and I had to go to three schools to try and understand it. You may not totally understand it, but all I am telling you is to buy this product. If you ever have a loss, you will be so glad you did." It is a testament to the way our clients trust us that we sold over 80% of our book of crop business on the new CRC product in the first year. When the dust settled we had sold over $400,000 of new premium.

In addition to the crop lines doing well, the commercial casualty lines were also doing well under my brother Casey's supervision. We came out of 1998 with written premium of $4,482,248 for an overall agency premium growth of 14%. The really big news was we had improved our contingency performance and written more profitable lines of insurance. By doing this we had raised our average commissions from a 1997 low of 15.7% to 16.8% at year end 1998. This was a significant move upward. Keep in mind that we did not increase our cost of production. By paying salary instead of commission, I did not see all of this excellent profit go down the road. I gave bonuses to the sales staff and put most of the extra store income toward debt reduction. Western Agency, Inc., was finally getting solvent; 1998 was simply a stellar year. The beautiful thing about it was most insurance agents hate change as much as their clients, so virtually none of my competitors were selling CRC. By selling so much of it, we catapulted ahead of our competition so far in that year that they still have not caught up.

- **Considering part-time employees can get you some very good people.**

- **Getting plugged into new products can catapult you past your competition.**

I HATE LONG GOODBYES

The only problem with 1998 was I could see my staff was simply not performing smoothly. We were receiving more customer complaints over seemingly trivial things. The new bookkeeper we had hired to replace Linda was one of those people who is always keeping score; she was seeing how much money the agency made, and I think it really bothered her that she was not getting more of it. We had also hired a   CSR who had worked for a competing agency in their Minot office a few years prior, and all she wanted to work on were "her" own accounts. In addition, one of our best CSRs, who had been with us for many years, was having all kinds of family troubles. To top it off, our elderly secretary in Garrison was having more and more trouble keeping up with the automation advances we were making every day. All I knew by late 1998 was that instinctively I could sense that something was not right. As if that were not enough, Marlen's performance was continuing to deteriorate. In retrospect I realize we had serious staffing problems. I just could not put my finger on exactly what they were.

Linda and I took off for our yearly vacation to Hawai'i in early 1999. This year we had decided to try and stay for an entire month. However, while we were there things really started to come apart at home. The first indication was that the bookkeeper, the one who was so concerned with the income that we, the owners of the agency, were making, called to say she had taken a job in another state and would be quitting in February. She had given us no warning of this. It was just boom, "I am leaving." That was fortunate, though; I found out later she was one of the major disruptive forces on my staff.

Luckily, since I had been sensing problems on the staff ever since the early summer of 1998, I had started to talk to several people about going to work for me, even before we had left for Hawai'i. One of those people was a good friend of mine, Gene Curtiss, who was employed at the time as the assistant manager of the Minot Country Club. He had taken our employment test before I left for Hawai'i, and his score was perfect for the bookkeeping position that had just come open. I called Gene from Hawaii, and we talked about his going to work for us. As I remember it, the conversation was really not that long. At the end of it, however, we had decided on Gene's wages, his job description, and his start date. Even though he left our employ several years later, that was an excellent hiring decision.

Gene not only has a math degree; he is also a computer whiz. Within a matter of months, he had the bookkeeping position nailed and was also becoming our in-house automation person; we had hired a bookkeeper and gotten an automation man thrown in to boot. As this insurance business keeps evolving, you hear more and more that you do not need a full-time bookkeeper anymore. Possibly that is true. However, there is a new job description being created at the same time, and that is for an information technology (IT) person. Gene was soon happily covering both roles. Now we had someone on staff to input the programs, install the updates, and make sure the computer world at Western Agency, Inc., was turning smoothly. Of course, we occasionally had to bring in outside expertise to solve problems. But by having an in-house person, someone who was intimately aware of the mechanics of our system, available to help mentor the other employees on how to use it, we were really a huge step up on many other stores. Plus our reaction time and speed in solving the many little computer problems was far quicker than other stores.

It turned out that the bookkeeper's leaving was only the tip of the iceberg of my staffing problems and only one of the challenges that would come at us in 1999. The year was going to be one fast sleigh ride. A couple of weeks after the bookkeeper quit and Linda and I were back in the office, my longest-term CSR came into my office and quit. Other than her strange behavior for the past six months, I had no warning. She agreed to work two weeks before going. In retrospect it was a mistake to let her stay for that two weeks. We discovered she had been holding material in her desk, some of it for over two years; and she used the two weeks to ram all of it through the system. Late apps, late binders, coverage not bound: to this day I do not know what all she covered up. I do know that after she left the claims and problems really started coming in. It ended up costing me over $30,000 to pay losses on properties that she failed to cover, premiums that needed to be paid to get caught up, and claims on coverages she neglected to place. I wonder how someone who worked for us for 14 years could have gotten that far off base. To this day I have no idea what happened to her. She still lives in the area, and I understand she has had had five or six jobs in the past few years. However, what worried me most was that, other than a bit of customer grumbling, I had no indication that this employee was drifting completely off course. This brings up a staffing problem I still struggle with. If you have long-term employees, you really start to trust them, but that does not mean you should not check up on them once in awhile. I now periodically review the number of activities of my staff, occasionally sitting down with them and going over their suspense files so I can be absolutely sure I know where they are and whether they are getting buried. I also physically look in my CSRs' desks once in awhile to see if in fact they are holding material that should be going out. Automation is great but it is not the total answer to keeping up with everything. To stay on top of your store, you must still be looking at what is lying around.

Since this problem occurred, if I am going to terminate someone's employment, or if an individual gives me two weeks' notice, I just have her/him leave immediately with two weeks' severance pay. I want to find out about any problems myself without waiting for someone to cover them up even further.

We started looking for another CSR and were able to locate an excellent lady. She has proven to be outstanding and is now managing our personal lines department. This brings up a point concerning how to find capable people. Over the years I have tried to use employment agencies and the state job service but have never gotten even one employee from them that lasted very long. The system I use now is to put a note in my newsletter or just start telling people around town that we need to hire someone. Since our business is known for paying top salaries and we have a fine benefit plan, I never have to wait very long for people to inquire about the job. I start testing applicants that sound OK, and usually within short order we have located a good person. I find I am taking more and more time interviewing and testing in the ongoing attempt to locate the better employees. I honestly feel the extra time and effort spent to find the better people is far more profitable than making a bad hire.

We had just lost the second employee and started looking for a new one when a funny thing happened with the older woman in our Minot office. As you may remember, she had always been a difficult person to work with because all she wanted to do was devote herself to her old clientele, thus doing only "her" work. You know, in an agency such as ours, this attitude can be a big problem. There is no such thing as "your" work: it is all "our" work. They are not "your clients": they are "our clients." Very much set in her ways, this lady was extremely resistant to doing things differently. Now that we were short-handed, she really had to get with the program. I am sure this is the hardest she had worked for quite a long time, and within a week she came to me to complain about it. I told her as soon as we had the new people up to speed, things would get better, but in the meantime there was nothing I could do. We were all working hard--so what?

A week after that she came in to say she was quitting. I had already decided that would be fine with me. The longer I am at this job, the less sense it makes to me to have employees telling me how to manage my agency. Saying we would miss her, I got up, went right out to the front office, and announced to everyone that she would be leaving us and that I wished her luck. A couple of days before she was to go, she stopped by my office to say, "Well, you know, if you REALLY need me, maybe I could stay and help you out." The cute part was my brother Casey had worked with this lady years before when he was employed by another agency, and he had told me that she would offer to stay on at the last minute in the hopes that by "helping us out" she would get a raise or better hours. Glad to see her go and forewarned about this little scene, I just said, "Thanks anyway, but we have already hired your replacement." I have not seen her since.

Since I was now into getting my staff back on track for real, I drove to the Garrison office to talk to my elderly employee down there and try and get her to see that it was time for her to retire. She, not wanting to retire, did not see it my way. I did not expect her to, so I had a second plan, which I then put into effect: I gave her a severance package and laid her off. I know she did not like it, but it was the best and only thing to do.

To round out the year's employee challenges, Marlen had been building a house and it had gotten totally out of hand on costs. Since he needed to come up with some money to pay off the contractors, he asked me if I wanted to buy his stock out. I responded that I really hated to see him sell his stock as the agency was doing so well. But he said he wanted to cash out so I paid him off. He ended up getting over $3.50 back for every dollar he had invested in Western Agency, Inc. None-the-less, selling his stock was, I expect, the worst decision he ever made.

- **If you feel there is something wrong in your store, there most likely is.**

- **Modern agencies need an IT person.**

- **If employees want to leave, do not waste time letting them have their wishes.**

WHEN IT RAINS IT POURS :
Wet Weather, Big Losses, Great Opportunities

So far the new people were working out great, the office was starting to run better, and the crop insurance lines were going wild. We were pushing CRC and doing everything we could to get our clients the most coverage they would buy. It turned out we could not possibly have been doing a better thing. The spring of 1999 turned out to be the wettest one on record in North Dakota. Millions of acres were underwater, and farmers simply could not get into the fields to plant their crops. Early in the season I began to envision the possibility that we might have a huge number of multi-peril crop insurance claims and geared up for them.

Sure enough, it continued to rain and rain. Our farmer clients tried to get into the fields with very little success, and we started to file prevented planting claims on their multi-peril policies. There is a provision in the multi-peril policy that if the farmer cannot get the crop seeded by a certain date, it is his decision as to whether or not he will plant the crop at all. In other words, he can collect a certain amount of the face value of his policy and simply not plant a crop if conditions make it impossible to do so. Since if crops are not planted on time the yields are usually very poor anyway, many of my farmers elected to use this excellent option not to plant. To be doubly sure they could use the option, I had the division head of claims for my crop company come up to Minot to look at the situation. He and I got in an airplane and flew around for the better part of a day, taking pictures and looking at the totally flooded landscape. Literally millions of acres were underwater. If Minnesota is the land of 10,000 lakes, North Dakota in 1999 was the land of 100,000 lakes.

This head of claims agreed that yes, the farmers could use the prevented planting provisions of their policies if they wished. After flying around that day and looking the area over, it was very obvious the farmers were simply not going to be able to plant effectively before the seeding deadline. Of course, it was a huge decision to give the go-ahead for this many claims. By now Western Agency, Inc., was insuring several hundred thousand acres of crop; and if we started filing prevented planting losses, it was a foregone conclusion that there would be a ton of them. However, this claims head, Dick Pfilger, was the kind of guy who had the guts to make a tough call. He was one of the best crop people I have ever had the chance to work with. He never even wavered before he said we should start filing claims. Dick and I both knew that sending in this huge avalanche of prevent claims would trigger a bunch of controversy and literally millions of dollars in losses. The two of us had been in the crop business long enough to know that big decisions are never without conflict as people thousands of miles away try to second-guess what was done out in the field. I am still amazed, pleased, and awed that Dick did not hem and haw around. He just said sending in the losses was the right thing to do: get on with it.

Dick did get a bunch of heat for giving us the go-ahead on all of those claims. The company we were then doing crop insurance business with ended up a few years later replacing him as head of claims, and I have no doubt that his stand on the claims of 1999 had something to do with it. The guy who replaced him is a good little "yes man" for his company. He has no respect out in the field, and I no longer do any business with that company. I shudder to think how those farmers would have been taken care of back in 1999 without our having Dick in charge. He passed away this past year, and he will be sorely missed. There are still guys like him out there, but it seems they are fewer and fewer. When they are all gone, I honestly do not think the business will ever be the same again. For sure the clients will not be served as well. Rest in peace, Dick, you were one of the best.

Meanwhile, since our phones had been ringing off the hook with farmers trying to find out what in hell to do, we now had an answer for them. We told them that it was up to them if they wanted to continue to try and seed the crop or simply let the sodden land lie idle and collect the prevented planting portion of their multi-peril crop insurance policies. Many chose to collect the prevented planting payment. This proved to be the right thing to do, and our insureds came out very well on it.

Up to this time we were literally the only agency in the area pushing our clients to buy CRC policies. Now, with all the losses coming in since CRC was a superior product, our clients were collecting far more on their policies than the people with regular multi-peril poli-cies. When our clients started getting huge claim checks, they were very glad we had talked them into this excel-lent product. We ended the crop season up over $600,000 in premium, and we served our clients well by getting them the best coverage available. Everybody won.

What is still amazing to me to this day is, due to their lack of knowledge, many of my competitors were tell-ing their clients they "had to plant the crop." They were also telling their clients that they could not file claims under the prevented planting provisions of their multi-peril crop insurance policies. This was absolutely not true; and due to this misinformation, dozens of the cli-ents these agents insured suffered major financial losses by not filing claims under the prevented planting option on their crop insurance policies. What really torqued me off about some of my competitors was they were saying Western Agency, Inc., was a bunch of crooks for allowing their clients to file the prevented planting claims. Some of them even suggested we be investigated for allowing it. Investigated? Crooks? Hell, I think the clients of these other incompetent agents should have filed a class action

law suit against their know-nothing agents for not selling them the right policies and giving them the wrong
advice. By not having CRC and by not filing prevented
planting claims, those fool agents had cost their clients
millions. Ignorance is not always bliss.

- **Thank God for company people who have the
guts to make hard calls.**

- **Selling your clients excellent coverage will save
their financial lives.**

- **Not selling them good coverage could cost them
their financial lives.**

LEAVE NO MAN BEHIND:
Finding Out What Was Wrong with Marlen

Things were just settling down with the new employees when we won an incentive trip from the EMC
companies. It was a Mediterranean cruise. Since we usually give the incentive trips to the employees and it was
Marlen's turn, I thought he should have it. In addition,
because he seemed to be having more and more trouble with his work, it occurred to me that maybe he was
stressed out and just needed a vacation. Nothing could
have been further from the truth. The problem with his
health that we discovered later was that he had been
having increasingly severe headaches. As usual, he was
not saying anything to anyone about them.

On the appointed day Marlen and his cousin board-
ed a plane and headed for Europe. Once there, they got
on a big cruise ship and headed out into the Mediterranean. As they set out to sea, Marlen's headache became
unbearable. It got so bad he lapsed into a coma. As luck

would have it, there was a doctor on board who immediately could see he was suffering from a brain hemorrhage. She called for an air ambulance, and a helicopter flew out to sea and evacuated Marlen from the ship. He was taken to a hospital in the city of Palma, on the island of Majorca, off the coast of Spain. We first heard about it the next day. It was Sunday when I got a call from Marlen's sister Kim, telling me he was in the hospital in a coma and she was going over to see what she could do. I thought about it for an hour or so and told Linda I felt I needed to saddle up and head over there, too.

My niece is a booking agent supervisor for Northwest Airlines, so I called her and told her the deal. She had me booked right through to Palma in short order. I packed some bags, picked up my passport, and left. For an individual who had never been out of the United States before, traveling to Amsterdam, Madrid, and on to Palma was quite an adventure. I was amazed at how nice people were and how they helped see to it that this country boy got on the right planes at the right times. Next thing I knew it was the middle of the night, and I was at the Palma airport, looking for a hotel room. After a little nap I headed over to the hospital in one of the many cabs there. The fare for the cab was 3,500 pesetas: about $18, I believe.

Walking into the hospital next morning, I saw Kim. She had arrived there a bit ahead of me and was really tired. We went up to see Marlen, who was in very tough shape. If you have never been in hospitals abroad, you simply cannot fathom how good we have it here in the United States; this was a major medical facility, yet there were cigarette butts on the floors and in the old rickety elevator. Marlen was in the intensive care unit, which did not even have air-conditioning. The windows were open, Marlen was covered with a sheet, and a fan was blowing air under the sheet from one end. Because he

184

was in a coma, his body temperature was quite high, and they were trying to cool him down. Furthermore, his chest was heaving and rattling, for he had contracted pneumonia from fluid in his lungs. Rather than having a fun-filled trip on the Mediterranean, he was unconscious, twitching, thrashing around, and fighting for his life.

To make matters worse, there were no doctors in sight. It was to be a couple of days until we could sit down with a doctor and an interpreter to see what the diagnosis was. When this finally happened we found Marlen had a massive brain hemorrhage from a rare disease called Moya-Moya. Apparently he had been getting the headaches from the slow bleeding of his brain that this disease causes. It also causes drowsiness, which explained why Marlen had been so lethargic of late. The doctors there were not at all optimistic about his chances for recovery. They indicated through an interpreter, "He is disabled anyway--why not let him go?" Needless to say, neither Kim nor I felt this was an option. I asked if he could be moved, and they replied they did not see why not; they thought he was as good as dead, anyway. We knew to save his life we needed to get him back to the United States, and soon.

I called back to North Dakota and talked to Blue Cross and Blue Shield, where Marlen had his medical coverage. They told me that they would try to arrange for an air ambulance immediately. Dr. John Rice and his staff really put the wheels in motion, and a few hours later claim specialist Peggy Burman phoned to say a Lear Jet would pick Marlen up the following day. It was simply unbelievable how fast a rescue operation had been mobilized, and how simply marvelous our health care system works when the client purchases an adequate insurance program. When, through an interpreter, I told the doctors at this hospital that early the next day a Lear

Jet would be there to pick up Marlen, you would have thought I had told them I was going to launch him to the moon. No wonder everyone in the world wants to live in the United States--the power of an ordinary citizen in our country is absolutely unbelievable!

We agreed that Kim would accompany Marlen on the flight back to the United States, and I headed back home, tired and bothered by a persistent nagging cough. It was only when I returned and went to the doctor myself that I found out I had bronchial pneumonia. Anyway, Marlen was on his way to University Medical Center in Minneapolis, where he remained in a coma for six weeks. He has since come out of it and was eventually able to go to work again. He still has the disease but is now taking medication to treat it. So I finally found out why his work performance had been slowly deteriorating: too bad he had to go to the brink of death to show us why.

- **We leave no man behind.**

- **If you are ever going to be critically ill, do it in the United States.**

- **Excellent medical insurance can save your life.**

SOME PAIN, MORE GAIN:
Income Numbers Start to Rise

So far for the year, we had Marlen in the hospital and had lost four other secretarial staff, a total of five people out of a staff of 12. We had replaced several of them; but with the most crop claims we had ever had in one year, things were really hectic at the agency. I suppose you feel it was going to be a bad year; I felt so, too, at the time. Nevertheless, 1999 was our best, most profitable year in the history of the agency.

However, it surely did not look that way at the time. Also in the rush to get staffing back up to strength, I made the mistake of hiring someone in a hurry again. He was a former competitor of ours from a small town, and I erroneously thought that just because he had 23 years' experience he must know something. Man, was I wrong! Within a very short time we realized this. However, I did not let him go until almost a year later. I believed I needed him around because we were short-staffed, but I should have let him go within days. We are still finding messes he made. The older I get, the more I am aware that you must simply go with your instincts on people. I knew right away he was wasting our time and money. I should have dealt with it then. By waiting a year all I did was spend money, delay finding a good employee, and set myself up for a potential E&O loss. This lack of will to do something that needs to be done is one of the most problematic of the things that seem to plague all business ventures. I always strive to act on things I know need to be dealt with, but over the years I can see lack of will to act on things has hurt me more than once. Maybe as I get to be more of a grownup, I shall get the problem handled.

Late in 1999 I was again on a talent search since I was sure I would have to let the poor agent go. The search led me to a young man who was working for Scheels Hardware. He really did not dislike the job he had so much as he disliked the weekend hours and late evenings. Since our job offered stable hours, which would allow him more time with his family, he was ready to go to work for us. Although he did not have a strong sales curve, he was so good in all the other categories that we hired him. It was again a wonderful employment hit for us, right on the sweet spot. It just seems to me that if the hire is a good one you will know it within a couple of days. Such was the case with Brent, who has been with us ever since. He is a fine person. I would brag him up some more, but he will probably read this book, and you know where that might lead. Suffice it to say, he is one of our best organizational people. We have put him in charge of farm rewrites.

We rolled out of 1999 with one of the best year's production figures we had ever posted. The agency was up to $5,586,956 in written premium; this 20% growth made me very happy. However, we also pushed our average commissions up from 16.8% to 17.8%: this was huge news. Our contingency income was up, and we were concentrating on lines that paid higher commissions. Of the $1,104,708 in new premium, $600,000 was in crop lines and $400,000 was in commercial. I finally had staff members who would do what they were told. Furthermore, since I was paying wages, not commissions, the agency kept a lion's share of the profits. We now had all of our operating loans paid off: the SBA, the cards, and our home. Wow, this agency was really starting to rock and roll! We had turned over almost 50% of our staff, had the biggest number of claims going since the storm of 1995, and yet we were still caught up and on top of our game. Problems can really shake up your store, but they surely do not have to kill it. I was beginning to think that problems were not such a bad deal, after all. We had grown more in premium in 1999 than in the first 11 years of our existence. Maybe I need to get rid of almost half my staff more often…nah, just kidding.

To wrap the century up, naturally in 1999 the big computer crash in the year 2000 was a large worry. Everyone was quietly thinking we could have this monster Y2K computer crash, so all of us spent lots of cash making sure we had equipment in place to ride out the potential crisis. I hate to admit it, but in the 11th hour I went out and purchased three gas-powered generators:

one for my home, one for the office, and one spare. We had our electrician do the necessary hookups so that if the power failed we would be ready to go. In addition, to be sure I could keep the generators running, I stored a bunch of gas in the shop; and I had $20,000 in cash rat-holed to pay my staff if the world caved in. As the clock ticked down, things got a bit tense. Of course, as we all know, nothing happened; Y2K turned out to be the most gigantic non-event of the century. The night of December 31, 1999, Linda and I had a couple of glasses of good champagne, went out in the back yard, and lit a few fireworks off. I blew taps on my bugle for the end of the 1900s, and we went to bed. When nothing happened on January 2, 2000, we went on to other things. A day or so after the century's biggest non-event, I think I remember some moron saying that December 31, 1999, was not the big day for computers to crash, it was sometime in March. I told him to get a life and asked him if he wanted a good deal on a couple of unused generators.

- **Hire in haste; repent at leisure.**

- **Trauma in the agency can sometimes be a good thing.**

- **Y2K--want a good deal on a couple of generators that have never been used?**

NO GOOD DEED GOES UNPUNISHED:
Inexperienced Company People and Bad Auditors

The year 2000 was a time for us to catch our breath. First on the agenda was getting rid of the agent we had hired in a hurry to help with Marlen's workload. If there is a simple way to unplug someone, please let me know.

I had had many meetings with this guy to get him in gear, but it became very obvious that simply was not going to happen. Finally I went to the office, packed up his stuff in a couple of cardboard boxes, and met him in the parking lot early one frosty morning. As I was putting the boxes in his pickup, I told him we both knew it was not working and I hoped he would have better luck in his next job. I offered him my hand, but he refused it, driving off in a huff. As usual, after he had left, we found lots of mistakes and things undone. Why is it that as managers we usually wait too long to let a poor-performing person go? In all the years I have been in business, I have never let people go and wished I had them back. Invariably the only thought I have is Why in hell did I wait so long to do it?

We had a fairly good crop insurance year; in fact, things were going along fine in that department until one day I got a phone call that informed me the division manager for my main crop insurance company had been fired. This man, an excellent manager, was a very good friend of mine. The reasons for his departure were not clear, but he was gone. We held our breath to see who his successor would be. It was business as usual until hail season came along. We were short-staffed at the agency, as Marlen was not yet back in the game and I was trying to hold his job for him until his disability was better under control. (In retrospect I realize this was a mistake, for he would never completely recover.) It is always super hectic during the hail insurance season, and 2000 was no exception. In the hail insurance business we sometimes bind several hundred thousand dollars of premium in a single day, yet it takes several weeks to go out and get all the acres recorded. Needless to say, it gets pretty crazy, and 2000 was no exception.

We had always had a gentleman's agreement with our hail company that we would bind the risks, send

190

down a list of names and approximate acres, and do the apps as soon as we could finish them in the days to follow. Usually, we write our entire book of hail business within a few days; since we write around $1,000,000 in premium, things get very busy during this time. We were right in the middle of this process when a big storm front came across the state. We took dozens of calls from farmers wanting to get land covered and sent down a list of names for the day. However, one name did not get sent. The man had called to order coverage, and we had a record of the call, but his name was missing from our master binder list for that day. Realizing this could be a problem, I called the new division manager right away the next morning and told him we had a farmer who had called for coverage and somehow we had not put his name on the binder list. I also told the new manager the man we left out did have a loss from the storm the previous day. I said, "Will you people be able to accept this policy since we didn't have an official binder on it?" The man's exact words were "Sure, we'll take it." What a relief! However, in retrospect, I wish I had not even asked.

We turned in the losses, got all the paperwork completed, and had the losses settled in a few weeks: business as usual. We were just getting caught up for the summer when, lo and behold, a crop auditor came into town. Since audits are part of the business, certainly a necessary one, I thought nothing of it. The guy did not want us to go with him to find the fields, so away he went all alone to do his audits. He wanted to look at a couple of losses, one of which was the loss from when we had not had the binder in on time. Keep in mind that this client was a 9,000-acre farmer; and it had taken me and Duane Knutson, a very good hail adjustor, over a day to do the adjusting on the land that had been hail-damaged. The second farm was also over 7,000 acres, and it, too, had taken over a day to adjust. Furthermore, both of these farms were located over an hour's one-way drive from our office.

The auditor arrived at our office at 10 a.m. and left to do the audits about 11. He was back by five p.m. I was amazed that he could drive that far and hope to look at even a fraction of the crops in question. Never saying a word about any problems, he just got in his car and left town. I should have known we had trouble ahead. This genius was able to adjust 16,000 acres in only four hours all by himself: yeah, right. I found out later he supposedly had a quart-a-day booze habit; maybe that is what helped him move so fast. When "Speedy" turned in his report, he told the company we had vastly overpaid one of the losses. Things started to get ugly. In particular, he said we had overpaid the loss on the claim that had the late binder. Big surprise, huh? On that claim the adjustor had put a 51% loss on about 320 acres of Durum wheat, but the auditor believed it only should have been 25% or less. Never mind that the crop was badly mauled, I really wonder if that auditor ever even saw the field in question.

Eventually crop adjustor Duane Knutson's adjustment on the disputed crop settlement was totally validated. At the end of the season when the crop that was damaged was harvested, it yielded 18 bushels per acre, while this farmer's un-hailed crops yielded 36 to 40 bushels per acre. In other words, Duane's 50% damage assessment was right on target, as usual.

You would think after we got the yield figures on the disputed crop at year's end and communicated them to the new manager of the crop company, that would have been the end of it. In a perfect world this manager should have called "Speedy" the auditor and chewed his butt. No chance: it seemed after that particular hail loss, the new manager for this crop and hail company did not trust us and considered our store a bunch of crooks. Since I had worked for 30 years to have an agency with an impeccable reputation, this attitude made me angry. As the summer wore on, it became very apparent that this new manager's inexperience and the opinion he had of my agency were going to be major problems. I decided to move the crop hail book of business elsewhere the next year.

What made being labeled a crook even harder to take was that a few years before, this particular company had accidentally overpaid me $60,000 in commissions. I had found the error when I did my year-end production and earnings numbers, but they had not and very possibly would never have found it because it was an overpayment of an advance commission. On finding the error I had called my friend the division manager, the same guy who had just been fired, and told him about it. He was amazed I had even given them a heads-up on the overpayment, but the next day I cut the company a check for the $60,000 and sent it to them. Now, here these same people were insinuating I was less than honest-- I simply couldn't believe it! How about giving me back the $60K?

- **When companies rotate staff, it can have major implications for you, the agent.**

- **Crop auditors should actually look at the crops they are supposed to be auditing.**

- **Just because you are right does not necessarily mean it is OK.**

MOVING TO HIGHER GROUND:
Moving Our Entire Crop Insurance Book

As I have already said, at Western Agency, Inc., we sell a fairly large amount of multi-peril crop insurance and hail insurance. By the summer of 2000 we were covering over 350,000 acres. The multi-peril crop insurance product is designed to provide insurance coverage if a farmer's crop is damaged or destroyed by hail, untimely rains, disease, or virtually any other unforeseen event beyond the farmer's control. This product is supposed to be a risk management tool that will keep a farm going after one of these catastrophic events. As you probably know, because farming is a risky business, there can be quite a few losses on this type of insurance: so many losses, in fact, that these policies have to be underwritten by the government since no private company could take the terrible loss ratios produced by this insurance in a bad year.

As an agency we have, however, had many years in which our loss ratios on this type of insurance were very low, probably because we have always tried to insure the better farms in our area. But in 1999 our area was hit with constant rain during the seeding time of year, bringing about huge claims. We ended up having dozens of prevented planting losses; since we wrote about two million in crop premium that year, our claims were almost seven million. This, of course, added up to a very bad loss ratio. Luckily, we had taken many aerial photos of the water, because a federal auditor came up to see how we could spend so much of Uncle Sam's cash. Furthermore, as I have said before, many of the other local agents were telling their clients they could not file prevented planting losses when they actually could have. Due to this we had more losses than many of our competitors. This further eroded our stock with the new division manager for our crop company, the guy who was already convinced we operated a den of thieves.

Starting in 2000, the wheat crop was plagued with

194

a mould called Vomitoxin which generated more excessive claims, and, although not as bad as 1999, 2000 was still a big claim year. Things worked out, though, despite the problems the new manager of our crop company was causing us. We were getting our claims settled and our farmers paid. I was thinking maybe the new manager was all right, after all, when suddenly he fired the head of claims for our division. Dick was another good friend of ours who had OKed our prevented planting losses the prior year, an extremely knowledgeable person with years of experience who had been excellent to work with. Nevertheless, he was a no-nonsense person who would not suck up to anybody. This was a major shortcoming in the new management environment in which he now found himself. His replacement, however, was a person who understood well the fruits of kissing up. Unfortunately for us, whereas Dick had worked himself up from field adjustor to claims manager and was well acquainted with the crop insurance business, the new guy had virtually no experience out in the field. He had instead been an "inside-the-office" type of person for his whole insurance career. With this limited experience he had become head of claims for the entire division. Within weeks of this new man's taking over the claims department, we started having trouble getting things done. After the debacle with the binder the year before, I had already moved our hail insurance book of business to another company. Now I started to look in earnest for another company for my multi-peril crop insurance book.

My friend, the former division manager, had gone to work for another company, and I had gotten in touch with him to start the negotiations for moving at least part of our 350,000 acres of crop insurance to his new employer. It just so happened in the spring of 2001 that his new company and the one I was having all the trouble with had their spring multi-peril crop insurance agent meetings in the same hotel, at the same time, on the same day. The new division manager, who considered me a crook, showed up. However, even though we were by far his biggest agency in the area, he did not even stop into our office the day of the meeting. Instead he made a point of going over to see our biggest competitor. At the meeting I did see him in the halls, but not much was said. His cold attitude and the fact he had been to visit my biggest competition helped me decide to attend the meeting for the company I was thinking of moving part of my crop book to. Of course he noticed this, which, of course, did not make his day, either. I left the room to take a cell phone call, and here the guy was, pacing up and down the hall like a mad bull. Already angry that he had snubbed me by going to visit my biggest competitors, yet still thinking of moving only half the book to another carrier, when I went back into the meeting I decided to see what kind of deal I could make if I moved the entire book. Since the president of my prospective new company was actually attending the meeting, I called one of the field reps over and asked him if the president and I could have a little chat. A few minutes later the field rep tapped me on the shoulder and said I should follow him out of the meeting. I left to go into another room. My 15-minute conversation there would culminate in one of the very best contracts I have ever been able to work out.

I informed the president of the reason I was interested in moving the book, emphasizing our reputation in the crop insurance business. I told him I wanted a three-year contract and certain specific commissions. He, in turn, told me what he expected out of the deal and how and what he needed from us. In a short quarter of an hour we had the entire contract basically drawn up. As any of you know who sell multi-peril crop insurance, this is not a line with which you want inexperienced people involved. It is probably one of the most complicated coverages sold, and you absolutely have to deal with a company that has deep knowledge of what they are selling. To my relief, it soon became obvious I was talking to solid people once more. It was also wonderful to talk with someone who knew what he was doing, knew when he had a good deal in hand, and had the horsepower to act on it. We shook hands, and he said he would have contracts and terms to me in a couple of days. He was as good as his word. What a relief! We would move our entire multi-peril crop insurance book of business to this new company for the 2001 crop year. We got our crop book back on solid ground, and the new company got over $3,000,000 in premium.

In 2000 I also took a different route than normal and got involved in politics. I did not run for any office; but in North Dakota the insurance commissioner is an elected official, and I had an opportunity to help get a very good man get elected to that post. Since I was on the board of the Professional Insurance Agents Association (PIA) and the incoming president, I was in a position to help get some grassroots support organized. Our PIA executive officer, Kent Olson, is a dynamo of energy. He, the board, and I started writing letters, soliciting campaign contributions, and generally doing everything we could to help this excellent person get elected. Up until then I had never gotten political with my newsletter but ended up doing two articles in support of our candidate in that. The reason I took the chance of making a few of my insureds mad by getting politically involved, and the reason I really got fired up about this election, was that the other person running was a product liability attorney. Can you imagine someone with those credentials being an insurance commissioner? Neither could we. The result was that our candidate, Jim Poolman, won the election and has been doing a spectacular job of serving the people of North Dakota ever since. It reaffirmed my belief in grassroots politics, and I was proud to help a good man get into office.

We exited 2000 with fairly steady production figures. We had actually exceeded the number of crop acres we insured in 1999 by over 100,000 acres. This was a phenomenal production year for us. In any other 12-month period it would have meant a tremendous increase in premium. However, since the premium on crop insurance is set by the per-bushel price of grain and the price of grain was down, we had a pretty flat year premium-increase-wise with a gain of only 5% for the entire store. No matter, I was still happy because I knew the price of grain would not stay down forever. When it came back all of the new acres would translate into a ton of new premium.

- **Inexperience should not be considered a plus when companies appoint claims managers.**

- **Good connections help you make good deals.**

- **You can still do handshake deals in the Old West.**

- **Once in a while you can get involved in politics for a good-enough cause.**

• CHAPTER TEN •

THE PINK PANTHER, PRINCE FARQUART, AND THE KEYSTONE COPS

The real problems with the 2000 crop claims started early in the year of 2001, shortly after we announced we were moving our book of multi-peril crop insurance to another carrier. This was to prove a wise decision in that our service vastly improved and we were again dealing with people who knew what they were doing. It turns out I was not the only agent who was tired of the new manager with the prior company; after the dust settled for the 2001 sales year, the company we had moved our multi-peril crop insurance book away from had lost over 30% of its volume in our division. This amounted to a decrease of over 12 million in premium: the couple of million we had moved and 10 million of premium other disgruntled agents had moved to other carriers. You would think at this point the company would have gotten rid of this terrible manager, but, true to the form of most companies, they did not.

I knew that the manager who had caused this exodus of agents and premium was very mad at me and other agents for leaving his company, and I had a bad feeling that he was going to make me pay for it. As time would tell, this feeling of mine was right on target. Early in the spring of 2001 we began to get audits on the 2000 crop year claims. Of course audits are necessary and normal, but we were getting more than our share. Then I started to hear rumors that this manager and his buddy, the inexperienced claims manager he had appointed, were out to get my agency. Sure enough, we got a call from two guys who were "fraud investigators" for his company. They set up a day to come visit, and we sat down with them to see where the problem was.

By then I had been in business for almost 30 years and had never had anyone imply I was less than an honest agent. Now here I was, face-to-face with two guys who made a big deal out of telling me they were "fraud investigators." Inside I was so damn mad at having to be put through this simply because of moving a book of business away from a poor-performing company. But I decided the best way to get through it was simply to prove to these people our agency was not the den of thieves their boss believed we were.

I got the agent involved on most of the accounts, the adjustor who had done the losses, myself, and the two "fraud investigators" (who, incidentally, knew basically nothing about multi-peril crop insurance) together within a few minutes of their getting to town. We sat down in my office and started to review files. The first thing the investigators told us was that they were retired FBI men; I suppose this was done to scare us. Actually, all I can remember thinking was Great, now I'm going to be investigated by two guys who're clueless about the most complicated insurance we sell. Sure enough, in case after case the questions were simple and easily answered. However, trying to explain what we had done and why we had done it to two people with the equivalent of a third-grade education in crop insurance made it twice as difficult as it should have been. Actually, I was surprised at how simple the questions were. It very quickly became apparent that the new claims manager did not know much about the multi-peril product, either, or he never would have sent such trivial stuff in for "investigation." It took us an entire day to go through all of the files in question. By late afternoon virtually every issue had been answered, with the exception of a couple for which we needed to provide more information.

In the end only one account had a problem that bothered the investigators. Farmers receive a scale ticket on every load of grain they deliver to the grain-buying facility where they are selling their grain. These grain-buying facilities are called grain elevators. When the farmer is done harvesting his crop, the amount of grain recorded on tickets he gets at these elevators determines how much he is paid for his crop because the tickets show the bushels of grain delivered. On this one particular claim, the amount of damage on the grain had been changed on one of the scale tickets, which made a difference of $395 dollars in the claim. It seemed to me that on a book of business of over $3,000,000 in premium and in a year where we had about $6,000,000 in claims, $395 would be no big deal, but it sure was to these guys.

However, after a few days they had what they wanted from us, went home, and filed their report, a copy of which, of course, we never received. They simply could not put that $395 loss to bed; they left still feeling it was a big problem. The joke of the whole deal is that the scale ticket is not used to settle the crop loss, anyway, if it is a quality loss. With a quality loss, which is what this farmer had, the grain has to be sampled and tested by a federal grain-testing facility. This had been done according to regulations. Thus the amount of damage written or "changed" on the elevator scale ticket in question really had no relevance to the claim at all. If these guys had known anything about crop claims, they would have known this. No matter: facts should not confuse the issue, right? Sure as hell, there was more to come.

In a few more weeks we got a call from the "head of fraud investigations" for the company, who wanted to fly out from the East Coast to see us. I was getting disgusted and remember telling him he was going to spend far more in airfares than the $395 claim. Nevertheless, out he came. His big news was that he had analyzed the ink on the scale ticket that had been changed, and found it came from two different pens--my God, you would have thought he discovered fire! I asked the man if he had ever visited a grain-buying facility; he said no he had not. I told him maybe he should go over to one of the local grain elevators, where he would notice that on the counter, like every other elevator in the country, there is usually a large container of ink pens for people to use. It would be perfectly understandable if two different pens had been used on the same ticket. Again, thinking that possibly because he was the "head of fraud investigations" for this particular company and therefore might know something about multi-peril crop insurance, I reminded him that the damage listed on the scale ticket was unimportant, that the only thing on the scale ticket that mattered was the amount of the gross bushels and that number had not been changed. I figured he would have known that only the damage grade done by the federal people was used or for that matter could have been used to settle the loss. But he was utterly unaware of that. My suspicions were being confirmed that these "investigators" knew next-to-nothing about crop insurance. They were actually just accountant types who had little idea of what the crop product even was. Scary, is it not?

So the "Pink Panther" continued on his mission. He was here to investigate, and investigate he did. He looked into our client, the elevator people, the adjustor, our agency, and most likely the maid who cleaned his room the several days he was in our little town. I cannot imagine how much money these idiots spent studying a $395 claim that was perfectly legit. However, as I was to find out, this was still only the beginning.

Once more I asked them to send me a copy of the big report, but to this day I have never received a page of information on what they supposedly uncovered. What I wanted to do was sue the division manager of this company for causing all this needless trouble. I did not, however, because I was worried he would turn us into the real federal investigators and we would have to go through the same song and dance with them. I was hoping since we had by now cleared up all their questions, things would be OK. Of course, nothing could have been further from the truth.

Agents in the multi-peril crop insurance business can make a tremendous difference to the people they insure. Designed and marketed as a risk management tool, the product is exactly that; but to perform properly, it must be correctly written. Here is the rub. The multi-peril crop insurance policy is most likely one of the most complicated insurance instruments ever developed. Many agents selling this product do not know much about it. Time and again they do not set the policy up correctly, and the client then cannot collect as much on a loss as someone who had an agent who put the policy together correctly. Over the years we have seen clients of these poor agents lose literally hundreds of thousands of dollars by having a carelessly written contract fail them. In most cases these people and the agents who are writing their business have no idea they have even been screwed or have screwed up. It is just that these agents' clients get smaller claim checks.

As I said in previous chapters, a classic example of this was the 1999 crop year. We had sold virtually all of our clients a new crop product called CRC. A revenue-based product, on Durum wheat it paid nearly 30% more than the standard multi-peril crop insurance policy. The problem was that CRC is really a complicated product, and most agents were not even selling it since they did not understand it. In 1999 we were literally the only agency for miles around pushing this excellent policy. Furthermore, at that time I had more Durum wheat farmers insured than any agent in North Dakota, and in that year

CRC paid an especially high claim on Durum wheat. Sure, it was hard to get the clients to see the benefits of purchasing this policy instead of the usual multi-peril contract. However, CRC was such a good policy and it was so relevant for the times that I aggressively pushed it and had my staff do likewise. Many times I simply told my clients, "Just buy this product; you have to trust me that it is the thing to do. Believe me, if you ever have a claim, you will be glad you did."

Sure enough, as I said before, in 1999 we had more rain in North Dakota than we have ever had since records have been kept. Literally hundreds of thousands of acres of cropland were underwater, which set the stage for a tremendous number of prevented planting losses. The combination of all these losses plus our selling a product that paid 30% more caused us to have huge losses, hence a horrible loss ratio for the 1999 year. Since in that same year we had sold over two million of premium, most of it the CRC product, we subsequently had many more dollars in losses than other agents in our area, who had not taken the time to understand and sell CRC. In a situation like this the government may say, "Why do you have a higher loss ratio than the average agency in your area?" The implication is, of course, if you have more losses than other agents in the area, you must be running a crooked shop; it is the classic "push me, pull you" syndrome of multi-peril crop insurance. Farmers are supposed to be able to use the crop product to lessen the risk of farming; the product, as previously stated, is supposed to be a risk management tool. You, the agent, are supposed to deliver a quality policy that the farmer can use and show him how to use it. However, as soon as you start doing a better job, you will most likely have a higher loss ratio than your peers.

The government thinks all agents are the same. All of us have to pass a crop insurance knowledge test, so we must all be the same, right? Using this logic, if your agency has a higher loss ratio than your peers, the sales practices of your store should be looked into. Since we had a higher loss ratio than other agencies in our area because of the 1999 claims and our selling CRC, we were thus suspect as far as fraud was concerned. I knew this and that is why the last thing I wanted or needed was a bogus whistle-blower telling the feds my store was crooked. Of course, sure as hell, that is exactly what happened.

Being relatively pleasant to the prior company's investigators had done little good. Early in the summer of 2001 we got a call from two real, live federal investigators; if you think they did not have my attention now, you can think again. A chill went down my spine: I knew we were in for a fight. Why did these two federal investigators show up? Although I couldn't prove it, the rumor was that to get back at us for moving our entire book of crop insurance away from his company, the manager I could not stand had turned us in to the Fraud Investigation Unit of the Federal Crop Insurance Corporation for "suspicion of fraudulent insurance practices." This was exactly what I had been worried about because I knew we were already on the federal radar for having such high losses in 1999. It was not bad enough that it had cost me a bunch of money to move an entire book of business away from this fool. Now I was going to have to fight for my financial life because of it. By now he knew damn well we were not doing anything fraudulent. He was just trying to make my life miserable because we had moved our book of business to someone else. It didn't matter if the rumor was true or not, the Feds were in town, they were in my office, and they were going to go through me 'like bad beef through a senior citizen's center'.

When you are an agency selling multi-peril crop insurance, you quickly find out that the federal people in the multi-peril crop insurance world have the power of God walking on the earth over you. This product is backed by government dollars; therefore, if they find you deficient, fraudulent, or bad in any way, they can and will pull your license to sell crop insurance. They can literally put you out of business--hell, for that matter, they can put you in jail! When you realize I had over $3,000,000 in crop premiums, had a staff of three who basically did nothing but service crop insurance, and had made this product a major part of our agency revenues, you can get a sense of how concerned I was. The only thing that was preventing a huge panic attack was I knew damn well we were in the right, we were on solid ground, and we had the records to prove it. Not only that: I was, by now, also furious and ready for a fight.

The two federal guys were both nice-enough fellows. However, it soon became obvious that once again we were to be investigated by a couple of people who did not really know too much about the multi-peril crop insurance policy. Due to the growth of sales in crop insurance, the feds were badly in need of more crop insurance investigators, putting auditors from other areas into that one as fast as they could. During the interview one of them told us he had been a federal meat inspector only a few months before. I thought, Great--once more I am being grilled by a couple of guys who don't understand how the policy works! The only difference was that now we had a couple of guys looking at us who could literally put us out of business if we did not come away with a clean slate. I probably have never been more focused in my life about being sure we proved our sales practices were sound.

That first day we sat down with the inspectors, the files, the agents, and the adjustors, trying to place all the square pegs in the square holes. We only had one tense moment, and that was when I got angry over a question one of the investigators was asking. He asked, "Chuck, why are you getting mad?" I replied that when you start a business from scratch, grow it to the size of ours, and spend 30 years getting an excellent reputation in the business community, it pisses you off to have a couple of guys come in insinuating you are a crook. He laughed and said maybe he would be mad, too.

The two investigators talked to me, many of our insureds, and the adjustors, in addition to focusing on my farm insurance manager, Craig Johnson. They grilled him for the entire next day; he told me later that as they asked question after question, he could feel the sweat dripping down his back. What saved us was we were in the right, we had good records, we had good clients, and we could prove the work we had done was not only good work but also correct work. I was thinking to myself, Why in the hell don't they go investigate the agents who haven't sold good policies? These guys cost their clients literally millions in lost claims but, due to having lower loss ratios, never seem to get checked up on: so much for government logic.

After a few days they left. Again, I asked for a copy of their report but never received a response. You know, that is the problem of dealing in a government-backed product. If this had been a private company, no way would I have put up with this BS. I would have called until I got somebody's supervisor on the phone, and there would have been reasons given for actions taken (or not taken). Failing that, I could have called the Insurance Commissioner to make someone give me some answers. However, with a government product you find yourself in kind of a quasi-neverland of "who is regulating whom." It can make you feel very lonely sometimes.

When the big investigation was over, the only response we received from the federal people was that they felt my agents' should not go out on claims with the adjustors. Not only did they forbid us to do this; but the next crop year, they called many of our clients to be sure we were not. The reason they gave for not wanting us to go out on losses was they felt it was possible we were influencing the adjustors to pay too much on claims. Obviously they were not acquainted with our main adjustor, Ron Oplund. If they had been, they would have known there was no way in hell we--or anybody else, for that matter--could influence Ronnie to pay a dime more than what he felt the actual claim was worth. I guarantee you that not we, not they, not anyone could make Ron pay more than he felt was due on any loss. Nonetheless, I was glad it was finally over. I was happy we had vindicated ourselves and glad to agree to their terms (as if I had a choice, anyway). Now, I thought, this stupid investigation is finally done. Not.

The next round in the war of the idiots was a letter sent to 28 of my insureds on October 25, 2001. Of course, it was from the company we had gotten rid of, basically stating that these 28 losses had been overpaid so this company wanted their money back. The total of these supposed overpayments, which the company was demanding refunds for, was almost $300,000. The company was contending that improper documentation was provided with the losses to prove that, in fact, the farmers had been discounted for the presence of Vomitoxin in their grain. Luckily, elevators keep records of what price was paid for what quality of grain on any given day. For God's sake, if the new claims manager of this company had known anything; anything at all about multi-peril crop insurance, he would have known this! Naturally, he did not.

To prove our clients had been discounted on the price paid for their grain, we contacted the grain elevators in question, picked up the price sheets from the disputed days during the prior year, and sent this proof to the company. It should have stopped the problem cold, putting things to bed, once and for all. Did it? Hell, no!

I had moved my entire book of crop insurance to escape that idiot division manager and his know-nothing claims manager, and here I was, still fighting them a year-and-a-half later! They simply would not budge. I got on the phone to have a talk with the best crop insurance lawyer in the state of North Dakota. After I had explained our problem to her, the attorney felt that we had an excellent case. So on November 21, 2001, my crop insurance manager Craig Johnson and I drove the 115 miles to the town where she had her office to have a visit with her.

To make a long story short, we filed a class action arbitration on behalf of our 28 farmers. We agreed to pay for the up-front cost of the litigation; then we simply billed our clients for their share of the costs, based on the amount of their claims. We provided the attorney and her team with the information, and they sent it off to the insurance company. On February 14, 2002, the insurance company sent a letter out to the 28 farmers, informing them that they were dropping their request to send back the money. That finally put the matter to bed, right? Well, not quite--remember the farmer who had the grain ticket on which the amount of damage had been changed? The one for which they sent an investigator all the way from the East Coast to look into this $395 claim? Well, guess what, a full year after that the "head fraud investigator," who had already made the special trip to North Dakota once to look into this $395 problem, again called, this time leaving a message on the farmer's answering service. He wanted the farmer to call him back to answer some questions he still had concerning the changed scale ticket. When the farmer told us about the call, all we advised him to do was ignore the SOB. That is what he did, and now, a year later, he has not heard from him. Maybe, just maybe, the whole mess is finally over.

If this is to be a "how to" book, I honestly do not know what I can tell you that will help you avoid a problem such as this. Companies change personnel; often they replace a perfectly good manager with a horrible one. Usually, bad managers fill their staffs with more people just like themselves. The only recourse is to move the book of business, which in this case is exactly what we did. Possibly, having someone such as this poor manager falsely accuse us with the feds is just one of the pitfalls of the game. I guess what I am most proud of is that we did fight it out and vindicate ourselves. We did help our clients successfully fight the ridiculous request for the claim money to be returned. Best of all, we shed ourselves and our clients of an incompetent company. It was like getting over a bad case of constipation--feels great, does it not?

- **Investigators do not necessarily have to know much about what they are investigating.**

- **In selling multi-peril crop insurance, one problem with providing better policies than your competitors, and hence getting more claims paid on them, is that Uncle Sam will want to talk to you.**

- **In an investigation, keeping and maintaining good records can save your neck.**

GROWING PAINS:
More Stores, More Staff, Commission Cuts

Other than the time it took to settle the investigation into our multi-peril crop insurance sales and practices,

2001 was a great year. We had super growth in both crop and hail insurance sales and purchased another small book of business in a town 200 miles away from us. The net result was our overall agency growth in 2001 was over 32%; we were now writing $7,737,485 of premium. Also, we saw our average commissions increase from 17% to 17.7%: this was due to moving the multi-peril crop insurance book. The company we had moved it to had given us a 2% rollover bonus on $2,700,000 of premium. While the higher commission would be temporary, it sure looked good on the bottom line at the end of the year.

After the stock market crash, the lower interest rates, and the 9/11 disaster, it was very obvious that insurance rates were going to go up. Therefore, with higher insurance premiums being a virtual certainty, I knew it would be the perfect time to purchase some more agencies. In late 2001 I really started polling my field reps as to who had an agency for sale. The agency for sale in Dickinson, North Dakota, was located in this way. About 200 miles from our town, Dickinson had an excellent airport; and I knew that, with automation and being able to fly the plane down there, we could hook the agency up with our main office and make it sing. After a 30-year hiatus from flying, I had begun to fly again in 2000. Now I could put my pilot's license and the twin-engine airplane I had purchased to work. Plus, Dickinson is a very nice, progressive little town where I felt we could do some good work. The book of business was solid, and the owner was a very nice person. Since the store was not automated, however, it was struggling to keep markets. I reasoned that Dickinson's good airport would enable me to move staff members and myself down there quickly from time to time if need be. The plane, coupled with our efficient automation, would negate the physical distance of the store from my main agency in Minot, so we had gone ahead and done the deal.

As in so many small agencies, the owner felt he was working his butt off going nowhere. Without a vacation in over five years, he was just worn out; I could see that he badly needed a break. After the purchase had been completed, I told him I would send one of my people down to cover the store so he and his wife could take at least a week off, go on a little trip, and get some much-needed R&R. A few weeks later we hired a secretary for him who proved to be an absolutely excellent employee. It was actually an advantage that she knew little about the insurance business because she had not learned to do things wrong. We were able to train her correctly, right from the start, and before long she was putting information into the computer as if she had been doing it for years. A quick learner, she was soon taking care of all the secretarial duties in Dickinson, as well as doing a substantial amount of work sent down to her from the Minot office.

This little agency we purchased in Dickinson was to prove both a challenge and a good deal. The biggest problem was that we agreed to hire the store owner/manager, who had no automation skills at all and he had a terrible time learning to conduct the insurance business the way we did. As nice as he was, we found out he actually knew very little about how to handle things. Instead of filling out an application, taking pictures, getting loss run information, and really researching the account he was trying to write, his method was to just call an underwriter, tell him about the risk, and expect a quote back. Maybe this crap had worked in the soft market. But we had never done business that way, and it sure as hell was not going to work in the hard market we were now in. I literally had to threaten him with termination six months after the sale to force him to use the computers and learn how to send in professional submissions.

To improve and develop the Dickinson book in the course of 2002, we canceled a bunch of poor accounts. However, we replaced them with good healthy commercial, crop, and farm business. This, plus rate hikes, saw us come out of the first year in that community with over 100% of the premium we had purchased, even though the sales figures for the book we had bought were somewhat overstated. The big message to me was that if I was going to be purchasing agencies and the staff was going to go with the deal, I had to factor in some time to retrain them into how a modern store runs. The model was working, though, so I went searching for more stores to buy.

The year 2002 was an adequate, average year. We went through the book of business of the Dickinson store, inputted it all, got it online to Minot, and used the purchase to develop a model of how to buy and assimilate an agency. The territory had looked good to me, and it WAS good. We put $170,000 of new premium on the books in the first 14 months. In our world this is not too bad, proving we had made a solid investment.

Based on the success of the Dickinson store, I continued to look for more agencies for sale, soon locating one in the small town of Oakes, North Dakota. Although Oakes is 300 miles away from Minot, it has a nice little airport; and, due to the success we were having in Dickinson, I put the Oakes deal together on September 1, 2002. It, too, was a good hit, and in a few months it was also cruising along. Both of these books of business sold for about 1.5X renewal commissions. The Dickinson store was probably overpriced at the 1.5X figure, but still, since we had five years to pay for it at a low interest number, plus the new production, it was a solid buy at the 1.5X number, as was the Oakes location. It seems that, in most cases where small buys are concerned, you will end up pretty close to this old 1.5X multiplier of commissions to do the deal. I looked at nine agencies for sale in 2002, only purchasing the one in Oakes. We continued to refine the model we had developed with the Dickinson purchase; and in the assimilation of the Oakes agency, we had the local secretary do all the inputting chores. This helped her learn how our automation worked without creating any extra work for the Minot office.

Although I looked at five more agencies in 2003, we only bought one. We have a good chance of picking up two others, but a year or so will probably pass until they are ready to do the deal. An important capability I am discovering is that we can export work from the main office in Minot to these outlying agencies. This helps keep the staff in the small agency busy and takes lots of workload off my main office staff, enabling us to afford to pay good salaries in the small towns and still get enough work out of these people to justify keeping them on the payroll. The added benefit is I am keeping a business open in a small town, which creates a tremendous amount of goodwill in these smaller communities. The negative is that, in many cases, the people in these little stores are not at all used to putting out as much work as we expect from them. I do not mean they are lazy; it is just that their pace of work is simply not as intense as ours. They want to earn big-city wages, but they are not aware right away of how much work I must have in return.

In 2002 I was expecting premiums to go up agency-wide. The big surprise when I did my year-end break-outs was that our overall premium growth for 2002 had only been 6%, probably because, for the past couple of years, we had been out educating our clients to higher deductibles, dropping unneeded coverages, and removing full coverage on older automobiles. We had done quite a thorough job teaching our clients how to lower their insurance costs; once done, it had cost us quite a bit of production. However, due to this purge of our book of business and increase in deductibles, I really expected to see later benefits and earnings in the form of better loss ratios and higher contingency income. In fact, in 2003 we did see a dramatic rise in our contingency incomes. Another thing that impacted our 2002 growth was a drop of $300,000 in premium in the crop lines, which we attributed to lower price elections on the crop products. The largest and nastiest surprise in 2002 was that the companies had been cutting commissions, so we saw the average for the store drop a full 1.1%. This commission drop was the most significant thing to come out of 2002. Although I was not happy about it, at least I knew how it had happened, how much it had cost us, and how we intended to fix it. It is incredible how few stores do year-end production and income numbers to figure things out. End result for the year was we wrote $468,000 in new premiums and saw our earned commissions drop $6,000. Signs of things to come, were they?

I do an Excel spreadsheet on all of my companies at year end showing four years of production by company. This spreadsheet also shows written premium, earned commission, contingency income, average commission by company, and my three and five year loss ratios. I categorize the companies by Casualty, Brokerage, Crop Insurance, Bonds, and Life Insurance. I get the premium numbers off the 12/31 year end statements the companies put out. The income numbers are from the 1099's that the companies send out each year. When I am done with this I can take the number of accounts I have and come up with most of my management numbers, such as average account size, average commission per account, average earnings per employee and so on. It would be nice if our automation could give us these numbers and to some degree they can, but to find out actual numbers of clients, number of people cancelled, why they left and so on, takes a fair amount of legwork. Most agencies don't take the time to do it. I think that is a big mistake.

• When buying new agencies and keeping their staffs, it can be hard to teach old dogs new tricks.

• Exporting work to your outlying offices helps justify paying and keeping staff in the satellites.

E & OH, OH:
The E & O Crises

The year 2003 started out normally enough; So in early January, Linda and I left for our annual vacation in Hawai'i. We had sold our condo and purchased a house over there, and I set up an office in one of the bedrooms. By installing a DSL line, I was now able to pipe right into my automation, which turned out to be a spectacular deal. We were set up to be on the Big Island for two months and most of my insureds had no idea I was even gone. Again, ain't automation grand? Between golfing and going to the beach, I sat down to do my production breakouts for 2002 and set up my goals and plans for 2003.

Every year I do a complete breakout of premiums written by company, average commissions, loss ratios, earnings per employee, average account size, and agency retention ratio. What I discovered that surprised and worried me about the results of 2002 was a slip in our retention ratio. We have had a retention ratio of 95% or better at Western Agency, Inc., for years, yet in 2002 this had dropped to 89%; I was shocked. At least in breaking the numbers out, I found the reason: we had lost over 125 accounts in the Dickinson store when we cleaned the junk out of the book. The accounts we had cleaned out had mainly been a bunch of poor-risk auto in which the clients bought policies that they let lapse every month or so. The prior owner of the store had always reinstated these accounts or rewritten them, whatever it took to get them back up and running. We just do not do business that way, so losing this type of account did not disturb me much. However, I also saw an increase in people leaving the main book of business in our other stores. I had let two secretaries go who had not been particularly people-friendly a few months prior, and I thought that might have been a small part of the problem. In addition, it appeared my employee who had suffered the stroke was still not letting us help him on accounts, so people were moving their business away from him. In his case it seemed that they were embarrassed to say he was not getting things done. Rather than requesting another agent in our store, they simply were moving their business to another agency. I had not been aware of how much this was costing me. Also, I suppose the hard market was costing us more than we realized since it was pushing people to shop accounts. At any rate, after taking a hard look at the numbers from 2002, I resolved in 2003 to intensify our customer contact even more, informing our clients about keeping insurance costs in line while still maintaining a viable insurance program. As usual, I felt the best strategy to get back up to the 95% or better retention ratio was to continue to educate our clients and work even harder in 2003 to earn our keep. Maybe it is a tired old phrase, but when things start to slip, I always go back to basics. As it turned out, we got right back in the game with a retention ratio of 94% on our core book of business by the end of 2003.

Another project I had started in 2002 and wanted to finish up in 2003 was getting my commercial single- and multi-engine pilot's ratings in Hawai'i. I had taken the written test the previous November and was taking lessons so I would be ready for the practical test at the end of January. I have found that when I am in Hawai'I, if I work on my insurance business half the day and then vacation the rest of the time, I can have a super vacation and still stay in touch with the office. The flying was fitting right in with my half-work and half-play kind of vacation. After a few weeks of being worked over by Chad Alexander, my single-engine instructor, and Roy Mann, my multi-engine instructor, I earned the commercial endorsements on my pilot's license.

I suppose some people would not agree with this formula of working and playing while on vacation in Hawai'i, but it works for Linda and me. I usually am able to update my business plan for the coming year, bring all of my production numbers for the past year together, and visualize where I have been and where I intend to go in the next year. I have found over the years that if I put in a half-day on business, it leaves me plenty of time to have fun on the Big Island. Plus, by playing at least half the day, I am having a great vacation and keeping on top of my business simultaneously. I was having a steaming cup of Kona coffee and thinking this was the best vacation Linda and I had ever taken when one perfect tropical morning a bombshell dropped.

We had gone for 29 years without having an E&O loss. (For those of you not involved in the insurance industry, E&O stands for Errors and Omissions.) In 2001, however, we had a farmer who forgot to tell us about 159 acres of seeded crop when he reported his acres to be insured for that year. It was a perfectly innocent mistake. These acres are taken off of maps of the individual acres of land; and since he had two landlords on this same section of land, there were two maps. He accidentally only gave us the acres off of one map. Every year a few acres slip through the system in this way. This would have been no big deal if he had no loss on the unit; but, sure as hell, he had a claim on these 159 acres that made it quickly become apparent that we were short by 159 acres on the policy. Even though the mistake was the farmer's, it was probably partially our fault for not crosschecking well enough. Consequently, I filed an E&O loss. Since the claim was only about $6,900 and we had a $2,500 deductible, I reasoned it would be no big deal. I thought, Hell, we've been insured with this company for over 28 years without a loss: it won't be any problem. We sent the claim in, it was paid, and that was the end of it. Or so I thought.

To prevent another such loss, I did, however, set up a new checklist for the 2002 crop year. We used this throughout 2002, and it prevented several other losses such as this from occurring again. Our checklist was so good it was used for the PIA crop insurance E&O seminars in 2003. I came out of 2002 thinking we had solved the problem. At least for this problem we had found the checklist to be the solution.

But another E&O claim showed up the next year. On this one our client farmed land for an older gentleman. Due to a bit of a problem in how it was rented, we were unable to place multi-peril crop insurance on the land for our insured, the tenant farmer. To protect both their interests, the landlord placed his own hail insurance policy on the land in question, and everyone went on his merry way. Of course, you guessed it; there was a major hail loss on the crop. This was fine, a policy was in place, and all was well. There was only one little problem: the landlord left all the paperwork with the tenant farmer while he went on vacation. The tenant farmer called in to file a loss on his own crop, incorrectly assuming we were clairvoyant and would know we needed to file a loss on the absentee landlord's policy as well. Well, we were not and we did not. To make matters even worse, when no claim was filed and no adjustor showed up to settle the loss, the tenant farmer did not bother to call us and see what the delay was in getting the claim settled. Only three months later did he stop by the office and inquire what was going on with the big hail loss on his landlord's land. We incredulously asked, "What big hail loss?"

It turned out the tenant farmer client had called and talked to my agent who had had the stroke, telling him about the loss several months earlier. Whether or not he mentioned the loss on the landlord's policy to this agent, we shall probably never know. The agent, as I said before, was using proper office procedure less and less, had a problem with short-term memory, and did not prepare a loss report. He simply wrote a note on a sticky-pad piece of paper and put it on my crop insurance manager's desk, informing Craig that the tenant had had a loss. Seeing the note, the next day Craig had simply done a full loss report for the tenant farmer and sent it in. He did not remember the landlord's hail policy, so the landlord's loss was never filed.

Who knows the proximate cause of this E&O claim? Probably it was the stroke-affected agent's customary incomplete work. Probably it was my fault for keeping this man employed when I knew damn well he should not have been in the insurance business any longer. Whatever the reason, we were looking at another E&O loss. Hoping common sense would prevail, we called the company that had insured the landlord, told them of the mishap, and reminded them we had literally millions of dollars in losses in the area in question. We got an adjustor up to the area to assure us that yes, the crop had indeed had the hell hailed out of it. There was one big problem, though. On hail insurance policies you are supposed to report the loss within 10 days. Sure, this can be stretched out, but not for three months, for heaven's sake. Furthermore, this little mistake had a large price tag of $21,000. I was praying for a miracle, that the company would step up to the plate and do the correct thing. It was an innocent mistake; it was a verifiable loss: come on, guys. No deal. Claim denied. Times are tough, reinsurance costs are up, and profits are down. You have had tons of claims already. Grow up and clean up your own mess. Well, it does not hurt to ask.

I called up to file another E&O loss. In my own mind I was thinking that this uninsured loss also, was not really our fault; the client had not given us correct notice of loss on the land in question, letting things drag for over three months without giving us a heads-up that something was not getting done. However, this particular client happened to be a $140,000 annual premium account. I was smart enough to know we probably could not win in court on the deal. Furthermore, if we told him tough bounce, no coverage, it would have cost us the account. That is why I turned in the claim. I was hoping the E&O carrier would at least fight it. No dice: they just paid the loss.

Remember, my reasoning in turning in the loss was hey, only two E&O losses in 29 years, right? Over the years I have paid more than $170,000 in premiums; now I need you to help me out. Stupid me, I was thinking like a consumer, not an insurance agent in a hard, unprofitable market. After this loss I put yet another checklist in place and changed a couple of other procedures to prevent this type of loss from occurring again. But I did not tell my E&O carrier about what I was doing to avoid these further losses; for that matter, I had not told them about the other checklist and procedures we had developed to prevent more losses of the type we had in 2001, either: big mistake.

The company did not spend much time investigating this second loss. I was thinking they should fight the claim and at least go to the courthouse steps before sending money; but, as I said, they just cranked out a check, and that was it. The next thing they did a few weeks later almost gave me a heart attack that morning in Hawai'i: they sent out a non-renewal notice on my E&O policy. I got the call from Gene as Linda and I were having that nice hot cup of Kona coffee on the lanai. As he spoke, the hairs stood up on the back of my neck, things closed in, and the cool Pacific wind seemed suddenly hot. How in hell was I going to run a $8,500,000 premium agency with no E&O coverage? It was time for some serious begging.

I called our underwriter at our E&O carrier and started doing some fancy talking. I told him I would take any deductible up to and including $100,000 on my E&O policy; I told him how we had developed new checklists and procedures to prevent further losses of the type that had cost us the E&O claim; I reminded him of all the claim-free years; I told him I was on the E&O prevention committee of the North Dakota PIA and was going to teach crop insurance E&O at our meetings that year. He agreed to talk to his boss and the head of claims for Utica's E&O program. Faxing him eight pages of documentation for the procedures we had prepared to prevent more losses, I held my breath over the weekend.

No word from him Monday, none Tuesday: finally Wednesday I could not stand it anymore. I called the underwriter. We made small talk for a few minutes until he said, "Chuck, with all the things you have done to prevent further losses, we feel we can offer you a renewal with a $10,000 deductible and a surcharge." I felt as if an elephant had just gotten off my chest. I assured him I would be more than happy to go with the $10,000 deductible and surcharge. That night I took Linda out for supper at the Martini Yacht Club to celebrate being back in the game.

E&O insurance has been under a tremendous amount

of pressure from claims in these past years, especially in the crop insurance sector. It is more critical now than perhaps ever before to be on good terms with your E&O carrier. The short message here is that if you have done something to prevent an E&O loss, it really pays to let the underwriter handling your account know about it.

• **Never stop working on retention; if it slips, know why it slipped and take steps to correct it.**

• **If you have an E&O loss, take steps to prevent its reoccurrence, and tell your E&O carrier what steps you have taken.**

• **Now is a great time to go to a huge E&O deductible. What have you got to lose? If you put in too many losses, you will be canceled anyway.**

• CHAPTER ELEVEN •

ICE ON THE WING, THE ANGELS MAY SING

I finished qualifying for my single- and multi-engine commercial pilot's license. Linda and I hit the beach, played a few more rounds of golf, and headed back to North Dakota. It was time to put on our farmer meetings for multi-peril crop insurance and get the spring's sales effort kicked into high gear.

Shortly after returning to North Dakota and putting on my crop meetings, I was scheduled to go to Aquity's yearly agents' meeting in Rapid City, South Dakota. Since it is around 500 miles from Minot to Rapid City, I was going to be flying the Twin Comanche. Piloting the plane was fun. Furthermore, it reduced the time it took to get there from seven or eight hard hours of driving one way to an hour-and-a-half magic carpet ride. Casey was too busy to go, and my friend Craig Oxalt in Williston could not make his schedule work, so I ended up flying down by myself. Parked up at 12,000 feet above the clouds with no bumps, no stop signs and a beautiful sky of robin's-egg blue, the flight was simply terrific.

Because I had flown down the night before the meeting, I was able to have a few cocktails with my friend Gene Reiling from Western Dakota Insurers. Afterward I tried to get some sleep before our meeting the next day. The only problem was that I do not sleep well in motels, so I did not get much of a nights sleep.

The meeting was a good one, as usual. Aquity had plenty of new information and things to talk about. Ben Saltsman and his guys really know how to fire you up. I must admit I had another motive for going to this meeting. Gene's agency had sold part of their operation to The Leavitt Group out of Cedar City, Utah. The Leavitt

224

Group wanted to expand into North Dakota and had expressed interest in doing a similar deal with me. Since they have such an excellent reputation and since the idea appealed to me, I had agreed to meet them after the Aquity meeting at the offices of Western Dakota Insurers. This was to set up a chain of events that would push my piloting skills to the absolute limit.

A big fat low pressure weather system had come into North Dakota that morning, and the front end of it was due to be in Minot late that afternoon. The difficulty with flying in the clouds in North Dakota that time of year is that often those clouds in the spring of the year cause severe icing conditions. As any of you pilots know, ice and small planes do not mix; this can be a fatal combination. I did a quick flight plan calculation that morning at the hotel that told me I had better be in the air and headed home by around two that afternoon in order to be safe.

As planned, after the Aquity meeting, I went down to Western Dakota Insurers to meet with the people from Leavitt; and, of course, that took too much time. I really enjoyed talking to these people and absolutely hated to cut the meeting short, but I had been determined to leave in the Twin by one, and it was already two. I headed for the airport and checked the weather. As I saw the front approaching Minot, a chill shot through me. I was too slow getting out of Rapid City, and the front was moving too fast. At any rate, the route to Bismarck, North Dakota, which is 100 miles south of Minot, looked fine, so I filed an IFR flight plan and headed in that direction. My reason for leaving and not just staying over another day was that Linda and I were scheduled to head for Washington, DC, the next day for the PIA legislative conference. If any of you reading this are pilots, remember the warnings about "Get-there-itis"? I was about to find out why those warnings exist. In addition, my three hours' sleep the night before was about to jump up and bite me.

About to do some serious instrument flying, I was dead tired.

The flight from Rapid City to Bismarck was a pleasure. I filed for 13,000 feet and got a super tailwind. I found myself descending into Bismarck through a few scattered layers of clouds after barely an hour. Intending to fuel the airplane and stay overnight in Bismarck because of the bad weather, I called flight service anyway, just in case it might be OK to go on into Minot. The report was not too bad: the current conditions in Minot seemed to be fine, with reported cloud ceilings of 4,500 feet. Quickly filing another IFR flight plan for a flight to Minot at 4,100 feet, I jumped into the Twin and headed home. The first clue that the forecast was not as predicted was when, less than 15 miles from Bismarck, at my assigned altitude of 4,100 feet, I was totally in the clouds; it was raining, and I was definitely in the soup. Since I am instrument-rated, this was not too big a problem. A huge danger, however, was that, as I said before, in North Dakota in the spring many times rain in the clouds will turn into ice when it hits your airplane. In icing conditions the worst place to be flying into a large low pressure system is in the northeast portion of it. Where was the northeast portion of this big low? Where else: right over Minot, my destination. My plane was not equipped to fly in icing conditions. If I had had a brain in my head, I would have turned back and stayed in Bismarck a couple of days. What did I do--what else? I kept going.

Even though I was in total instrument conditions and rain, things went along well for the first half hour of flight. I was talking to flight service off and on the whole way to find out what the weather was doing in Minot. They told me that the cloud bases had dropped to 3,100 feet. Although this was quite a bit lower than the 4,500 feet of an hour ago, conditions were still very workable. I was just starting to think flying in the soup was not

226

too bad when, about 15 minutes from Minot, suddenly I noticed big globs of ice starting to hit my windshield. At times like this it is imperative to climb up out of the forming ice or turn around and fly back the way you came. I did neither. Reasoning that I was nearly home, I thought when they started vectoring me for the approach to Minot and approved my descent to 3,500 feet, I would escape from the ice. I advised approach I was getting ice, and, as expected, a few minutes later I was being vectored down. Conditions were better there, but I was still getting some more ice accumulation. Not having flown much in ice in my short career as a pilot, this certainly got my attention. Most likely the smart money would have still been to request vectors for a return to Bismarck, where I knew conditions were better; instead, I accepted a vector to take me over the airport runway to see if I could just do a visual approach. No deal: in those few minutes the cloud ceilings had dropped to 600 feet with blowing snow. Furthermore, I could not see a thing out of the windshield, for by now it had totally iced over. I was starting to realize I had better concentrate or end up dead. Luckily, I had done one thing right: I had all of my approach plates on my clipboard, ready to read. Tension was building; I could feel sweat start to run down my back. I was beginning to realize with dread that a trap was closing. The trap was the rapidly developing low pressure system. Getting home had been the bait, and I was getting set up to be the rabbit.

I was thinking "There's ice on the air frame, it's slowing me down; Keep power up, Air speed up, Keep scanning the gauges, Keep wings level, Watch your altitude."

Cutting into my thought, the voice of the Minot approach controller, the only friend I now had, seemed to come from far away when I heard, "7949Y, I am giving you vectors to the runway 13 localizer back course.

Turn heading 308 degrees." My tired mind seemed to be mired in mud. I was so busy just flying the airplane that I was hard-pressed to remember what to do next. Instead of proper readback of the clearance, I simply replied, "OK for 13." At least I turned the plane to the 308-degree heading. What to do then? For just a fraction of a second, it was as if my mind was in low gear; my head buzzed. It was all I could do to control the airplane, and just for a few terrible moments I could not think. The lack of sleep, the worrying about not being able to see out of the windshield, the ice on the plane: all of this was piling up on me. I felt the beginning of a terrible, paralyzing panic coming on. Most likely it was one of the times in my life when I was very close to death.

Then reason and training started to take over. Hell, I had done this approach many times in practice. I could not change the windshield, I could not change the ice on the airframe, but I could fly this plane. My mind started to work, and I got the aircraft configured to land: boost pumps on, mixtures to rich, tanks on mains. Fly the approach: 3,500 feet, 120 miles per hour, and outbound two minutes on 308 degrees from Oxhol intersection; then left procedure turn 263 degrees outbound for one minute, left turn inbound to 083 degrees, and intercept the inbound 128 degree localizer to the runway. Training and good instructors are priceless; and it was as if they were all with me that night: Leo Jostad, Phil Aldridge, Chad Alexander, and Roy Mann. All of them and all of the knowledge they had given me over the years were with me that night.

As the motors droned on, I could hear Roy saying, "If you ever get in the ice, keep your airspeed up. Remember, your stall speed will increase with the added drag and weight of the ice. Most likely you won't use flaps at all. Be extra-careful of stalling the airplane." True to his teaching, instead of keeping 15 inches manifold pressure, I was holding 21 inches just to maintain my 120 m.p.h. approach speed. Phil Aldridge's high-pitched Texas twang was telling me to keep an eye on all the gauges: "You know, Chuck, be careful you don't fixate on any one. Remember, when you intercept the localizer, it will happen quickly." Right on schedule, in came the localizer back course. I was headed directly for the airport on a heading of 128 degrees, looking for Oxhol intersection five miles from the airport. At Oxhol I could drop down from 3,500 feet to the lowest permissible altitude of 2,080 feet.

With cotton in my mouth I radioed Minot Approach, "Minot Approach, 7949Y is established on the localizer inbound." They came back, "7949Y, missed approach instructions will be as published. Contact Magic City tower on 118.2." I called Magic City tower, was cleared to land, and began my descent. The only thought I had was if I got to the airport, could not see the runway, and had to go missed approach, I was going to get my stupid butt back to Bismarck and stay the hell out of icing conditions the rest of my life. As I started down again, my instructor Leo Jostad's voice was right there in my head: 3,500 feet for 2100; 3,100 feet for 2100; 2,700 feet for 2100; until finally at 2,400 feet I could see lights on the ground out my side window--my God, I was happy to see them! Since Minot is my home airport I now knew exactly where I was: right over one of my insured's, John Pitner's, farm. I put the plane in a slight sideways skid so I could see out the side window, confirmed gear down, props forward, boost pumps on, tanks on main, and headed in. The only difference was that, instead of staying at 365 feet above the ground, I dropped down to about 150 feet. I knew where I was; I finally had the runway in sight and was not going to lose it. This cowboy was headed for the barn.

Actually, the landing was pretty uneventful. It was

a good one, and the snow-covered runway was no big problem at all. It was heavenly to feel the wheels start rolling. I cannot remember my mouth ever being that dry as I taxied through the blowing snow toward the hangar. It was dark as I cut the engines and listened to the whine of the gyros spinning down. I took a few pictures of 7949Y and the ice she had all over her, thanked God for giving me great instructors who had taught me what to do in these types of situations, and drove thankfully home. I told Linda when I got there, "Daddy needs a new toy." I explained that if I was going to use airplanes for business, I needed an airplane that had de-icing capabilities. It turned out the weather got so bad that the airlines were not even flying the next day. I may as well have stayed in Rapid City and had a few beers with my buddy Gene Rieling! But how do you know?.

- **Flying is fun, but flying into a cold weather low front can be deadly.**

- **Good instructors can save your life someday.**

- **If you fly in icy conditions, get a "known ice" equipped airplane.**

"BABY, BABY, YOU KNOW YOU LOVE ME, BABY"

The 2003 crop year was shaping up to be an excellent one. The price of crop insurance was up a bit, the farmers got in the field on time, the situation was superb. The farmers purchased a record amount of hail and multiperil crop insurance. By the time the dust settled in July, we had written over 1.3 million of new crop premium. Folks, in my little world up here in the Dakotas, that is a ton of new production--I was elated! The only downside was that commissions had been drastically cut on hail insurance and, although not to such a severe degree, on multi-peril crop insurance as well. Hail was the worst hit with commission cuts of nearly 50%. We increased our hail production by almost $400,000 of premium, yet ended up actually losing $8,000 in commission on the hail portion of the book. Scary, is it not? Of course, the companies simply reminded us how with sales up we were really OK, anyway. I asked a couple of them why in hell they did not raise the premium enough to keep from killing the agency force. Of course, that was like talking to the side of my office building.

Nonetheless, with the huge increase in multi-peril crop insurance writings, the increase in hail production, and the steady increase in commercial and other lines, we were still heading for a stellar year. Furthermore, we fortunately did not get killed by any major hailstorm in 2003 and thus were headed for a super low loss year in crop lines. Since this had not happened for some time, I was elated that we were going to be able to say we had an excellent loss year in these lines, too, for a change.

As a result of beginning conversations with the Leavitt Group, they stopped up to see me later that spring, and Linda and I went to their annual meeting in Vancouver. I really liked these people and was very busy sending them information on the agency so they would be able to give me an offer on the store. Sitting in on their annual meeting would be an excellent way for us to see how their agency operation worked. It would also be fun to see Vancouver.

The meeting in Vancouver was a huge hit with us. We hooked up with our friends from Rapid City, Gene and Ann Reiling, to tour the town. Gene and I were busy trying to eat all the raw oysters in town, while our ladies were busy shopping. The four of us had a memorable oyster-eating and wine-drinking afternoon at The Sandbar Restaurant on Granville Island. If memory serves me, on the way home, when we walked by a little street band that was playing, the four of us ended up dancing in the street. Just kids having fun…..

For the final night's entertainment, the Leavitt Group had hired Rita Coolidge as the main event. Linda and I sat with the folks from Western Dakota Insurers, and we had a couple of bottles of wine on the table. Dr. Hold of the Chartered Insurance Counselor (CIC) courses also sat at our table. It was a fun and interesting conversation. I remember thinking, God, how could I be so lucky to be in this place at this time with this much horsepower? As the night went on, I started saying the Lord's Prayer in my head: Our Father, who art in heaven…lead me not into temptation but….. Meanwhile, Rita sang, "Baby, baby, you know you love me, baby." What an evening!

Rita is one of Linda's favorite singers. As the show was ending, I happened to mention that to Mark Leavitt; and the next thing I knew, he was escorting Linda and me over to talk to Ms. Coolidge and get an autographed picture. The Leavitts are simply some of the finest and most accommodating people I have ever met.

- **You can mix business and pleasure.**

- **Dancing in the street is not a bad thing.**

- **Selling insurance is a good way to meet celebrities.**

NEVER TRY TO TEACH A PIG TO SING:
Chasing More Agencies

Ever heard of this old adage? "You should never try to teach a pig to sing. It wastes your time, and it annoys the pig." One of the problems with buying agencies is getting the existing staff up to speed so they can exist in the automated insurance world. Sometimes if you keep staff after purchases you find yourself attempting to train workers you would simply fire if they were not prior owners. This situation was cropping up again in another of the agencies I had purchased. Therefore, after I got back to Minot from the trip to Vancouver and we got the crop insurance season settled down, I started thinking of more ways I could get one of these problem employees up and running. We had purchased this little store December 1, 2001; and although the book was holding together fairly well and we were seeing some growth, it was totally obvious that the prior owner was never going to be a sales star. He was very much into drinking coffee and telling me how busy he was while not really getting much done, having his secretary do most of the actual work. We had done quite a few deals, but the promised prospect list and people to see were simply not materializing. The secretary I had hired for the office was getting four times the work done that he was. I began to consider promoting her, getting rid of him, and hiring another producer.

Perhaps this problem I was having with my producer in Dickinson was what caused me to get so interested when I heard of a small agency for sale in the little town of Regent, 35 miles to the southeast. Probably it was because buying good little stores is simply something I like to do. Whatever the reason, when I heard about the little agency for sale in Regent, I inquired about it and contacted the people who had it for sale. Unfortunately, it was owned by a man who was going to jail for insurance fraud. This made buying the store fairly scary. Normally, I would not have even pursued the deal; but this man had many agencies, and the one for sale (which looked about half OK) had been run by another person, who was a pretty straight shooter. It occurred to me that if I could get the store really cheap, it might just work out. However, I knew we would have to hire a local agent to run it, so I started asking around in the area as to whether or not anyone was interested in the job. As usual, I got a few names and started making calls. I had no success for several months until I got a call from a man in Regent. I had met him the previous year while on a pheasant hunt with North Dakota Governor John Hoeven. He was head of Cannonball Corporation, a pheasant-hunting company located in Regent. He and I talked on the phone about him selling insurance for Western Agency, Inc., part of the year; running his pheasant-hunting operation the rest of the time. It would solve the agent problem for me and develop another income stream for him: we would both win. Furthermore, the town of Regent is only 35 miles from Dickinson. If he turned out to be a good salesperson, possibly he could help pick up the sales slack in my Dickinson store.

Next thing I knew, I was sitting in my plane early in the morning for the 35 minute flight to meet with him at the little town of Mott, North Dakota. I dialed in the Mott identifier on my GPS navigation system, set up the autopilot, and headed out. What a beautiful morning! Dawn was just breaking as the plane climbed up through the haze to settle into a smooth, steady flight across southwest North Dakota. I had sold the Twin Comanche after the infamous ice flight in the spring, purchasing a fully known-ice-certified 340A Cessna. Its bigger twin engines got me around the state quite a bit faster, and the plane was able to handle any icing I might get myself into. Plus, it had far superior navigation aids, autopilot, and a bunch more goodies that helped me fly more safely.

After meeting with Pat he dropped me off at the Mott Airport for the flight back to Minot. However, be-

234

fore I headed back to Minot, I did a small detour over the Regent area. It was loaded with lovely farms and miles and miles of fine checkerboard fields. Clean, neat farms, a stunning blue North Dakota sky: we were going to do well here; this town and these farms were right down our alley. I know farms and farm business, and I could easily see that here was a definite opportunity. I was committed to purchasing the little agency. I had my agent lined up, the land looked good, all I had to do was get the sale completed. I dialed in MOT, the navigation identifier for Minot, set up a climb to 7,500 feet, kicked in the autopilot, and settled in for the ride home. I distinctly remember saying a prayer to God for just letting me be in this place at this time.

Next day I called up the owner of the agency, ready to begin final negotiations, when to my surprise he said he had already sold the store--bummer! I was mad I had missed the deal because I had no salesperson ready to go. After further reflection, however, I decided, Why not proceed to hire someone anyway and start a scratch agency? My reasoning was that the prior store's owner had such a bad reputation that bringing in our Western Agency, Inc., name with our good reputation and starting a book of business from scratch would probably pose no big problem. Instead of trying to bury the bad reputation of the prior owner, we could start with a clean slate and our unsullied name. In addition, the agency in Dickinson that had purchased the book ahead of me had a culture of not doing much with farm insurance. It appeared as if the opportunity was here for us to start a scratch store, pick up only good accounts, and build a solid book of business in the Regent area.

I tested Pat the way I do all of my job candidates, and he scored super as a salesperson. Also, he was and is very smart--great! Now all we had to do was meet with the board of directors for Cannonball Corporation, where he was presently employed, and convince them that Pat's having two jobs could work for both of us.

I flew down to have an evening meeting with the Cannonball board and Pat--what a nice bunch of people! A group of farmers and ranchers who had started Cannonball Corporation several years ago, they created their company to sell pheasant hunts to people from all over the United States. By doing this they had helped to save their little town, bringing in a bunch of new money. They were now doing business in excess of $500,000 a year. Who says survival economics is not alive in North Dakota?

At the meeting I told them I had offices in eight different small towns around North Dakota. I told them how we would install our computer system in Pat's office and how we would help him develop a book of business in Regent. I told them we were the largest farm insurance agency in the state and would bring the most competitive insurance rates available in the state right to them. I told them I did not see any problem with Pat working exclusively for them during the pheasant-hunting season and for me in the off-season. They agreed to let Pat have the job and rent me an office in their building: excellent. People say you cannot make money in small-town North Dakota, yet I bet you that in less than five years we have a million or more premium on the books down there. Not only will we have an excellent book of business in place; also, Pat will have an excellent second income stream, the local people will have the best insurance products available anywhere, and we will all make money. The office rent was to be $150 per month, including a desk. See why I love North Dakota?

Around midnight I got done with the meeting with Cannonball Corporation. I was staying at Prairie Vista Bed and Breakfast, where owner Marlys said she would get up early to make me breakfast. What a deal, yet she apologized to me for the "high" nightly rate of $50--my God, things in North Dakota are such a bargain! Owners Lowell and Marlys Prince are a couple of the finest people you would ever want to meet. Today started out for me at 5:00 A.M. It had been another busy one, but I am still having fun. Am I crazy?

- **Never stop looking for good staff.**

- **Starting a satellite agency from scratch can be a good way to boost production in an area.**

- **Small towns do not mean small premiums.**

- **Again, flex-time helps me get quality employees.**

"WE CAN'T HEAR YOU, WE'RE TOO BUSY"

The 2003 North Dakota summer passed, with its heat, long days, and endless waves of grain. The wheat crop set a record, and we posted excellent loss ratios of only 22% on $4,000,000 of multi-peril crop insurance premium and only 46% on $1,000,000 of hail insurance. Everything was all right.

Fast forward to McPherson, Kansas: it is late August 2003, and the time is midnight. I am sitting in one more hotel room on one more thin mattress. The noisy air-conditioner is going to rob me of another good night's sleep, and I am getting ready to meet with one more advisory council in the morning, again attempting to tell a company what we agents think would improve things. Why in hell do we both put ourselves through this? The companies are, by and large, going to do what they are going to do, regardless of what we tell them. I suppose they have their own sets of different dynamics in this business, and it seems never the twain shall meet. Agents will continue to be their own worst enemies by time after time writing business they should not be writing, just to get another app. They will continue to work for too few commission dollars because they are too lazy to sit down and decide if they should move a book of business to a company that is still paying viable commission. Why do I keep letting myself get put on advisory councils? Probably for the camaraderie, probably to try and discover how companies really do operate, and probably because maybe, just maybe, some good does come from it. Also, I did get to fly the 340 down here all the way from North Dakota: fun. For this flight I parked myself up at 23,000 feet and arrived in three hours and 20 minutes; man, pilots love a tailwind. And wait, I have a bag of goodies from the company here. Let me see: six Hershey's Kisses, a package of Planter's Peanuts, a Members Mark bottle of water. Wow--I'm blessed!

I remember, back in the late 1970s and early 1980s, when advisory councils were just coming into fashion. I agreed to be put on the advisory council for a little company called Sunshine Mutual. Several of us North Dakota agents drove all the way to Sioux Falls, South Dakota, for the meeting. We were taken out for supper, then dropped off at our hotel, where they had rented us an extra room and left us a big supply of booze. There the 10 of us agents sat drinking and talking until the wee hours of the morning about the insurance business in general and in particular what, in our opinion, little Sunshine Mutual could do to be more successful at it. Hung over at next morning's meeting, we spent a few hours with the powers-that-be from Sunshine, gave them our recommendations, and went on our merry way, 500 miles back to North Dakota. I cannot remember what subjects we brought up, but one thing I do recall is that we really stressed they should leave their farm truck program

238

alone since they were doing well on it and making money. Guess what--can you believe it? The new farm truck rates were on my desk when I got home; the company had already decided what to do before we even got to Sioux Falls. We could have all saved ourselves the time, wasted days, and hangover. Hell, if an advisory council just consists of getting drunk and talking smart, I can do that at home.

I ended up writing an article for Agent and Broker magazine about advisory councils. I had written an article for them a year before on agency acquisitions and purchases; after the ill-fated trip to Sioux Falls, I was so disgusted with advisory councils I was prompted to write another one. It was a story about advisory councils in the form of an allegory entitled "The Legend of the King." It was fun to write, and it was nice to see my byline in print once more. My allegory told about a group of peasants who made a trip to give the King some advice on how to run his country. Of course, like the companies putting on advisory councils, the King did not take their advice, either. It had taken a whole lot of time to write the article. However, when I sent a note to the magazine asking how much they were going to pay me, I never heard from them again: so much for my early writing career. It was about as profitable as my early insurance career.

It seems sometimes as if the companies are saying to the agents on their advisory councils, "Don't tell us what the customer wants; we're too busy." I am well aware that companies cannot possibly do everything agents suggest, but some of this stuff has been troublesome for years and years. For example, have you ever known a company that had an understandable billing system, or an understandable help line? One that really, truly has efficient automation? How about getting paperwork back on time? Yes, it is popular now for companies to blame the long wait for endorsements on the "hard market" or "we're so busy doing this or that." But for heaven's sake, we have been hearing these same old tired excuses for over 30 years!

As to the issue with billing systems that no one can understand, I have a theory. My idea is that somewhere in America there is a computer programmer who has a nice little family and a nice little life, and he is the only person in the country who can consistently understand the insurance bill he gets from his carrier a couple of times a year. Why can he and no one else understand his bill? Because he is the genius who wrote the program! All the rest of us morons, who incidentally are paying the freight in the industry, have no idea what these wonderful bills mean. Hell, I (who have been in this business for over 30 years) got a bill a few weeks ago from one of my main carriers, on my own insurance policy. It was for $36, and I had absolutely no idea what to make of it. I had to take it up to the front desk and have one of my CSRs call the company to find out what it was for. People, when I am this upside-down, it is not a positive reflection on our billing systems.

I guess while I am ranting and raving on billing I would like to ask, "Who in hell is the person who designed the system that sends the client a bunch of policy information along with a big note to the effect that 'This is not a bill.' Then a month or two later, after the client has totally forgotten about what he even insured, the actual bill arrives?" I wonder what person or people saddled us with this monster. Whoever they are, they must be stupendous persuaders because they have sold this dumb, counterproductive, incomprehensible system to virtually every company billing system in the United States. Why can we agents set up our own management systems to put anything on a bill we want, but the companies cannot? Gee, on our bills we can put such things as "Bob, this is the bill for adding your new pickup": simple, cheap, easy to understand, effective. One little problem: the companies do not want agents doing billing anymore, do they? The companies have basically forced all us agents to go on automated "direct bill," totally taking us out of the billing equation. By the time we find out our customer is mad about getting an indecipherable bill, he has already left for another agent in the vain hope that agent's company will present him with a bill that is not printed in Chinese.

I believe the only way we can keep our clients, and the only way our clients can keep track of their insurance bills, is to educate them to call us agents when a question arises. You do not have the time to do this, you say? Just give your customer my phone number. After we complete the new application, my staff will be more than happy to help them keep their billing in order. What I mean here is that we as agents simply must take the time, develop the culture in our stores, and communicate to our clients that we are here to help them. We, the Independent Agents, are able to do this; we must do this. My store has been doing this, and it works. Possibly that is why Western Agency, Inc., has had 95% retention ratios for years and years. In this industry if we want to keep our books intact, it is time to work as hard on retention as we do on sales.

While we gripe about companies, "Let he who is without sin cast the first stone." We agents, too, make numerous mistakes that need to be corrected. Many of the same problems we have with companies can be traced to bad work we sometimes do. Also, I feel that on advisory councils we agents should understand up front that if the companies do not make a profit, they cannot exist. Just going to a council and whining that you want a better, cheaper product is a waste of their time and yours. Plus, in today's hard market it is really a stretch to expect a company to be expanding coverage without raising rates. We must try to point out things we think will help the client, the agent, and the company.

If there are gaps in coverage, for heaven's sake bring them up. Many times companies have a coverage gap of which they are unaware. Often they, just like us agents, get carried away with their own rhetoric about what a great job they are doing. I had one company with a major gap in coverage on ATVs. They were covering them for on-premises liability but not off-premises liability; the problem with this is that many times ATVs are off-premises. To omit this kind of coverage is nothing but an E&O time bomb for agents. This particular company's stated goal was "Being the leader in farm insurance." In the heat of trying to get them argued into putting better coverage on their four-wheelers I said, "It's going to be hard for you people to be the leader in farm insurance when you are selling a half-assed product." After I had said it, the room got pretty quiet. It was probably a poor choice of words for me to use, but the company did expand the coverage.

Also, be prepared that when companies add coverage, they must assess a charge. If they are taking more risk, they need to be paid. I imagine most of you are working on commission--what is wrong with charging for additional protection? I have a problem seeing premium increases as the end of the world; so should you. In spite my being a bit cynical about advisory councils, they do serve a purpose. Over the years I have seen companies, agents, and clients gain much from them.

At these councils I have met some very good people, both agency and company. Furthermore, I have made many lifetime friends, so I suppose spending time at advisory councils is an all-around win. I have to say that the council I am on now is one of the better ones. The only drawback is this council is two days long, twice a year. Figuring I have to leave a day early and spend a day to get home, it usually takes four to five days of my time to attend twice a year. Adding this up, I am donating more than a week a year to this. Not only that: they want you to serve on their council for four years—that is around 30 days, right? In my world a time commitment of 30 days is quite significant. I made over $400,000 net income last year. These guys do not get that if they remunerated me for this, they would be shelling out quite a bit of cash to pay for me being there. I have always felt it is a fundamental misunderstanding on the part of companies, that they feel by putting you the agent on their advisory council they are giving you a nice little paid vacation that compensates you for your time costs: not really.

However, I discovered that most agents do regard it as a holiday when I got elected president of the advisory council I am on now. I suggested we shorten the meetings to one day twice a year or two days once a year. Wow--you would have thought I had passed gas in church! Who knows, maybe I am the idiot. Let us move on.

- **Companies to agents: "Don't tell us what the customer wants; we're too busy."**

- **It is hard to make any money writing magazine articles.**

- **Advisory councils take a bunch of time, but over all they are probably worthwhile.**

SOME DON'T GET IT AND SOME REALLY DON'T GET IT:
Developing Small Agencies and Selling Business in Small Towns

As the summer of 2003 moved into fall, the Leavitt Group had visited me, and I had been sending production figures, tax statements, and reams of other paper their way. By late fall, after we had been on a couple of conference calls, I was very seriously thinking about doing a deal with them. They usually purchase 60% interest in an agency, and the active partner then has his perpetuation plan in place. When he is ready to retire, the Leavitt Group help either existing staff or someone they locate purchase the remaining 40%. It sounded so good that I really wanted to do a deal with these excellent people if it worked out. However, I still felt that they probably would not offer me enough money to convince me to sell Western Agency, Inc. Linda and I spent tons of time and energy talking about whether we should or could sell the agency. Both of us have always known that if we were to sell the store we would have to get enough money to set us up for the rest of our lives because who knows if I could work for someone else after being self-employed for over 30 years. If we sold the store, the worst had to be assumed: either that the deal would not work out or that they would fire me. Therefore, we had to have enough cash to be able to survive alone. Finally we had sent off all our numbers. The ball was in their court to come back with an offer.

As we moved into the fall of 2003, our commercial book of business became increasingly active. I found that by prospecting the small agencies we had purchased for commercial business, we were not only having a super hit ratio on sales, but we were also writing some very excellent $8,000 to $40,000 premium accounts. Quite a few small towns in North Dakota have little manufacturing companies, and we were developing a niche market in them. The way we would go after the accounts is have the local agent we had bought out get us expiration (ex.) dates on their current policies and then set up appointments for him and Casey to go see the people in charge. Our time frame was normally 60 days before renewal or, in the case of an account on which we were certain we could be very competitive, we went right after it and did a midterm cancellation. On the first appointment we would do an inspection, prepare an app, and get a proposal put together; then on the second appointment, when we were ready to close the deal, I flew Casey in, he would do the deal, and we were usually able to be back in Minot by late afternoon. Casey's ability to arrange deals and my skill at keeping the sales process moving made us a terrific team. Furthermore, we were having a ball using the plane to accelerate the development of a market that we simply would not have been able to develop as fast otherwise. We were definitely transforming our methods of selling commercial insurance.

Not only was it fun to be flying around the state doing deals; also, we were finding it was a super third- party influence to have our local agent tell his client that the commercial manager of Western Agency, Inc., was going to be flying into town in a twin-engine airplane to review this client's insurance program personally. These were clients who in many cases had not had a visit from their agent in years. Now they had a guy actually flying in to see them. It really emphasized that we considered their accounts important. The day's presentations done, Casey and I would get in the twin and head for home. Although we ended up flying over and through some bad weather once in awhile, it was entertaining and challenging. We both find we are enjoying the insurance business more than ever. Often the flight home has been an opportunity to decompress and go over the deal we are working on. Gee, am I starting to sound like an airplane salesman?

We were finding that in these small towns where we had purchased agencies, most of the good commercial insurance was being written by out-of-town agents. Now that we had purchased a local agency, we could come in as a local business. Because we had a local agent who had lived there for years, we had a solid leg up on those out-of-town agents. In fun Casey and I started calling this our "guilt trip pitch" because we were asking people to buy from us to help keep a local agent in business: it was important for all of us in the small towns to work together etc. However, truthfully, we were giving these clients a super product at a competitive price. Since we usually owned our offices in these small towns, we were in fact taxpayers and stakeholders in their community. In the town of Oakes, North Dakota, for instance, we purchased a small agency and an office building in 2002. Using these methods we knocked $87,000 of premium out of one insurance agency from Fargo, a big town 80 miles away, in just the next seven-month period after we had purchased the store.

The only difficulty that was developing was that I was having a hard time bringing the little agencies we had bought into the modern insurance world. It seemed to me that the staff members in these little agencies were so focused on writing anything, no matter what it was or what the loss ratio was, that they totally lost sight of what it is they SHOULD have been writing. For example, my agent in Dickinson was having one of his books of business that he had placed with a small mutual company re-underwritten by them. This little mutual was in a bit of a financial bind and it was a good idea for them to be cleaning out some bad business their various agencies had brought them. The president of this little mutual is a friend of mine; despite their drop in ratings to a Best's B, he and I had agreed that I would leave the premium we had with them intact. He assured me that they were not going to go broke and were taking the necessary steps to get back on solid footing. I agreed things appeared better for them after looking at what they were doing to get back on track. Maybe it is unwise not to move a book when a company gets in trouble, but as I said this president is a friend of mine, and many of the problems this company had stemmed from things that were done long before he came on board. They were raising their rates a bunch, cleaning out their book, and getting back in the insurance business--wow, what a concept! I totally agreed they had to go through their book and clean out any bad stuff they could get rid of.

My Dickinson agent, however, rather than work with this company to get rid of unprofitable accounts, was incensed that they were attacking 'his' book. He perceived it as a personal insult that they would get rid of all of this "good business." I called him and told him I totally agreed with the ones they were canceling. I had pulled loss runs on all of his bad accounts, and most of them had loss ratios of over 200%, for God's sake.

Things finally came to a head a few weeks later when I found out he had been badgering an underwriter to keep one of these junk accounts on the books. Luckily, I had a good enough relationship with the company that they called me about it. Incidentally, if you have never told a company or your key underwriters to give you a heads-up if one of your staff is doing something wrong, I feel it is a very good thing to do. Often companies seem to be afraid to offend owners, so they do not inform them when one of their employees is screwing up. I call my key underwriters and am very up-front with my field reps about letting me know if someone on my staff is getting in trouble.

Anyway, the account this agent was so focused on keeping was located in an area over 45 miles one way from our office. Furthermore, this client had claims in the past five years of over $60,000 with something like 14 claims--not only that, his total annual premium was not even $3,000! When I told this agent he was crazy to even think about writing this junk piece of business, rather than agreeing with me, he protested, "Yes, but the guy is going to start a hunting lodge, and we can insure that." I replied, "Why would we want still more business from a career claimer who is almost a 100-mile round trip away from us?" I elaborated that I now owned his agency and that if he wanted to continue to be employed by me, he would do things my way and stop going around me. Some people get it, some really get it, some do not get it, and some really do not get it. Remember about teaching a pig to sing?

The other problem I seemed to be having in converting the small agencies to our way of thinking was "Yes, Virginia, we are in the sales business." On one of my trips to my agency in Oakes, the prior owner and I were driving around town looking for business we could write and came across a nice little Honda dealer. Did he know the guy? Of course, he was a good friend, etc. "Gee, let's quote it," I said. To make a long story short, my agent got us the ex. date, and Casey did his usual super job of looking at what the prospective client had, what was missing, how we could do better. Our two different sit-downs with this guy determined that he was vastly underinsured. He had a garage policy from Auto Owners, a company that happens to be very good at that type of business, but his current agent had very little coverage in force for him; this agent did not even have either the Auto Owners Property Plus or Garage Plus endorsements on the policy. Both of these endorsements, which only cost about $500 per year, would have vastly increased his coverage. I told him that whether or not he chose us as his agent he should be sure to buy both of these excellent endorsements.

After we had gotten a good, solid quote on what he should have for coverage, Casey and his staff did a proposal showing the gaps in coverage and what coverage we felt would be adequate for the risk. We then flew down for Casey to give the Honda dealer a presentation on his policy. We told the guy he should stay with Auto Owners and that, due to rate hikes, he would be getting an increase of almost $2,000 on his current policy, even if he stayed with his current agent. With the rate hike and the extra coverage we were proposing, he would have a new premium substantially higher than the one he had before. After our second visit with him, our agent in Oakes seemed upset. I asked him what was wrong, and he said, "Well, I don't want to make Merle mad." I laughed and said I did not think Merle was mad, but whether or not he was really did not bother me. What I was interested in doing here was making a sale, and if we made the sale, I wanted it to be with the proper coverage. We went to see the Honda dealer one more time and--guess what--we sold him. The client got a super contract with the coverage he needed, the company now had a piece of business that was properly insured, we got a new insured, and our agent was amazed.

Again, the challenge in purchasing these small agencies is not in getting them automated; it seems we get them up to speed fairly fast on that. The challenge, as I see it, is to have them understand how to write the insurance product correctly and do it in a way that will be profitable to the agency, the company, and the client. If the man who owns the small agency you are buying is a good guy, then his book will be good also: it is just axiomatic. Good people write good business. What needs to be done is get the store automated, clean out the junk, get the policies in force correctly written, and get some new production going.

Maybe I am bitching too much about the problems with these stores. Suffice it to say, retention ratio on the last couple of these I have purchased is running in excess of 93%. My commission earnings per employee for Western Agency, Inc., are around $100,000 for 2003, so I am fairly comfortable in the conviction that, at least for our area, we are doing the right thing. Furthermore, we are finding that a significant segment of our new production in commercial lines is coming out of our outlying stores. As 2003 draws to a close, it is very apparent that I am happy with my purchases of these small agencies and have no plans for 2004 other than finding more of them to buy.

- **Contrary to popular belief, there is commercial insurance in small towns.**

- **Airplanes get you to a lot of places in a short time and are a great third-party influence.**

- **The guilt trip pitch works: try it.**

- **When you are buying little agencies, it is a challenge to get them up to speed on how the modern agency sells insurance.**

• CHAPTER TWELVE •

I STILL HATE LONG GOODBYES

While everything was going well on agency purchases, new business production, and loss ratio, I knew I still had big staffing troubles. Marlen, my agent, who had had the stroke was becoming a persistent problem that I simply could not solve. Now he rarely showed up for work on Monday; if he did, he was usually late. I had two CSRs checking his work daily to try and correct his mistakes before they went to a company and to prevent potential E&O losses. For a long time when he did not show up for work, we gave him a wake-up call, but it got to the point where it was easier when he was not there, so we let him sleep. It was heartbreaking to see this man, who had been such a super employee and had once been a partner in my agency, having such a hard time, through no fault of his own. Many days he would have to go home early, or would go home and not leave, if you know what I mean. I tried talking to him, I tried getting mad, I tried reasoning with him: nothing seemed to work. His procedures were slipping, and it seemed that, no matter what I did, I absolutely could not get him to do things the way they had to be done. It was as if, after his stroke, mentally he simply was not the same person he had been before. In retrospect, when it was obvious after the stroke he was not going to be able to get back up to speed, I should not have allowed him to return to the store.

In trying to help him, one of the main problems we had was, he absolutely would not let anyone else look at any of "his accounts." Agents like this simply end up so busy with trivia that they get nothing done. With someone who is already partially disabled due to a stroke, it

251

just gets impossible. I tried having his phone calls intercepted and having his work done by my CSRs in the front office. The next thing I knew, he was having people call him on his damn cell phone. He was behaving like a seventh-grade kid who would not mind.

Making it more confusing, now and then he put in a couple of weeks of working pretty well. He would come in on time and do quality work, and I would think that maybe, finally he was going to be back in the game. But after a few weeks he would slip into his old rut once more. Normally, I would have fired a person who would not work the way we needed to have things done. I kept remembering how he used to be before the stroke, though, which overshadowed my management judgment. I believed he was probably working harder than any of us to get anything done at all, and I admired him for trying so hard. He had worked for me for 16 years--how could I let someone go who had been unlucky enough to have a stroke? Thinking this way probably works in a vocational workshop. However, it is not effective in an Independent Insurance Agency. Sooner or later, people like this precipitate a huge E&O loss, which is easy enough to get anyway, let alone with someone who is not documenting or doing things that need to be done. I was in a panic about our recent E&O crisis, visualizing more potential E&O claims coming out of this man's office every day. I had to handle this; I just did not have the will to do it.

Eventually, he ended up binding a policy without sending the company a binder. In addition, it was a slow-pay account from which no premium was collected, a bad risk we should never have taken on in the first place. Before his stroke this employee would never have given the account a second glance. When I found out about it, I called him into my office to put him on notice. I had had enough. I repeated what I needed, how things had to be done. I warned him that the next major screw-up would be his last; I tried to point out the potential E&O problem. It was a very tense, uncomfortable time for both of us. What made it worse was I knew it would not help.

A couple of weeks later he saw me in the hall and said he wanted to talk to me. We both went in my office and closed the door. In a shaking voice he blurted out that he was handing in his two weeks' notice. He said, "I've found a job at an agency that doesn't have any of those damn computers, they don't expect me to be at work on time, and I don't have to meet all of these deadlines." I was flabbergasted. What I wanted to do was hug him and tell him, "Thank you, thank you, thank you for letting me off the hook!" But I knew what a traumatic thing it was for him to come in and resign after all these years. Basically, I wished him well, saying I was sure he would enjoy the change. Then I gave him two weeks' severance pay so he could go to work for the new agency immediately. I have found over the years that long goodbyes are not much good, and I was absolutely ecstatic that he was finally leaving. I felt as if a giant weight had been lifted off my chest. I was in a better mood than I had been in for months.

Of course, he took accounts away from us, most of them little homeowners, auto, high-risk auto, some brokered commercial. It is too early to tell how much premium will disappear, but I will be amazed if it is much above $150,000. When you consider this man's wages including benefits were quite significant, it was a colossal win for us when he quit; he did me the biggest favor of the year 2003. Furthermore, he wouldn't have to put up with those damn computers, being to work on time, and deadlines. What a deal.

The big joke was that the agency he moved to was run by a guy who had sold me an agency many years before. I had almost gone broke trying to pay for that piece-of-crap store. It was, by and large, a bunch of bar business, and most of it went away over the years. Although buying that store almost broke me, in many ways it probably made me successful because in trying to pay for it I really learned how to get efficient and stay alive in the business. The reason I still had so much ill will toward this guy was that years later, after I had paid him off in full for his junk book of business, he had told someone he owed money to that he was not paying him because that damn Chuck Tompkins was not paying him on time. Hearing that absolutely incensed me; even now, putting it into words makes me mad. Years later the guy had gone back into the insurance business, and he no doubt thought that by hiring my guy away he was really getting a shooter agent from me. Not so: he and his agency had just acquired a nightmare.

However, I was not done being surprised by my staff. My bookkeeper was a very good friend of mine; before going to work for me he had been the assistant manager of our local country club. Although he had no formal accounting training, Linda and I reasoned he would grow into the job, as we had. A super-smart person with a math degree, he did a superb job of handling our books. Furthermore, as our IT guy he was becoming an absolute expert at keeping our computer system working smoothly, getting to the point that he knew as much about how to make the Applied System software work as anyone in the state. Paying him more than twice what he had been making at the country club, I expected him to be with us for many years. That was not to be.

In early 2003 it became obvious that Gene was not as happy in his job as he had been before. In the four years he had worked for us, the company had doubled in size, and it seemed he could no longer deal with the stresses of keeping all the finances in order. A few things had been allowed to slip, a few mistakes had been made, and the signs of a deteriorating employee relationship were starting to show up. Possibly we as an agency were getting to the size where we needed both a bookkeeper/comptroller and an IT person.

Since Gene and I were such good friends, I really wanted to figure out a way to keep him in our employ. I was determined to make the job work so we would not lose this excellent guy. After a few long talks he admitted that, although he really liked the information technology part of his job, the books were driving him crazy. Since this was what I suspected, I had already been talking to another person about taking over the bookkeeper/comptroller job. I proposed to Gene that he become our IT guy. I would turn the other part of his position over to someone else, yet I agreed to leave his salary the same. He said it sounded like a good plan, but I could tell he wasn't totally sold on the deal.

I hurried up and hired another person I knew very well, one I had been talking to for over five years, who was a CPA in a major accounting firm in our town. We put a deal together with this excellent guy in a few weeks. Kelly went to work for us on October 1, 2003. I thought I had my problems handled until, out of the blue, Gene quit a few days later.

Now we were really in the shit: $10,500,000 of premium to keep track of and a new accountant with two days of training--damn! I couldn't believe that Gene, being the good friend he was, would do that to us. What I was unaware of at the time was that he was virtually in the middle of a walking nervous breakdown and completely unable to continue in the job. I need not have worried. Kelly, the CPA, simply settled in, got into the books, and in very short order had things humming. Funny, you always think people are irreplaceable, yet after they are gone, you find out that nothing succeeds like successors. In addition, Kelly was far ahead of his predecessor in most accounting matters.

In addition to my stroke-disabled agent, I had lost Gene and one unproductive agent. To replace these three, I had added Kelly, whom you already know about, and two other agents. The first one was a long-time bank agent who, although he was a bit bad on paperwork, brought a very nice book of business with him. He immediately wrote three times as much business as my stroke-challenged agent had removed. The third new hire was a long time adjustor friend of mine and Casey's, Lu Hanson. Training to be Casey's assistant in commercial lines sales, he is already becoming a very vital member of our team. The bottom line on staffing was that the new people were turning out to be many times more productive than the previous ones. It was good, solid progress.

- **If someone on your staff becomes disabled, this condition affects you, your staff, and your clients.**

- **People who are good employees will not necessarily be with you forever.**

- **Staffing will always be one of the biggest business challenges any employer has to deal with.**

SAYING NO TO A GOOD DEAL

We were just bolting Kelly into his new job with us when the Leavitt deal started to heat up. In the past few months we had sent enough information back and forth to the Leavitts to choke a horse. I wanted top dollar for the agency if I was going to sell it. I realized that I had to convince them this was the finest operation they would ever have a chance to get their hands on if I was going to get the money I wanted.

Early in November we agreed to meet in Rapid City, so Kelly and I jumped into the plane to fly down there. Again, I got lucky on weather, and we had a nice flight of a little over an hour to South Dakota. Buzzing along at 18,000 feet sure beat a boring, day-long drive. It seemed as if in no time at all Ellsworth approach was vectoring us for the landing at Rapid City. Since we had arrived a few hours early, we drove up to the casinos at Deadwood, South Dakota, a few miles from Rapid City, to see if we could be the first two people ever born to make a couple of bucks on the slot machines. No luck: we were just like everyone else. Two hours later we had peed away a few hundred dollars without making a thing. I told myself I had better stick to gambling my money on buying agencies; there I could control the odds a little better.

At this meeting the Leavitts laid out a rough estimate of what they would pay for the store, the terms they were willing to arrange, and the general layout of the deal. Of course, there were still more numbers to crunch, so the next day Kelly and I headed back home to finish up the deal.

What is it with my flying in and out of Rapid City? Sure as hell, the return trip was in weather with clouds and potential ice again. This time, however, my airplane was equipped for it. Since the 340 Cessna is pressurized, we stayed on top of the weather at 19,000 feet all the way back to Minot, having a beautiful ride. However, when we started descending through the clouds into Minot, Kelly asked, "What is that white stuff on the front of the wing?" I laughed and answered it was ice. I had the pitot heat, hot props, heated windshield, and the stall warning heat already on. The ice was minimal; I did not even have to cycle the de-ice boots on the wings. It was not nearly as serious as the ice I had gotten into in the spring, and it was a welcome change not to have to be in a panic about it. Also, by now I had flown so many more hours in clouds that I was actually starting to like the challenge of it. The descent and approach into Minot were no big deal--what a tremendous difference from a few short months before!

The Leavitts had offered me an excellent salary and benefit package. Furthermore, the sale would solve my perpetuation problem. But it seemed to me that I would not be making as much money as I was now after taxes; in other words, I would just be buying myself out with money I would have made anyway. The big advantage of my selling would apparently be that I could invest in the Leavitt operation, and this would probably not be too bad an idea. At the rate they are growing, it might possibly be like getting in on the ground floor of Wal-Mart.

I told Kelly I wanted him to do me a spreadsheet of what the Leavitts were offering, what I was now making after taxes, and where I would be after taxes if we did the Leavitt deal. He came back to me a couple of days later with an Excel spreadsheet of numbers that was a work of art; I was really starting to like having a CPA on staff. I had him send a copy over to Iver Eliason, my tax accountant, and Bob LaMont, my attorney, for their review.

After this last meeting with the Leavitts in Rapid City, I had to contemplate seriously whether or not I was actually going to sell 60% of my company. It was a huge decision, and for the first time I was really considering it. Linda and I discussed the sale endlessly, and the conversation would usually go something like "If we could get three million for the 60%, we would just have to sell it. But of course they are not going to offer us that much." Etc., etc., etc. Linda had heard it so many times it was starting to make her mad when I began blabbing on and on. Meanwhile, I also was talking to my long-time tax accountant CPA, Iver Eliason, and my attorney, Bob LaMont. All of my advisors, without exception, felt we would be better off keeping Western Agency, Inc., the way it was. The company was growing, we knew what we were doing, and it was making a ton of money. True, investing and going in with the Leavitt Group probably would be a wise decision, too. However, I owned all of my own company, which was doing outstandingly well just the way it was.

Probably two things prevented me from selling. First, after taking away the tax advantages of owning my own business, even with the price the Leavitts were offering, I would be making less than I was. They wanted to buy me out over a 10-year period with very little money down, and that was not a big enough payday to get me excited. Second, and probably more important, I simply was not ready to let go of running my own store. I had been signing my own paychecks now for almost 30 years, and I did not want to give up control of my own destiny just yet. I did not want to stop living the dream.

We did have two more conference calls with the Leavitt Group; the longest one ran over three hours. Before the final call I had Kelly, my tax accountant, and my attorney all look over their final offer. In the end, even though they offered us a package worth over two million dollars for 60% ownership of the agency, I turned them down. I am sure they thought I was crazy and I probably am, but as I said it seems to me that at age 53 I am just not ready to let go. Western Agency, Inc., grew in premium by over 24% in 2003. Revenues were consequently up, along with earnings per employee. Linda and I are still going to spend over three months at our house in Hawai'i.

But more than that, I guess I am just not prepared to quit. I told Linda we should double the agency again in the next few years, then perhaps sell it. Better yet, why not take a page out of Leavitt's playbook, selling 40% to the key employees and keeping the 60% indefinitely? We told the Leavitts thanks but no thanks, and I began negotiations to purchase an agency in Fargo that would be a good fit for us.

- **Possibly age 53 is too early to sell out.**

- **If you are considering a sale of your store, keep your CPA and your attorney close at hand.**

- **If you turn down a good offer, should you have your head examined?**

WHAT'S TOO MUCH?
Is Two times Earnings Too Much to Pay?

Even while we were in negotiations with the Leavitt Group, I had assumed from the get-go that they would not offer enough money to convince me to do the deal. All through 2003 I kept searching for more agencies to purchase and ended up looking at five different stores that year. After missing the one in Regent, I started the ball rolling on an operation in Fargo. I also spent some time talking to a friend of mine who had a small store up in Bottineau, a little town 100 miles northeast of Minot. I had wanted to get into the Bottineau area for years, but the main local agent, Larry Marchus, was such a fierce competitor that we had made no progress up until a couple of years ago, when he retired.

Larry and I knew each other quite well; but while he was an agent, there was no way he was going to let us get into his town. I did not blame him. Business is business, and as long as Larry was in the insurance business, Bottineau had been an impenetrable fortress to us. An agent for the bank, he had not owned his operation. If he had, we certainly would have been happy to buy him out when he was ready to quit. However, as I said, Larry had finally retired and was now actually sending us business, so we could move into this excellent territory.

As a result of Larry's being out of the business, we had picked up some choice commercial accounts in Bottineau and were looking to expand in the area. Furthermore, my friend wanted to sell his agency while keeping his HR Block tax business. His book had one of the finest loss ratios I had ever seen. The problem with his book, though, was that he really did not have a solid handle on how much volume he had, nor was he sure how much he wanted for it. We had been flirting around a sale for years, but I could not seem to come up with an idea that he liked. I decided he was not going to be doing anything for awhile.

However, as usually happens when you think no deal is going to happen, one does. One day a month or so later he called me out of the blue. We shot the breeze for a few minutes, and this time I said, "What do you want for that agency of yours?" He said he would get back to me in a couple of days, and when he did this was the offer he proposed. Two times commission for the agency was the price he wanted.

I know you are thinking I had to be out of my mind to pay two times earnings for a $50,000 revenue store with only two companies. Let me elaborate. The store had a five-year loss ratio of under 10% on 90% of his book, which was all farm, homeowners, and auto. There was huge potential to grow the book because he was not selling multi-peril crop insurance to his farm accounts. My friend just wanted to do his tax work and not be bothered by the insurance so, although he agreed to help us find new commercial business, he would collect no wages from us. He did want us to hire his CSR, who was excellent, so we were happy to do that. She was to do the entire inputting of the book into our automation system; when she was done with that, she could do inputting for our main office. But wait: it gets better. He rented us part of his office for $250 a month, heat and lights included. However, in return for being added to our medical policy, he waived the rent. Also, how about the terms of the sale? It was to be contract for deed, no personal guarantee, money to be payable over seven years at seven percent interest, payments to be made monthly, nothing down, with the first payment 30 days after closing. If the agency were half as good as I felt it was, we would never have any of our own money in the deal. I had the papers drawn up, the sale closed in a few days, and it was finalized November 11, 2003. Integrating his agency with our Western Agency, Inc., operation has been one of the most seamless additions I have ever done.

Still think I am paying too much for little stores? I shall take all of these deals I can get. I am interviewing prospective agents for the Bottineau store at this time. I feel when we get a good, hard-running agent up there we can take the Bottineau operation to $3,000,000 of premium in a few short years. As it is, until I do get that agent, the store will sit there paying for itself, anyway.

It had been quite a year so far. We now had locations in seven different towns, our loss ratios were absolutely super, production was up over 24%, and I had made some outstanding major employee changes. Linda and I had decided not to sell the agency, yet with the knowledge we had gained in the Leavitt negotiations had come away with a very good concept for how to set up the agency perpetuation plan we needed. Furthermore, I had a concrete idea of how to expand the store still further. We packed up our bags and headed for Hawai'i for another few months. I needed to hit the computer and get the 2003 numbers figured out, update my business plan for 2004, lay out my plans for the new year, and finish writing this book.

- Let the seller of the store tell you what he wants for it; if the terms are right, you may find it is cheaper than you think.

- If you buy the agency right and it is a good store, you do not have to locate a super salesman immediately; all you have to do is get the store on line so you can began managing it and take your time looking for a salesman to step in.

• CHAPTER THIRTEEN •

A CRYSTAL BALL FOR SMALL AGENCIES

While I realize this book can be only so long, it seems there is so much still to say. To begin with, the battle in building a midsize Independent Agency is winnable. Profit can be bigger than you will believe, and the tools, many of them in this book, are available to help you succeed in this business. When I look back over the past 30 years, it seems to me that the more we change, the more we must stay the same. In the way we deliver the insurance product and process, the paperwork has changed so much it is unbelievable. We have seen companies go through huge internal alterations, and the premium volumes they are requiring from the agencies seem now to be astronomical compared to years ago. The way we use computers right at the point of sale and when doing renewals and audits in clients' offices would have been a thing of dreams in the not-too-distant past. The proposals we can generate at the push of a button are works of art that would have cost hundreds of dollars to produce before.

Yet the basic, fundamental premise of our business has not changed at all. To sell this product you still have to sit down with clients, answer and deal with their insurance needs and questions, and persuade them that the person they should be buying insurance from is you. Maybe we are now using nice computer-generated proposals; maybe we can do renewal audits and apps on shiny laptops. But the bottom line is that clients must be convinced that they should be doing business with you. Working a prospect list and keeping the sales process moving still has to be done: day after day, all the time.

Rather than feeling disappointed with the Independent Agency business, I feel that right now there is an absolutely unbelievable opportunity in this area. Many agencies are not going to make the leap in technology that will be required to capitalize on the changing times. These agents can be told, shown, or sold a management system, but due to long-ingrained habits, they simply are not going to use it to make that leap. Therefore, they are becoming illiterate in the eyes of the companies because the companies wish to communicate with them electronically. The companies are saying, "Send me an e-mail," and these out-of-date agents are saying, "What's an e-mail?" They hate change, and they will not change. In very short order it will be costing them their stores. Maybe it is sad, maybe it is tough, but it is the reality of the market today. It is business evolution at work.

Although I am an incurable optimist, a huge negative I see in the current insurance world is that the companies are again cutting commissions. Why? Because they can get away with it, due to the present hard market and increased premiums. Please remember that companies have the visual acuity of a rhino, which is to say they are shortsighted and stupidly arrogant on this matter of commission cutting. They tell us that since premiums have gone up, at the end of the year, even with the commission cuts, we shall have the same revenue. In the current market that is possibly so. But what about when this hard market softens, as it is now in the process of doing--do you think they will then give us those lost commission dollars back? Not. It is then, when we see the premiums falling, that these cuts of 15-20% of the available commission are going to put still more struggling agencies out of business. Of course, it would be too easy to raise the premium enough so commissions could be left alone and we could all survive better; companies will give you a wealth of reasons why this is not possible. The only defense we Independent Agents have is not to be our own worst enemies and put up with this by working for free. We must not forget that if we accept continually lower commissions from certain companies, in effect saying we are willing to continue working for less and less, why would the companies pay us anything more? I know it is a popular idea to think we can work more efficiently with computers: we have done so and we still do. However, this only goes so far. To give our clients the level of service they are now demanding, to continue to expand and even to keep our market share, we must provide very high-touch service. This a computer simply cannot do. It takes people talking to people, and people need to get paid. The Independent Agency system cannot do it for free, even if some of these companies think we can.

What we must do is look at companies that are not cutting our commissions and place our volumes with them. Naturally, we cannot move a volume of business to a higher-paying carrier in minutes. But the movement of your best agency volume toward the better carriers is something you should be doing every day: it is the only way out of this maze. Yes, there are companies out there that are paying viable commissions. Use them and direct your best volumes toward them. They will win, your store will earn higher commissions, and we shall all survive better. This steady glacial movement of the good business to the good companies is real. It is happening in this country, and the companies and agents that recognize it will end up with the majority of quality premium dollars. Putting the best business with the best carriers will benefit everybody.

Every year, after I get all of my year end numbers together, I sit down and figure out the average commission I receive from each of my companies. I keep this information on a four-year spreadsheet, which obviously shows me trends. To get the average commission number, I simply take the 1099 for income against the written premiums for each company; note that the prior year's contingency is included in the 1099. With contingency income included I see that this year I have companies with an average commission of 18.2% and companies with a low of 11.2%, with the median average for my agency being 15.8%. I know these average commissions seem quite high; but remember that in North Dakota the state has a monopolistic workmen's compensation insurance system, so we agents cannot sell it. Back to my point, though—do you have any doubt where my good premium is going? Meanwhile, occasionally we must write business that is not the best. Where does it go? Junk business goes to junk companies.

If we want top commissions as agents, then we must do everything we can to work efficiently with companies. They want to upload, download, e-mail, and scan. Efficient and fast, this technology is a win for both the agents and the companies. Agents who do not see this are going to be gone. Furthermore, it is the very agents who need to get automated who are not doing it. These smaller-volume agents will gradually lose their company contacts. Usually, the company will cite too-low premium production as the reason. However, if these same agents were automated so the companies could efficiently download and upload to them, the companies could afford to do business with him. If these agents would just embrace these new tools, instead of resisting them, they would see their profits go up, their problems go down, and the clouds of worry start to dissolve.

But just watch: these agents will not get automated. Therefore, their stores will be purchased by agents who are. Remember, I never said these little un-automated agencies had bad books of business. Far from it, in many cases they have wonderful, solid, low loss ratio books that will hold together for years. It is just that they need to be brought into the new century.

If they refuse to purchase an agency management system, the only way I can see for them to survive is for them to partner up with one or two companies. That way, using the proprietary automation that some companies provide, they possibly can provide enough volume to one or two companies for those companies to continue to do business with them. You see companies like Progressive, Allstate, Grinnell, and State Auto doing this. But will the majority of these smaller guys do this? Probably not. As I said in prior chapters, they feel they have to write every single policy they can get their hands on. Contrary to popular belief, rather than having too few companies, usually they have too many companies because, "Well, gee, Timbuktu Mutual writes a couple of donkey carts I have insured; and if I didn't have good old Timbuktu Mutual, I wouldn't be able to write those donkey carts." How much premium is on the donkey cart deals? Probably a couple thousand dollars a year. How much commission do they make on these few orphan deals? "Gosh, I guess virtually nothing." I rest my case.

I should interject here that I do not consider Western Agency, Inc., to be a big agency by any means. I should say I think we are large enough to be able to relate to companies with little problem and keep up with the times, but I do not mean we are a large agency. When I talk about small agencies, I probably mean the ones with under two to three million in premium at this time.

I do implore you, if you are one of these small agencies, to get automated. Partner up with a few companies to get the necessary volumes to keep your contract safe and keep your costs in line. In many cases you will be able to find companies with proprietary automation you can use to help with your automation issues. If you do this I am convinced you will survive and prosper. However, if you are not going to take the above steps, you probably will be selling out to someone like me in the near future. Perhaps you will do it because your store is upside-down on expenses. Perhaps you will do it because you no longer have any companies. Perhaps you will do it because you want to retire. Maybe it will be because you are simply too tired and worn out to continue the fight. But you will be doing it. Not only that: being non-automated will really decrease the value of your store when you do sell.

The joke of the year is that after the sale, if you expect to stay in the business at all, you will have to do the very things you refused to do in the first place. You will have to become computer-knowledgeable, you will have to work your prospect list, and you will be expected to do a good job of inputting data. You will most likely be working on bigger, better, more complicated deals. In many cases you will be spending a bunch less time in the coffee shop telling everyone how busy you are, or you will become unemployed. Most of all, it will require a culture change on your part. Do not think it will be easy, I guarantee you it will not. Maybe by being affiliated with a larger shop, you will find the training easier, but to stay in the business you will have to do it.

If you have an agency you are looking to sell, be sure you are selling to someone who will be a good match. If you are selling to a person on a contract for deed, try to get a personal guarantee and be sure the buyers are solvent enough to do the deal. Remember, if you sell out to a person who is nothing but a bunch of hot air and no knowledge, possibly this individual will trash your book and end up not paying you. When you try to recover either the agency or the money, you may well find out you have lost both. Your accountant and attorney can help you here, as can your own good instincts. Trust them both. If you intend to work with the buyer, honestly ask yourself if you can keep up the pace. Ask him what he thinks. Go look at his store, spend a few days there, and see what the culture of a modern agency is. All of this will help you make a good, solid decision as to whether or not you feel the deal will be compatible.

If you are a growing store such as mine and have not gone out and purchased some of these good smaller books of business, I urge you to take a look at this. They will be bought up in the next few years, and possibly you will miss out on a super way to accelerate your growth if you do not act soon. Buying smaller agencies can help inject you into new markets and new areas. In more cases than not, it can give you a complete new crop of largely undeveloped accounts to work on. It can give you the needed increase in revenue to hire more producers. Over the years I have only made one bad buy, and if I had used my common sense, I could have avoided that one, too. If you have not looked into purchasing additional agencies, you should.

The same thing a seller should be looking for is the same thing a buyer should be looking for: a compatible book of business. If the person you are buying out is a good person, the chances are extremely good he will have put together an excellent book of business. If he is a drunk, there is a virtual certainty he will have written a book of drunk business. I strongly feel that now is the time to be picking up agencies. With automation at our fingertips, it is an easy task to combine books and integrate them. Experimenting with buying stores for years, I feel it is one of the ways agencies can really accelerate their growth profitably.

• **To survive, small agencies must automate themselves or partner up with a company that has automation they can use.**

270

- Take every opportunity to place your best business with your best carriers.

- Do not work for low commissions.

- The opportunity to purchase additional stores presents an excellent chance for automated agencies to expand.

- If you sell your store, be sure you sell it to someone who will be able to pay for it.

- If you are buying a store, be sure it is morally compatible with yours.

• AFTERWORD •

SOME PEOPLE NEVER KNOW WHEN TO SHUT UP

In wrapping up this book, I found there were still many things I had left unsaid, so here are a few more thoughts that I have on this wonderful business. Consider things like Business Ethics 101. This involves being fair to the client and the company, as well as yourself. All agents approach this in individual ways. People will be more or less fair to each party, depending on their own consciences. What is the answer? I do not know. I tell you that when you send in an application and forget to tell a company about a bunch of claims, that is one of the reasons why we agents are now are having to do loss runs on virtually all commercial applications. I tell you that taking a picture of only the good side of a roof is why agents are now plagued by audits and inspections. I tell you that not telling companies about traffic violations is why motor vehicle reports have to be sent in on virtually everyone. You see, so many of our compatriots in this business have lied, cheated, and stretched the truth to companies so many times that it has gotten to the point that companies feel about agents the way I feel about software salesman. Remember the part about their lips moving? And really, can we blame the companies?

I will tell you this. When I was a new agent, I wrote an income disability policy on a young married man with a couple of kids and a small business to run. When the income policy came back, it had a minor little endorsement to sign, which had to do with this client's middle name being misspelled; it had nothing to do with insurability. However, the policy was not in effect until the insured signed the endorsement. Lo and behold, the policy came in Friday, and the insured suffered a serious broken thigh injury the next day. I stopped up to the hospital, had him sign the endorsement, and sent it in. He later filed a loss, and the policy helped keep him, his family, and his business together. Was it wrong? Was I being un-ethical to the company? I do not know. But I sleep like a baby over it.

I have had companies overpay me by $60,000 and sent them back their money. Of course many times we have gotten refunds the clients never would have known about and sent the money back to them. One spring Linda and I were at a party at our lake cabin; during the party one of my farmers called me on my cell phone, wanting to buy more hail insurance coverage. I was pretty sure the man had suffered a hail loss that same afternoon on the crops he wanted the additional insurance on, so I told him I was unable to raise the coverage. He was so mad he chewed me out and went elsewhere with his business the next year; I do not miss him. Several farmers attended that party, and they were aware the guy had called. If I had rolled over and given that man coverage after the fact, it would have materially affected how all of those honest insureds felt about my integrity. However, even if they hadn't of been there I would not have raised the guy's coverage until I was sure the crop had not been previously damaged.

I have had companies refuse to do a deal when I told them about the claims an account had. Then I have watched another unscrupulous local agent write the same account with the same company, getting the company to accept the policy because this agent lied on the app. It is discouraging when you see this happen, and it makes me wonder sometimes if the companies really want to know all the information on an account. It is a sad fact that in this business we are saddled with some bad agents. They make life miserable for us, the companies, and, at claim time, the clients. They cost all of us lots of money with their extra E&O losses, they cause us to lose credibility with the companies, and they hurt the reputation of this wonderful industry. In my own mind, the companies should be working harder to get rid of these bad agents. Possibly the hard market we now find ourselves in will help. However, bad agents have been in this business since the beginning and probably will be with us forever.

I feel that at the end of the day it is far better to do good submissions, talk about the challenges of the account, and try to work with the underwriter to see if the account can be engineered enough to be written. You may be surprised how many times something as simple as going with a higher deductible will solve the problem. Instead of complaining about having to get a loss run, why not just get one so you can prove to the company that with a higher deductible the loss ratio would be far better. I keep track of how companies are accepting or rejecting our submissions, and sometimes when it is just obvious that a company is not in the mood to write, I quit trying to use them until they are. Business ebbs and flows like the tides, and not surprisingly, companies do also.

I can tell you that, having been in this wonderful industry for over 30 years, it has been: exciting, mentally as well as financially; rewarding; and far from dull. Also, once you finally figure out how to run your store and move ahead, it seems so simple that you cannot figure out why everyone else does not get it. I was talking to a young agent who is learning how to get his store up and moving, and he told me, "I just wish I knew what to do more of the time." I told him when I look at how I am supposed to run my store it is as if the rules were carved in granite. One of the reasons I have written this book is to try and help people like him succeed. I want to continue to hire and train good staff, continue to write the better accounts, continue to look for good solid stores to buy, continue to push my earnings per employee up, continue to set up a good solid plan for my key employees to be able to buy into the agency, and continue to refine our automation for maximum efficiency. Maybe that is what being in the saddle for 30 years does to you.

The rules and the way to run my store look simple to me now, but that certainly was not always the case. I do not mean to say there is any one quick way to own, operate, and succeed at building a good, solid independent agency without first paying your dues. If there is a simple, easy way, I have not heard of it; and in my mind a simple, fast way to create a successful store does not exist. Borrowing an idea from the book First, Break All the Rules by Buckingham and Coffman, I do think that people coming into this industry, especially those who aspire to own or run an Independent Agency, should be acutely aware that in order to RUN one of these agencies, you must first UNDERSTAND what an Independent Agency is all about, what makes one tick and grow. Similar to mountain climbing, it is not enough simply to say you are going to climb a high mountain and head straight for the summit. You must work your way up to the higher elevations gradually, or the altitude sickness will kill you.

Although it would be nice if one or more of our kids wanted to go into the insurance business with us, they all seem to have found good careers elsewhere. Linda and I thought it would be unfair to push them into our business, even though we believe it is the greatest one in the world. In addition, with their various degrees and MBAs, I do not think they would understand what I just said above: "To be able to RUN one of these agencies, you must first UNDERSTAND how they work." In other words, if they really wanted to take over the agency, they would have to start at or near the bottom to reinforce their foundations in this business.

I am proud of this career, I am proud of being in the insurance business, and I am proud of the job my staff does every day. Having pride in the work you do is probably one of the golden keys to having a good store, and my staff is one of the best. Without them, of course, the store simply would not be the size it is and could not run the way it does. Contrary to popular belief, having a successful Independent Insurance Agency has far less to do with having a great sales organization than you may believe. What builds great, enduring agencies is having a staff that understands, and is committed to, writing a good, solid book of clients. Whether you have one agency or 10, procedures throughout your organization must be consistent and adhered to. Your staff must know that the client needs to be taken care of first, foremost, and always. They must know if a problem comes up which they cannot fix, they must get in touch with someone who can fix it: not a month from now, but as soon as is humanly possible.

Furthermore, your staff must know it is imperative that clients be provided with the best policies that it is possible for them to have. If the client will not purchase a policy that is adequate, tell your staff it is perfectly permissible to walk away from the deal or at the very least have the client sign a statement saying he or she understands that coverage was left out of the contract. Always remember this: at the end of the day, good insurance protection and good claims service, not price, are instrumental in your agency's success, not shoddy products and "always being cheaper." The agencies that use a quality approach versus a quantity approach will up their profitability and retention, guaranteeing very acceptable sales growth.

Many people seem to think the insurance business is a dull, go-nowhere career. I can assure you that this is absolutely not the case. In addition to running the agency, for a long time I have been able to do my year-end books and update my business plan while on vacation in Hawai'i. Also, I soon want to see about learning to fly a jet. To me this business is anything but dull; the opportunities in it are limitless and bigger now than ever before. As I wrap up this little book, I am looking out over the cobalt blue Pacific. I never get over how beautiful the view from the house is, and I still cannot believe I am able to be here for part of each year. If I have any fear about putting this book out, I guess it would be possibly I was too candid about some of the people Linda and I have had to deal with over the years. I suppose I had better be sure I don't need to borrow money from certain banks, or ever do business with a couple of companies mentioned. However this book is real, it is the last 30 years of my life, and the story had to be told the way it happened to have any meaning.

I thought I would conclude my book with a little story about a client I had when I first got into the insurance business. His kids were all friends of mine, and this man had given me his auto insurance business a few months earlier. On this particular cold spring morning, I had driven 15 miles through the mud and slush to meet with him. I was trying to round out his account by writing his farm insurance in addition to the auto policy I had already sold him. It turned out I could not make a sale to him that day because he was way underinsured. He had his home insured for only half what it was worth, and I just could not convince him to raise his coverage. I realized that without raising his coverage, if he ever had a loss, there was no way I could make the policy work, so I did not do the deal. His kids had mostly all moved away from our little town, had gotten 'good jobs' and I suppose he, like many people, thought insurance was a dull, dead-end way to make a living. I imagine he was feeling sorry for me when he patted me on the shoulder as I was leaving and remarked, "Chuck, don't worry, someday you'll find a good job, too." Well, you know what, Bernard? I think I did.